Accelerating MATLAB with GPU Computing

Accelerating MATLAB with GPU Computing
A Primer with Examples

Jung W. Suh
Youngmin Kim

AMSTERDAM • BOSTON • HEIDELBERG • LONDON
NEW YORK • OXFORD • PARIS • SAN DIEGO
SAN FRANCISCO • SINGAPORE • SYDNEY • TOKYO

Morgan Kaufmann is an imprint of Elsevier

Acquiring Editor: Todd Green
Editorial Project Manager: Lindsay Lawrence
Project Manager: Mohana Natarajan
Designer: Matthew Limbert

Morgan Kaufmann is an imprint of Elsevier

225 Wyman Street, Waltham, MA 02451, USA

First edition 2014

British Library Cataloguing-in-Publication Data
A catalogue record for this book is available from the British Library

Library of Congress Cataloging-in-Publication Data
Application Submitted

ISBN: 978-0-12-408080-5

For information on all MK publications
visit our web site at *www.mkp.com*

Contents

Preface

MATLAB is a widely used simulation tool for rapid prototyping and algorithm development. Many laboratories and research institutions face growing demands to run their MATLAB codes faster for computationally heavy projects after simple simulations. Since MATLAB uses a vector/matrix representation of data, which is suitable for parallel processing, it can benefit a lot from GPU acceleration.

Target Readers and Contents

This book is aimed primarily at the graduate students and researchers in the field of engineering, science, and technology who need huge data processing without losing the many benefits of MATLAB. However, MATLAB users come from various backgrounds and do not necessarily have much programming experience. For those whose backgrounds are not from programming, GPU acceleration for MATLAB may distract their algorithm development and introduce unnecessary hassles, even when setting the environment. This book targets the readers who have some or a lot of experience on MATLAB coding but not enough depth in either C coding or the computer architecture for parallelization. So readers can focus more on their research and work by avoiding non-algorithmic hassles in using GPU and CUDA in MATLAB.

As a primer, the book will start with the basics, walking through the process of setting MATLAB for CUDA (in Windows and Mac OSX), creating c-mex and m-file profiling, then guide the users through the expert-level topics such as third-party CUDA libraries. It also provides many practical ways to modify users' MATLAB codes to better utilize the immense computational power of graphics processors.

This book guides the reader to dramatically maximize the MATLAB speed using NVIDIA's Graphics Processing Unit (GPU). NVIDIA's Compute Unified Device Architecture (CUDA) is a parallel computing architecture originally designed for computer games but is getting a reputation in the general science and technology fields for its efficient massive computation power. From this book, the reader can take advantage of the parallel processing power of GPU and abundant CUDA scientific libraries for accelerating MATLAB code with no or less effort and time, and bring readers' researches and works to a higher level.

Directions of this Book

GPU Utilization Using c-mex Versus Parallel Computing Toolbox

This book deals with Mathworks's Parallel Computing Toolbox in Chapter 5. Although Mathworks's Parallel Computing Toolbox is a useful tool for speeding up MATLAB, the current version still has its limitation in making the Parallel Computing Toolbox a general speeding-up solution, in addition to the extra cost of purchasing the toolbox. Especially, since the Parallel Computing Toolbox targets distributed computing over multicore, multiple computers and/or cluster machines as well as GPU processing, GPU optimization for speeding up the user's code is comparatively limited both in speeding-up and supporting MATLAB functions. Furthermore, if we limit to Mathworks's the Parallel Computing Toolbox only, then it is difficult to find an efficient way to utilize the abundant CUDA libraries to their maximum. In this book, we address both the strengths and the limitations of the current Parallel Computing Toolbox in Chapter 5. For the purpose of general speeding up, GPU-utilization through `c-mex` proves a better approach and provides more flexibility in current situation.

Tutorial Approach Versus Case Study Approach

As the book's title says, we take more of a tutorial approach. MATLAB users may come from many different backgrounds, and web resources are scattered over Mathworks, NVIDIA, and private blogs as fragmented information. The tutorial approach from setting the GPU environment to acquiring critical (but compressed) hardware knowledge for GPU would be beneficial to prospective readers over a wide spectrum. However, this book also has two chapters (Chapters 7 and 8) that include case examples with working codes.

CUDA Versus OpenCL

When we prepared the proposal of this book, we also considered OpenCL as a topic, because the inclusion of OpenCL would attract a wider range of readers. However, while CUDA is more consistent and stable, because it is solely driven by NVIDIA, the current OpenCL has no unified development environment and is still unstable in some areas, because OpenCL is not governed by one company or institution. For this reason, installing, profiling, and debugging OpenCL are not yet standardized. As a primer, this may distract the focus of this book. More importantly, for some reason Mathworks is very conservative in its support of OpenCL, unlike CUDA. Therefore, we decided not to include OpenCL in this edition of our book. However, we will again consider whether to include OpenCL in future editions if increased needs come from market or Mathworks' direction changes.

After reading this book, the reader, in no time, will experience an amazing performance boost in utilizing reader's MATLAB codes and be better equipped in research to enjoy the useful open-source resources for CUDA. The features this book covers are available on Windows and Mac.

1 Accelerating MATLAB without GPU

1.1   Chapter Objectives

In this chapter, we deal with the basic accelerating methods for MATLAB codes in an intrinsic way — a simple code optimization without using GPU or C-MEX. You will learn about the following:

- The vectorization for parallel processing.
- The preallocation for efficient memory management.
- Other useful tips to increase your MATLAB codes.
- Examples that show the code improvements step by step.

1.2   Vectorization

Since MATLAB has the vector/matrix representation of its data, "vectorization" can help to make your MATLAB codes run faster. The key for vectorization is to minimize the usage of a for-loop.

Consider the following two m files, which are functionally the same:

```
% nonVec1.m                              % Vec1.m

clear all;                              clear all;
tic                                     tic

A = 0:0.000001:10;                      A = 0:0.000001:10;
B = 0:0.000001:10;                      B = 0:0.000001:10;

Z = zeros(size(A));                     Z = zeros(size(A));
y = 0;                                  y = 0;

for i = 1:10000001                      y = sin(0.5*A) * exp(B.^2)';

    Z(i) = sin(0.5*A(i)) * exp(B(i)^2); toc
    y = y + Z(i);                       y

end
toc
y
```

The left `nonVec1.m` has a `for-loop` to calculate the sum, while the right `Vec1.m` has no `for-loop` in the code.

```
>> nonVec1
Elapsed time is 0.944395 seconds.

y =
  -1.3042e + 48
>> Vec1
Elapsed time is 0.330786 seconds.

y =
  -1.3042e + 48
```

The results are same but the elapsed time for `Vec1.m` is almost three times less than that for `nonVec1.m`. For better vectorization, utilize the elementwise operation and vector/matrix operation.

1.2.1 Elementwise Operation

The * symbol is defined as matrix multiplication when it is used on two matrices. But the .* symbol specifies an elementwise multiplication. For example, if x = [1 2 3] and v = [4 5 6],

```
>> k = x .* v
k =
    4   10   18
```

Many other operations can be performed elementwise:

```
>> k = x .^2
k =
    1 4 9
>> k = x ./ v
k =
    0.2500  0.4000  0.5000
```

Many functions also support this elementwise operation:

```
>> k = sqrt(x)
k =
    1.0000  1.4142  1.7321
>> k = sin(x)
k =
    0.8415  0.9093  0.1411
```

```
>> k = log(x)
k =
    0  0.6931  1.0986
>> k = abs(x)
k =
    1  2  3
```

Even the relational operators can be used elementwise:

```
>> R = rand(2,3)
R =
    0.8147  0.1270  0.6324
    0.9058  0.9134  0.0975

>> (R > 0.2) & (R < 0.8)
ans =
    0  0  1
    0  0  0
>> x = 5

x =
    5
>> x >= [1 2 3; 4 5 6; 7 8 9]
ans =
    1  1  1
    1  1  0
    0  0  0
```

We can do even more complicated elementwise operations together:

```
>> A = 1:10;
>> B = 2:11;
>> C = 0.1:0.1:1;
>> D = 5:14;
>> M = B ./ (A .* D .* sin(C));
```

1.2.2   Vector/Matrix Operation

Since MATLAB is based on a linear algebra software package, employing vector/matrix operation in linear algebra can effectively replace the for-loop, and result in speeding up. Most common vector/matrix operations are matrix multiplication for combining multiplication and addition for each element.

If we consider two column vectors, **a** and **b**, the resulting dot product is the 1×1 matrix, as follows:

$$\mathbf{a} = \begin{bmatrix} a_x \\ a_y \\ a_z \end{bmatrix}, \quad \mathbf{b} = \begin{bmatrix} b_x \\ b_y \\ b_z \end{bmatrix}$$

$$\mathbf{a} \cdot \mathbf{b} = \mathbf{a}^T \mathbf{b} = \begin{bmatrix} a_x & a_y & a_z \end{bmatrix} \begin{bmatrix} b_x \\ b_y \\ b_z \end{bmatrix} = \begin{bmatrix} a_x b_x + a_y b_y + a_z b_z \end{bmatrix}$$

If two vectors, **a** and **b**, are row vectors, the **a** · **b** should be **ab**^{T} to get the 1×1 matrix, resulting from the combination of multiplication and addition, as follows.

```
A = 1:10   % 1×10 matrix          A = 1:10   % 1×10 matrix
B = 0.1:0.1:1.0   % 1×10 matrix   B = 0.1:0.1:1.0   % 1×10 matrix

C = 0;                            C = 0;

for i = 1:10                      C = A*B';   % A·Bᵀ

    C = C + A(i) * B(i);

end
```

In many cases, it is useful to consider matrix multiplication in terms of vector operations. For example, we can interpret the matrix-vector multiplication $\mathbf{y} = \mathbf{Ax}$ as the dot products of x with the rows of A:

$$\begin{bmatrix} : \\ \mathbf{y} \\ : \end{bmatrix} = \begin{bmatrix} \dots a_1 \dots \\ \dots a_2 \dots \\ \dots a_3 \dots \end{bmatrix} \begin{bmatrix} : \\ x \\ : \end{bmatrix}$$

$$y_i = a_i \cdot x$$

1.2.3 Useful Tricks

In many applications, we need to set upper and lower bounds on each element. For that purpose, we often use if and elseif statements, which easily break vectorization. Instead of if and elseif statements for bounding elements, we may use min and max built-in functions:

```
% ifExample.m                     % nonifExample.m

clear all;                        clear all;
tic                               tic
```

```
A = 0:0.000001:10;                      A = 0:0.000001:10;
B = 0:0.000001:10;                      B = 0:0.000001:10;

Z = zeros(size(A));                     Z = zeros(size(A));
y = 0;                                  y = 0;

for i = 1:10000001                      A = max(A, 0.1);
                                        % max(A, LowerBound)
                                        % A >= LowerBound

   if(A(i) < 0.1) A(i) = 0.1;           A = min(A, 0.9);
   elseif(A(i) > 0.9) A(i) = 0.9;       % min(A, UpperBound)
   end                                  % A <= UpperBound

   Z(i) = sin(0.5*A(i)) * exp(B(i)^2);  y = sin(0.5*A) * exp(B.^2)';
   y = y + Z(i);
                                        toc
end                                     y

toc

y
```

```
>> ifExample
Elapsed time is 0.878781 seconds.

y =
   5.8759e + 47

>> nonifExample
Elapsed time is 0.309516 seconds.

y =
   5.8759e + 47
```

Similarly, if you need to find and replace some values in elements, you can also avoid `if` and `elseif` statements by using the `find` function to keep vectorization.

```
% ifExample2.m                          % nonifExample2.m

clear all;                              clear all;
tic                                     tic

A = 0:0.000001:10;                      A = 0:0.000001:10;
B = 0:0.000001:10;                      B = 0:0.000001:10;

Z = zeros(size(A));                     Z = zeros(size(A));
y = 0;                                  y = 0;

for i = 1:10000001                      % Vector A is compared with scalar
                                        % 0.5

if(A(i) == 0.5) A(i) = 0;               A(find(A == 0.5)) = 0;
end
```

```
    Z(i) = sin(0.5*A(i)) * exp(B(i)^2);
    y = y + Z(i);                           y = sin(0.5*A) * exp(B.^2)';
end                                         toc
                                            y
toc

y
```

Vector A is compared with scalar 0.5 in elementwise fashion and returns a vector of the same size as A with ones for matched positions. The find function gives the indices of matched positions then replaces the original value.

1.3   Preallocation

Resizing an array is expensive, since it involves memory deallocation or allocation and value copies each time we resize. So, by preallocating the matrices of interest, we can get a pretty significant speedup.

```
% preAlloc.m

% Resizing Array
tic

x = 8;
x(2) = 10;
x(3) = 11;
x(4) = 20;

toc

% Pre-allocation
tic

y = zeros(4,1);
y(1) = 8;
y(2) = 10;
y(3) = 11;
y(4) = 20;

toc
```

```
>> preAlloc
Elapsed time is 0.000032 seconds.
Elapsed time is 0.000014 seconds.
```

In the preceding example, the array x is resized by reallocating the memory and setting the values more than once, while the array y is initialized with zeros(4,1).

If you do not know the size of matrix before the operation, it would be a good idea to first allocate an array that will be big enough to hold your data, and use it without memory reallocation.

1.4 For-Loop

In many cases, it is inevitable that we need to use a `for-loop`. As a legacy of Fortran, MATLAB stores matrix in a column-major order, where elements of the first column are stored together in order, followed by the elements of the second column, and so forth. Since memory is a linear object and the system caches values with their linear neighbors, it would be better to make the nested loop for your matrix, column by column.

```
% row_first.m                        % col_first.m

clear all;                           clear all;

A = rand(300,300,40,40);             A = rand(300,300,40,40);
B = zeros(300,300,40,40);            B = zeros(300,300,40,40);

tic                                  tic
for i = 1:300                        for j = 1:300
  for j = 1:300                        for i = 1:300

    B(i,j,:,:) = 2.5 * A(i,j,:,:);       B(i,j,:,:) = 2.5 * A(i,j,:,:);

  end                                  end
end                                  end

toc                                  toc
```

```
>> row_first
Elapsed time is 9.972601 seconds.
>> col_first
Elapsed time is 7.140390 seconds.
```

The preceding `col_first.m` is almost 30% faster than `row_first.m` by the simple switch of the `i` and `j` in the nested `for-loop`. When we use huge higher dimensional matrices, we can expect greater speed gain from the column-major operation.

1.5 Consider a Sparse Matrix Form

For handling sparse matrices (large matrices of which the majority of the elements are zeros), it is a good idea to consider the use of the "sparse matrix form" in MATLAB. For very large matrices, the sparse matrix form requires less memory because it stores only nonzero elements, and it is faster because it eliminates operations on zero elements.

The simple way to create a matrix in sparse form is as follows:

```
>> i = [5 3 6] % used for row index
>> j = [1 6 3] % used for column index
>> value = [0.1  2.3  3.1] % used for values to fill in
>> s = sparse (i,j,value) % generate sparse matrix

s =
   (5,1)    0.1000
   (6,3)    3.1000
   (3,6)    2.3000

>> full = full(s) % convert the sparse matrix to full matrix

full =
        0        0        0        0        0        0
        0        0        0        0        0        0
        0        0        0        0        0   2.3000
        0        0        0        0        0        0
   0.1000        0        0        0        0        0
        0        0   3.1000        0        0        0
```

Or simply convert the full matrix to a sparse matrix using the sparse built-in command:

```
>> SP = sparse(full)

SP =
   (5,1)    0.1000
   (6,3)    3.1000
   (3,6)    2.3000
```

All of the MATLAB built-in operations can be applied to the sparse matrix form without modification, and operations on the sparse matrix form automatically return results in the sparse matrix form.

The efficiency of the sparse matrix form depends on the sparseness of the matrix, meaning that the more the zero elements the matrix has, the speedier the matrix operation will be. If a matrix has very little or no sparseness, speeding up and memory saving benefits from using the sparse matrix form no longer can be expected.

```
% DenseSparse.m              % RealSparse.m

% Dense matrix               % Sparse matrix

A = rand (5000,2000);        sp_A2 = sprand(5000, 2000, 0.2);
                             b2 = rand (5000,1);
```

```
b = rand (5000,1);                    % Convert sparse matrix to full
tic                                   % matrix
    x = A\b ;                         full_A2 = full(sp_A2);
toc                                   tic
% Convert to sparse form in MATLAB        y = full_A2\b ;
sp_denseA = sparse(A);                toc
tic                                   tic
    x = sp_denseA\b ;                     y = sp_A2\b2 ;
toc                                   toc
```

```
>> denseSparse
Elapsed time is 5.846979 seconds.
Elapsed time is 41.050271 seconds.

>> RealSparse
Elapsed time is 5.879175 seconds.
Elapsed time is 3.798073 seconds.
```

In the `DenseSparse.m` example, we tried to convert the dense matrix (A: 5000×5000) to the sparse matrix (sp_denseA). The operation with sparse matrix form takes much more time than that of dense matrix calculation. In the `RealSparse.m` example, however, we speed up a lot from the sparse matrix form. The function `sprand(5000, 2000, 0.2)` generates 5000×2000 elements. The third parameter, `0.2`, means that about 20% of the total elements are nonzero elements and other 80% are zero elements within the generated matrix. The sparse matrix with even 20% nonzero elements can achieve much greater speed in matrix operations.

When we look at the memory size required for each matrix, as in the following, the sparse form (sp_A2) from the sparse matrix requires much less memory size (about 29 MB) than the full matrix form (80 MB). However, the sparse form (sp sp_denseA) from the dense matrix requires much more memory (about 160 MB) than its full matrix form (80 MB), because the sparse matrix form requires extra memory for its matrix index information in addition to its values.

```
>> whos('A', 'sp_denseA','full_A2','sp_A2')
```

Name	Size	Bytes	Class	Attributes
A	5000×2000	80000000	double	
full_A2	5000×2000	80000000	double	
sp_A2	5000×2000	29016504	double	sparse
sp_denseA	5000×2000	160016008	double	sparse

1.6   Miscellaneous Tips

1.6.1   Minimize File Read/Write Within the Loop

Calling functions involving file read/write is very expensive. Therefore, we should try to minimize or avoid its use especially within a loop. The best way for handling file read/write is to read files and store data into variables before the loop, and then use those stored variables inside the loop. After you exit the loop, write the results back to the file.

It seems simple and obvious to avoid file reading/writing within loop, but when we use many functions over multiple files, the file reading/writing parts can inadvertently reside within the deep inner loop. To detect this inadvertent mistake, we recommend the profiler to analyze which parts of a code significantly affect the total processing time. We deal with the use of a profiler in Chapter 3.

1.6.2   Minimize Dynamically Changing the Path and Changing the Variable Class

Similar to the file reading/writing, setting a path is also expensive. So it should be minimized. It is also recommended to set the path outside the loop. Changing the variable/vector/matrix class is also expensive. So it should also be minimized, especially within loops.

1.6.3   Maintain a Balance Between the Code Readability and Optimization

Although we emphasize the code optimization so far, the code maintenance is a very important factor for designing/prototyping algorithm. Therefore, it is not always a good idea to trade off code readability with heavy optimizations. Please try to make a balance between code readability and optimization, from which we can get more benefits by saving costly debugging times while spending more on creative algorithms and living a happier life.

1.7   Examples

When you run `myDisplay.m`, you see a figure like Figure 1.1. In this example, we are going to search for a black book (template image on the left) out of 12 objects (right). Since both the template and object images are in color, the dimensions of both images are three dimensions (x, y, and color). Although the original size of the object image on the right is $1536 \times 2048 \times 3$ and the size of the template image on the left is $463 \times 463 \times 3$, each object in the right image is picked already to have the same size as the template image (Figure 1.2) to reduce

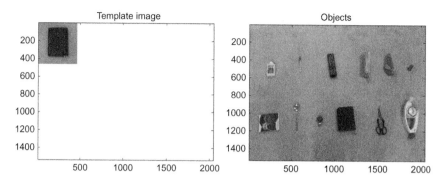

Figure 1.1 Object detection example using a template image. In this example, the black book on the left is used as a template image to search the 12 objects on the right. Notice that a black book on the right is rotated slightly and has some shading around its background.

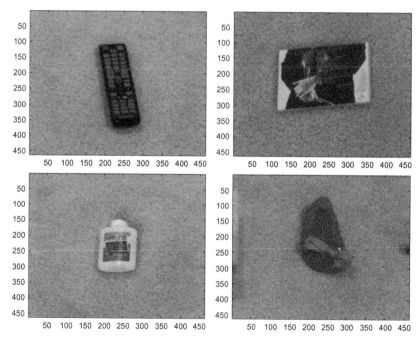

Figure 1.2 Every object is already picked to have the same size as the template image for simplicity.

unnecessary details for the purpose of demonstration. Also those 12 objects are stored in a big matrix **v** in the `compareImageVector.mat` with "unrolled" forms. So the $463 \times 463 \times 3$ matrix for one object is unrolled to a 1×643107 row vector, and the matrix **v** has 12 rows for a total of 12 objects (12×643107 matrix).

Our first naïve m code follows:

```
% compareVec_LoopNaive.m
load('compareImageVector.mat');
[sizeX, sizeY, sizeZ] = size(template);
tic
mean_v = mean(v')';
std_v = std(v')';
mean_template = mean(template_vec);
std_template = std(template_vec);
for i = 1:12
  y(i,1) = 0;
  for j = 1:size(v,2)

    normalized_v(i,j) = (v(i,j) - mean_v(i));
    normalized_template(j,1) = template_vec(j,1) - mean_template;
    y(i) = y(i) + (normalized_v(i,j) * normalized_template(j,1))/...
        (std_v(i,1)*std_template);

  end
end

toc
y
```

This m file tries to calculate the normalized cross-correlation to compare each image with the template image.

$$\text{Normalized Cross-Correlation} = \sum_{x,y} \frac{[I(x,y) - \bar{I}][T(x,y) - \bar{T}]}{\sigma_I \sigma_T}$$

Here, $T(x, y)$ is each pixel value for the template image, $\bar{T}$ is the average pixel value for the template image, and σ_T is the standard deviation, while $I(x, y)$ is each pixel value for each object image to be compared. So, when we have a higher normalized cross-correlation value, it means that the two images being compared are more similar. In this example, we will try to find the object with the highest normalized cross-correlation value, as it is most similar to the template image.

compareVec_LoopNaive.m results out like this:

```
>> compareVec_LoopNaive
Elapsed time is 65.008446 seconds.

y =
   1.0e + 05 *

   0.2002
```

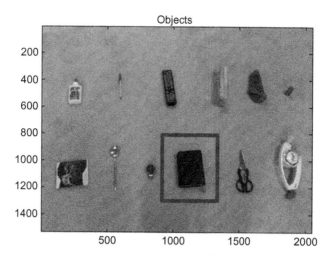

Figure 1.3 Comparing the result with the template image using the normalized cross-correlation. The 10th object was chosen to have the highest normalized cross-correlation value.

```
  1.2613
  2.9765
  2.6793
  2.6650
 -0.0070
  2.7570
  0.7832
  0.3291
  5.0278
  2.8071
 -0.5271
```

From this result, the 10th line of the normalized cross-correlation has the highest value (5.0278 * E05), which is the 10th object in the Figure 1.1. Although the result was good enough to find the right object (Figure 1.3), we may do a few things to improve its speed. Before going to next pages, please try to find the parts that can be improved from the compareVec_LoopNaive.m file by yourself.

Let us start to look over the code carefully. Do you remember that the preallocation can speed up MATLAB code? Let us do memory allocations for the variable y, normalized_template, and normalized_v by putting the function zero() before they are used (see compareVec_Loop.m below).

```
% compareVec_Loop.m
load('compareImageVector.mat');
[sizeX, sizeY, sizeZ] = size(template);
```

```
y = zeros(12,1,'double');

tic
mean_v = mean(v')';
std_v = std(v')';

mean_template = mean(template_vec);
std_template = std(template_vec);

normalized_template = zeros(size(template_vec));
normalized_v = zeros(size(v));

for i = 1:12
  for j = 1:size(v,2)

    normalized_v(i,j) = (v(i,j) - mean_v(i));
    normalized_template(j,1) = template_vec(j,1) - mean_template;
    y(i) = y(i) + (normalized_v(i,j) * normalized_template(j,1))/ ...
        (std_v(i,1)*std_template);

  end
end

toc
y
```

The results follow:

```
>> compareVec_Loop
Elapsed time is 58.102506 seconds.

y =
    1.0e + 05 *

    0.2002
    1.2613
    2.9765
    2.6793
    2.6650
   -0.0070
    2.7570
    0.7832
    0.3291
    5.0278
    2.8071
   -0.5271
```

From this simple memory preallocation, we save a lot of running time (from 65 seconds to 58 seconds) easily. Let us tweak the first operation within loop.

Since `normalized_v(i,j) = (v(i,j) - mean_v(i));` is the simple subtraction from each row, we can put that line out of loop by vector operation:

```
mean_matrix = mean_v(:,ones(1,size(v,2)));
normalized_v = v - mean_matrix;
```

Here, `mean_matrix` has the same size as the matrix with `v` by repeating `mean_v`. From this simple change, we can reduce the running time.

```
% compareVec_LoopImprove.m

load('compareImageVector.mat');

[sizeX, sizeY, sizeZ] = size(template);
y = zeros(12,1,'double');

tic

mean_v = mean(v')';
std_v = std(v')';

mean_template = mean(template_vec);
std_template = std(template_vec);

normalized_template = zeros(size(template_vec));
normalized_v = zeros(size(v));

mean_matrix = mean_v(:,ones(1,size(v,2)));
normalized_v = v - mean_matrix;

for i = 1:12
  for j = 1:size(v,2)

    normalized_template(j,1) = template_vec(j,1) - mean_template;
    y(i) = y(i) + (normalized_v(i,j) * normalized_template(j,1))/ ...
        (std_v(i,1)*std_template);

  end
end

toc
y
```

```
>> compareVec_LoopImprove
Elapsed time is 51.289607 seconds.

y =
   1.0e + 05 *

   0.2002
   1.2613
   2.9765
   2.6793
   2.6650
  -0.0070
   2.7570
```

```
 0.7832
 0.3291
 5.0278
 2.8071
-0.5271
```

Let us go further. We use the elementwise operation and vector/matrix operation to avoid using the for-loop. For the elementwise operation, we have

```
mean_matrix = mean_v(:,ones(1,size(v,2)));
normalized_v = v - mean_matrix;

mean_template = mean(template_vec);
std_template = std(template_vec);
normalized_template = template_vec - mean_template;
```

These parts can be effectively used to replace the for-loop.
From the vector/matrix operation, we can completely remove the for-loop:

```
y = normalized_v * normalized_template;
```

Our final vectorized m-code looks like this:

```
% compareVec.m

load('compareImageVector.mat');

[sizeX, sizeY, sizeZ] = size(template);
y = zeros(12,1,'double');

tic

mean_v = mean(v')';
std_v = std(v')';

mean_matrix = mean_v(:,ones(1,size(v,2)));
normalized_v = v - mean_matrix;

mean_template = mean(template_vec);
std_template = std(template_vec);
normalized_template = template_vec - mean_template;

y = normalized_v * normalized_template;
y = y./(std_v*std_template);

toc
y
```

Its result follows:

```
>> compareVec
Elapsed time is 0.412896 seconds.
```

```
y =
   1.0e + 05 *

   0.2002
   1.2613
   2.9765
   2.6793
   2.6650
  -0.0070
   2.7570
   0.7832
   0.3291
   5.0278
   2.8071
  -0.5271
```

This shows that the optimized code is much faster (from 65 seconds to 0.41 seconds without losing accuracy) than the original m code, which had two nested for-loop's and no preallocation.

2 Configurations for MATLAB and CUDA

2.1 Chapter Objectives

MATLAB functions written in C/C++ are called `c-mex` files. The `c-mex` file is the basic starting point for using CUDA and GPU in MATLAB. These functions are dynamically loaded as a function during MATLAB sessions. We write our own `c-mex` files for many reasons:

1. To reuse C/C++ functions in MATLAB.
2. For increased speed.
3. For endless custom extensions

Although the parallel computing toolbox from Mathworks and other third party CPU toolboxes provide CUDA interface, many constraints and limitations inhibit fully utilizing CUDA and GPUs. However, the generic way of using the `c-mex` file has endless custom extensions and is flexible in using the CUDA libraries provided by NVIDIA and other companies. In this chapter, we learn the following:

- To configure MATLAB for `c-mex` programming.
- To make the simplest `c-mex` example, `Hello, c-mex`.
- To configure CUDA for MATLAB.
- To make simple CUDA examples for MATLAB.

2.2 MATLAB Configuration for `c-mex` Programming

2.2.1 Checklists

MATLAB Executable (MEX) is intended to directly use C/C++ and FORTRAN codes within the MATLAB environment to accomplish higher executing speed and avoid application bottlenecks. We call `C-MEX` for the C/C++ MEX, and focus on `C-MEX` only in this book for the purpose of deploying a GPU device. Since `c-mex` requires building C/C++ executable and CUDA requires hardware-specific (NVIDIA GPU) codes, we need extra installation steps in addition to a standard MATLAB installation. We first check the C/C++ compiler installation followed by CUDA installation.

2.2.1.1 C/C++ Compilers

When it comes to C-MEX programming, MATLAB makes use of the C/C++ compiler installed in your system in order to create a MATLAB callable binary. You should be aware of what compilers are available in your system and where they are located. You first have to make sure your MATLAB version supports the compiler in your system. For this, you may have to visit the Mathworks website and check the version compatibility for your MATLAB and compiler at http://www.mathworks.com/support/compilers/R2013a/index.html. Typically, in a Windows, the Microsoft Visual C++ compiler, cl.exe, is installed at

- C:\Program Files (x86)\Microsoft Visual Studio x.0\VC\bin   on 64 bit
- C:\Program Files\Microsoft Visual Studio x.0\VC\bin   on 32 bit

In Mac OS X and Linux distributions, the gcc/g++ compiler is supported by MATLAB and its installation location depends on Linux distributions. Common installations are at, for example,

- /Developer/usr/bin   Mac OS X
- /usr/local/bin   Linux distributions

At this point, verify you have your compiler installed properly and take a note of its location if it is installed in a different location.

2.2.1.2 NVIDIA CUDA Compiler nvcc

To compile CUDA codes, we need to download and install the CUDA toolkit from NVIDIA's website. This toolkit is available as free. For the steps and information on the downloading and installing the CUDA toolkit, please refer to Appendix 1. Download and Install the CUDA Library.

The nvcc translates CUDA-specific codes and invokes the C/C++ compiler to generate executable binaries or object files. Therefore, we need both a CUDA compiler and a C/C++ compiler to build a GPU-enabled executable.

It is very helpful to know beforehand where these are located. Also, you need to know where the CUDA runtime libraries are located.

Often times, most compilation errors come from incorrectly defined or undefined compiler and library locations. Once you identify those locations and set their paths in your system environment accordingly, your sail through C-MEX and CUDA programming will be a lot easier and smoother.

2.2.2 Compiler Selection

We begin by selecting our C compiler from MATLAB. In MATLAB command window, run mex -setup. Once you are greeted with the welcome message, continue by pressing [y] to let mex locate the installed compilers (Figure 2.1).

In this example, two Microsoft Visual C++ compilers are available; we choose Microsoft Visual C++ 2010 as our C++ compiler by selecting [1].

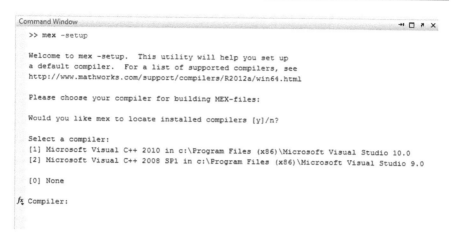

Figure 2.1 The c-mex configuration message in MATLAB command window.

MATLAB asks you to verify your choice. Confirm it by pressing y. Once MATLAB updates the option files, we are done with our compiler selection. The updated c-mex option file contains information about which C++ compiler we use and how we compile and link our C++ codes.

This option file was actually generated and updated from the template that is supported by mex. All the template options files supported by mex are located in the MATLABroot\bin\win32\mexopts or the MATLABroot\bin\win64\mexopts on Windows, or MATLABroot/bin folder on UNIX systems. Figure 2.2 shows an actual example session on c-mex setup in MATLAB command window.

MATLAB uses the one from the built-in templates for the chosen compiler. MATLAB provides a list of compilers supported by the given MATLAB version. The final option file stores all the compiler-specific compilation and linking options to be used for a c-mex compilation. You can edit this option file for specific compilation needs, such as warning and debugging options.

You can find the local copy of the option file, for example, at

• For Window 7,

    C:\Users\MyName\AppData\Roaming\MathWorks\MATLAB\R2012a\mexopts.bat.

• For Windows XP,

    C:\Documents and Settings\MyName\Application Data\MathWorks\MATLAB
    \R2012a\mexopts.bat.

• For Mac OS X,

    /Users/MyName/.matlab/R2012a/mexopts.sh.

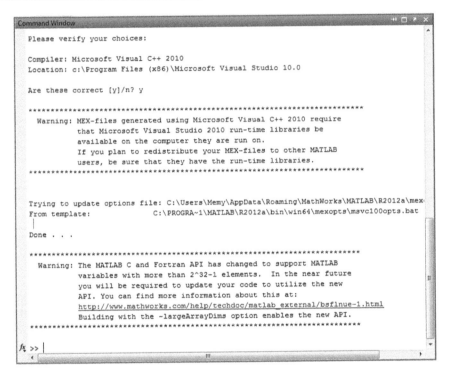

Figure 2.2 C/C++ compiler verification during c-mex configuration.

If you open this option file in Mac, you also can specify what SDK you would like to use for the compiler. You simply edit SDKROOT and save (Figure 2.3).

- For Linux distributions,

$$\sim/.matlab/R2012a/mexopts.sh.$$

The supported compilers for MATLAB vary from operation system to operation system and different MATLAB versions. Again, you have to make sure your installed compiler is supported by the version of MATLAB installed in your system.

2.3 "Hello, mex!" using C-MEX

Now, we go step by step to say 'Hello' to our c-mex.

Step 1. First, create an empty working directory, for example, at

$$c:\junk\MatlabMeetsCuda\Hello.$$

Step 2. Now, open MATLAB and set the working directory as our current folder in the MATLAB toolbar, as shown in the Figure 2.4.

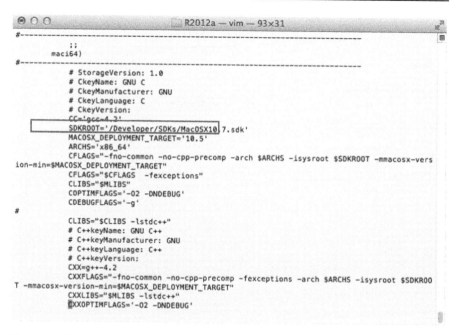

Figure 2.3 The `mexopts.sh` file for Mac OS X SDK selection.

Figure 2.4 Set a working directory as a current folder.

Step 3. Open the MATLAB editor and create a new script by choosing `File > New > Script` from the menu. Then, save this new script as `helloMex.cpp` in the editor (Figure 2.5).

Step 4. Type the following codes into the editor window and save the file by choosing `File > Save`:

```
1  #include "mex.h"
2
3  void mexFunction(int nlhs,
4                   mxArray *plhs[],
```

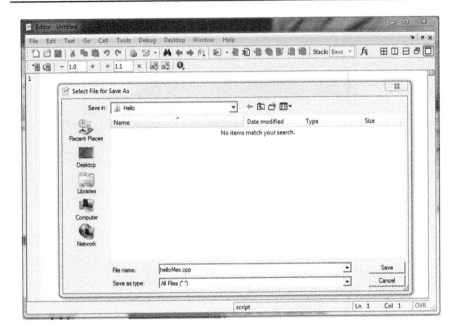

Figure 2.5 Save a new script as a C++ code.

```
5                          int nrhs,
6                          const mxArray *prhs[])
7  {
8      mexPrintf("Hello, mex!\n");
9  }
```

The mexPrintf(..) is equivalent to printf(..) in C/C++. Unlike printing to stdout in pritnf, this prints your formatted message in the MATLAB command window. You will find its usage is same as printf.

Step 5. Go back to the MATLAB. MATLAB now shows our newly created file, helloMex.cpp in the MATLAB current folder. We then compile this code by running the following command in the command window,

```
>> mex helloMex.cpp
```

The c-mex invokes our selected compiler to compile, link, and finally generate the binary, which we can call in our normal MATLAB session.

Step 6. On success, this will create a new mex file, hello.mexw64 (or hello.mexw32) on Windows system, in the same directory (Figure 2.6).

Step 7. Now, it is time to say hello to our c-mex by entering the command in the command window (Figure 2.7).

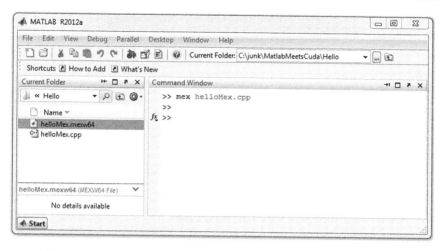

Figure 2.6 Creating a `c-mex` file from the C++ code.

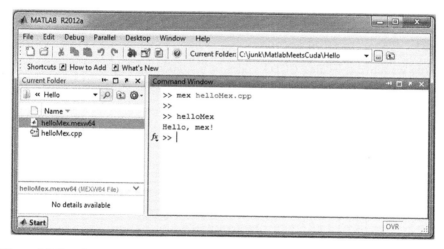

Figure 2.7 Running `Hello, mex` in the command window.

```
>> helloMex
```

With just a couple of lines, we have just created our first C-MEX function!

2.3.1.1 Summary

In this example, we created one special function called *mexFunction*. It is referred to as the *gateway routine*. This function provides the entry point to the mex-shared library, just like the `main(...)` function in C/C++ programming. Let us take a brief look at the function definition and its input parameters:

```
void mexFunction(int nlhs, mxArray *plhs[], int nrhs, const
mxArray *prhs[])

nlhs:  It is the number of output variables.
plhs:  Array of mxArray pointers to the output variables
nrhs:  Number of input variables
prhs:  Array of mxArray pointers to the input variables
```

We visit this in more detail in the following section.

2.4   CUDA Configuration for MATLAB

Let us now turn to CUDA. To compile CUDA codes, we need an `nvcc` compiler, which translates CUDA specific keywords in our codes and generates machine codes for GPU and our host system. The `nvcc` under the hood uses our configured C/C++ compiler.

2.4.1   Preparing CUDA Settings

Before we move to adding CUDA codes, it is a good idea to check if our CUDA has been installed properly. The CUDA Toolkit is installed by default to

- In Windows:

  `C:\Program Files\NVIDIA GPU Computing Toolkit\CUDA\v#.#`,
  where #.# is version number 3.2 or higher.

- In Mac OSX:

  `/Deverloper/NVIDIA/CUDA-#.#`.

- In Linux:

  `/usr/local/cuda-#.#`.

If properly installed, you should be able to enter command `nvcc` using a "`system`" command from the MATLAB console:

```
>> system('nvcc')
```

If we run this, we get an error message, "`nvcc : fatal error : No input files specified; use option -help for more information.`" As the message indicates, we sure got the error since we did not specify which input file we want to compile. However, if MATLAB complains with a message, "`nvcc is not recognized as an`

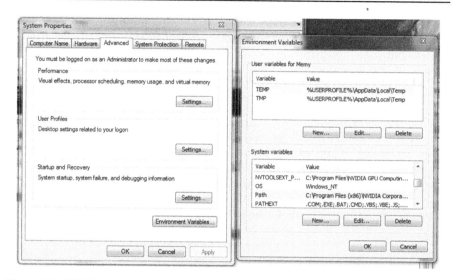

Figure 2.8 NVIDIA compiler path in the `PATH` variable.

`internal or external command, operable program or batch file`", then it indicates that our CUDA has not been properly installed. You will most likely want to refer to http://docs.nvidia.com/cuda/index.html to make sure your CUDA is properly installed on your system before taking the next step.

Here are some tips as to how to make sure the CUDA environment is configured properly.

In Windows, check your path by entering `path` at the command prompt.

```
C:\> path
```

You should see the NVIDIA compiler path in the `PATH` variable as follows

```
PATH = C:\Program Files\NVIDIA GPU Computing Toolkit\CUDA\v#.#\bin\;C:
\WINDOWS\system32;C:\WINDOWS;C:\WINDOWS\System32\Wbem;C:\Program Files
\MATLAB\R2010b\bin;C:\Program Files\TortoiseSVN\bin;
```

Or, open `Control Panel > All Control Panel Items > System > Advanced System Settings` (Figure 2.8). Further information for Windows can be found at http://docs.nvidia.com/cuda/cuda-getting-started-guide-for-microsoft-windows/index.html.

In Mac OS X, open the Terminal application in the Finder by going to `/Application/Utilities`. In the shell, enter as

```
imac:bin $ echo $PATH
/Developer/NVIDIA/CUDA-5.0/bin:/usr/bin:/bin:/usr/sbin:/sbin:/usr/
local/bin:/usr/X11/bin
```

You find path where your CUDA is installed. Further information for Mac OSX can be found at http://docs.nvidia.com/cuda/cuda-getting-started-guide-for-mac-osx/index.html.

In Linux, in bash, for example, enter as

```
[user@linux_bash ~]$ echo $PATH
/usr/java/default/bin:        /opt/CollabNet_Subversion/bin:/bin:/sbin:/
usr:/usr/bin:/usr/sbin:/opt/openoffice.org3/program:/usr/local/cuda/
bin:/usr/java/default/bin:/usr/local/bin:/bin:/usr/bin:
```

And look for the nvcc path. In this case, nvcc was installed at /usr/local/cuda/bin. Further information for Linux can be found at http://docs.nvidia.com/cuda/cuda-getting-started-guide-for-linux/index.html.

2.5   Example: Simple Vector Addition Using CUDA

We start with very popular and simple example of vector addition. In this exercise, we create a CUDA function to add two input vectors of the same size and output the result to a separate output vector of the same size.

Step 1. Create AddVectors.h in the working directory. Enter the following codes and save:

```
1  #ifndef __ADDVECTORS_H__
2  #define __ADDVECTORS_H__
3
4  extern void addVectors(float* A, float* B, float* C, int size);
5
6  #endif // __ADDVECTORS_H__
```

In this header file, we declare our vector addition function prototype which we will use in our mex function. extern indicates that our function is implemented in some other file.

Step 2. We now implement our addVectors function in AddVectors.cu. The file extension .cu represents the CUDA file. Create a new file in the MATLAB editor. Enter the following codes and save it as AddVectors.cu:

```
1  #include "AddVectors.h"
2  #include "mex.h"
3
4  __global__ void addVectorsMask(float* A, float* B, float* C, int
   size)
5  {
6      int i = blockIdx.x;
7      if (i >= size)
8          return;
9
10     C[i] = A[i] + B[i];
```

```
11  }
12
13  void addVectors(float* A, float* B, float* C, int size)
14  {
15      float *devPtrA = 0, *devPtrB = 0, *devPtrC = 0;
16
17      cudaMalloc(&devPtrA, sizeof(float) * size);
18      cudaMalloc(&devPtrB, sizeof(float) * size);
19      cudaMalloc(&devPtrC, sizeof(float) * size);
20
21      cudaMemcpy(devPtrA, A, sizeof(float) * size,
            cudaMemcpyHostToDevice);
22      cudaMemcpy(devPtrB, B, sizeof(float) * size,
            cudaMemcpyHostToDevice);
23
24      addVectorsMask << <size, 1>> >(devPtrA, devPtrB, devPtrC,
            size);
25
26      cudaMemcpy(C, devPtrC, sizeof(float) * size,
            cudaMemcpyDeviceToHost);
27
28      cudaFree(devPtrA);
29      cudaFree(devPtrB);
30      cudaFree(devPtrC);
31  }
```

Step 3. In this step, we compile the simple CUDA codes using the -c option into the object
file, which we then use later for linking to our mex code. To build an object file
from this code, enter the following command in the MATLAB command window.

```
>> system('nvcc -c AddVectors.cu')
```

On success, you see a message similar to the following message coming from
nvcc in the command window:

```
AddVectors.cu
tmpxft_00000dc0_00000000-5_AddVectors.cudafe1.gpu
tmpxft_00000dc0_00000000-10_AddVectors.cudafe2.gpu
AddVectors.cu
tmpxft_00000dc0_00000000-5_AddVectors.cudafe1.cpp
tmpxft_00000dc0_00000000-15_AddVectors.ii
ans =
     0
```

If, however, you get the error message, "'nvcc' is not recognized as an
internal or external command, operable program or batch file" in the
Command Window, this means the C++ compiler path is not set in your system.
You can add the C++ compiler path to your system environment or pass it explicitly by using —ccbin option:

```
>> system('nvcc -c AddVectors.cu -ccbin "C:\Program Files\Microsoft
Visual Studio 10.0\VC\bin"')
```

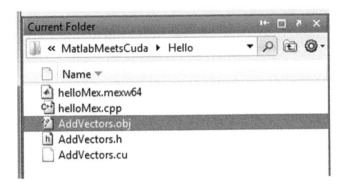

Figure 2.9 The created object file.

Step 4. You now notice that we just created the object file in the same working directory in the MATLAB current folder window (Figure 2.9).

Step 5. In this step, we create our mex function, which we call our AddVectors function. Just like our helloMex function, we start with mexFunction. Create a new file in the MATLAB editor. Enter the following codes and save it as AddVectorsCuda.cpp:

```
1   #include "mex.h"
2   #include "AddVectors.h"
3
4   void mexFunction(int nlhs, mxArray *plhs[], int nrhs, mxArray
    *prhs[])
5   {
6       if (nrhs != 2)
7           mexErrMsgTxt("Invaid number of input arguments");
8
9       if (nlhs != 1)
10          mexErrMsgTxt("Invalid number of outputs");
11
12      if (!mxIsSingle(prhs[0]) && !mxIsSingle(prhs[1]))
13          mexErrMsgTxt("input vector data type must be single");
14
15      int numRowsA = (int)mxGetM(prhs[0]);
16      int numColsA = (int)mxGetN(prhs[0]);
17      int numRowsB = (int)mxGetM(prhs[1]);
18      int numColsB = (int)mxGetN(prhs[1]);
19
20      if (numRowsA != numRowsB || numColsA != numColsB)
21          mexErrMsgTxt("Invalid size. The sizes of two vectors must
            be same");
22
23      int minSize = (numRowsA < numColsA) ? numRowsA : numColsA;
24      int maxSize = (numRowsA > numColsA) ? numRowsA : numColsA;
25
26      if (minSize != 1)
27          mexErrMsgTxt("Invalid  size.  The  vector  must  be  one
            dimentional");
```

```
28
29      float* A = (float*)mxGetData(prhs[0]);
30      float* B = (float*)mxGetData(prhs[1]);
31
32      plhs[0] = mxCreateNumericMatrix(numRowsA, numColsB,
        mxSINGLE_CLASS, mxREAL);
33      float* C = (float*)mxGetData(plhs[0]);
34
35      addVectors(A, B, C, maxSize);
36  }
```

From line 6 to 13, we make sure that our inputs support data type and correct vector size. We then acquire the size of the input vectors. In line 32, we create the output vector that will hold the result of the two-vector addition. In line 35, we call our CUDA based function to add two input vectors.

Step 6. To compile our mex and link to the CUDA object file we created, enter the following command in the MATLAB command window. For a 64-bit Windows system and CUDA v5.0,

```
>> mex AddVectorsCuda.cpp AddVectors.obj -lcudart -L"C:\Program
Files\NVIDIA GPU Computing Toolkit\CUDA\v5.0\lib\x64"
```

If you have CUDA v4.0, replace v5.0 with v4.0. For 32-bit Windows, replace x64 with Win32; for example,

```
>> mex AddVectorsCuda.cpp AddVectors.obj -lcudart -L"C:\Program
Files\NVIDIA GPU Computing Toolkit\CUDA\v4.0\lib\Win32"
```

The -lcudart tells mex that we are using CUDA runtime libraries. The -L"C: \Program Files\NVIDIA GPU Computing Toolkit\CUDA\v5.0\lib\x64" tells the location of those CUDA runtime libraries.

For Mac OS X,

```
>> mex AddVectorsCuda.cpp AddVectors.obj -lcudart -L"/Developer/
NVIDIA/CUDA-5.0/lib"
```

And, for Linux Distributions,

```
>> mex AddVectorsCuda.cpp AddVectors.obj -lcudart -L"/usr/local/
cuda/lib"
```

Step 7. On success, a new mex file, AddVectorsCuda.mexw64, is created in the same working directory (Figure 2.10).

Step 8. Now, it is time to run our new mex function in the MATLAB. In the command window, run

```
>> A = single([1 2 3 4 5 6 7 8 9 10]);
>> B = single([10 9 8 7 6 5 4 3 2 1]);
>> C = AddVectorsCuda(A, B);
```

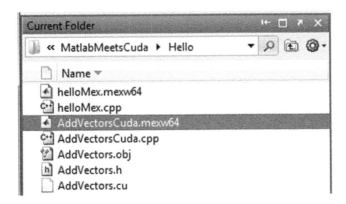

Figure 2.10 The c-mex file created,

Step 9. Verify the result stored in the vector C. When you add each vector element, you get 11 in the resulting vector C:

```
>> C
C =
    11   11   11   11   11   11   11   11   11   11
```

You can run this whole process using runAddVectors.m, as follows:

```
% runAddVectors.m

disp('1. nvcc AddVectors.cu compiling...');

system('nvcc -c AddVectors.cu -ccbin "C:\Program Files (x86)\Microsoft
Visual Studio 10.0\VC\bin"')

disp('nvcc compiling done !');

disp('2. C/C++ compiling for AddVectorsCuda.cpp with AddVectors.
obj...');

mex AddVectorsCuda.cpp AddVectors.obj -lcudart -L"C:\Program Files
\NVIDIA GPU Computing Toolkit\CUDA\v5.0\lib\x64"

disp('C/C++ compiling done !');

disp('3. Test AddVectorsCuda()...')

disp('Two input arrays:')
A = single([1 2 3 4 5 6 7 8 9 10])
B = single([10 9 8 7 6 5 4 3 2 1])

disp('Result:')
C = AddVectorsCuda(A, B)
```

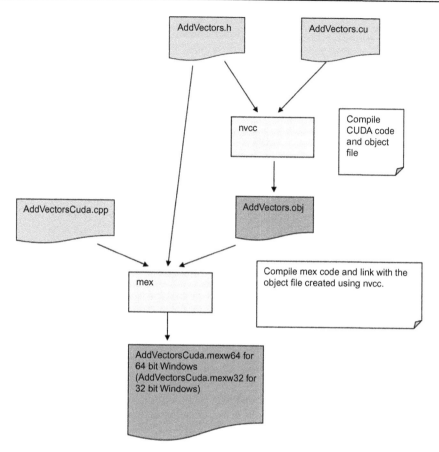

Figure 2.11 The summarized block diagram for CUDA related `c-mex` compilation (▨: input source files, ☐: commands, ▣: generated files).

2.5.1.1 Summary

We put CUDA related stuff in `AddVectors.cu`. `AddVectors.h` contains the function prototype defined in the `AddVectors.cu` file. Our `mex` function (the gateway routine in `AddVectorsCuda.cpp`) calls the CUDA function through `AddVectors.h`. Once we compile CUDA code (`.cu`) into an object file (`.obj`) by `nvcc.exe`, we use the `mex` command to compile our C/C++ code (`.cpp`) and to link it to the CUDA object file (`.obj`). We finally obtain the binary `mex` executable (`.mexw64`) file, which combines the regular `cpp` file and the `cu` file. This process is depicted in Figure 2.11.

2.6   Example with Image Convolution

We now try to create a more complex example. First of all, we define our `mex` function. We read one sample image from MATLAB and pass it onto our `mex` function

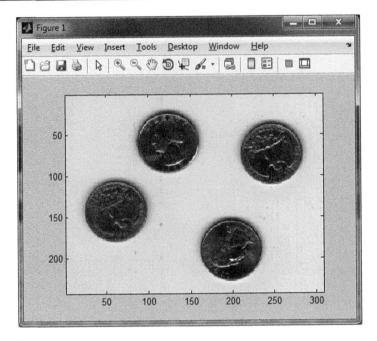

Figure 2.12 Input image as an example.

which then does simple two-dimensional convolution using a 3×3 mask. The result is returned to MATLAB. It will be interesting to show how we do this in three cases:

1. Use the MATLAB function, `conv2`,
2. Do the same in pure C++ code.
3. Do the same using CUDA.

In this section, we focus on how we do this in each case with sample codes. For all cases, we use the same image (Figure 2.12), whose date type is *single* and the same 3×3 mask of *single* data type. The example mask follows:

$$\begin{pmatrix} 1 & 2 & 1 \\ 0 & 0 & 0 \\ -1 & -2 & -1 \end{pmatrix}$$

2.6.1 Convolution in MATLAB

MATLAB has a built-in function, `conv2`. It computes the two-dimensional convolution of two input matrices using a straightforward implementation. It is very simple to use. Let us first see how we do this in plain MATLAB.

Step 1. Read the sample image of coins in the MATLAB command window:

```
>> quarters = single(imread('eight.tif'));
>> mask = single([1 2 1; 0 0 0; -1 -2 -1]);
>> imagesc(quarters);
>> colormap(gray);
```

Note that we cast the input image and mask to the *single* data type. When we read an image using imread, it returns the image in *uint8* data type. Since we will work with a *single* data type in CUDA, we are preparing the input data as *single*.

Step 2. Do two-dimensional convolution using conv2:

```
>> H = conv2(quarters, mask, 'same');
```

For now, we chose to do the convolution with the shape parameter, 'same' By specifying the third parameter same, we ask MATLAB to return the output of the same size as the input image. Now, plot the output image H, to see the result of gradient image.

```
>> imagesc(H);
>> colormap(gray);
```

You can run this whole process using convol_matlab.m as follows:

```
% convol_matlab.m

quarters = single(imread('eight.tif'));
mask = single([1 2 1; 0 0 0; -1 -2 -1]);
imagesc(quarters);
colormap(gray);

H = conv2(quarters, mask, 'same');
imagesc(H);
colormap(gray);
```

Figure 2.13 shows the resulting image.

2.6.2 Convolution in Custom c-mex

We implement the same conv2 function using our custom c-mex function. Before we start implementing, let us revisit the gateway routine introduced in the previous example. The gateway routine takes four input parameters. The first two are used

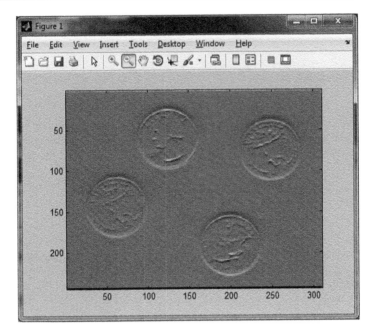

Figure 2.13 The resulting gradient image.

to pass outputs from our `c-mex` function to MATLAB. The last two are for passing inputs from MATLAB to our `c-mex` function:

```
void mexFunction(int nlhs, mxArray *plhs[], int nrhs, const mxArray
*prhs[])
```

Step 1. Create a new file, add the following code and save it as `conv2Mex.cpp`:

```
1    #include "mex.h"
2
3    void conv2Mex(float* src, float* dst, int numRows, int numCols,
     float* mask)
4    {
5        int boundCol = numCols - 1;
6        int boundRow = numRows - 1;
7
8        for (int c = 1; c < boundCol; c++)
9        {
10           for (int r = 1; r < boundRow - 1; r++)
11           {
12               int dstIndex = c * numRows + r;
13               int kerIndex = 8;
14               for (int kc = -1; kc < 2; kc++)
15               {
16                   int srcIndex = (c + kc) * numRows + r;
```

```
17                         for (int kr = -1; kr < 2; kr++)
18                             dst[dstIndex] + = mask[kerIndex--] * src
                             [srcIndex + kr];
19                     }
20             }
21       }
22  }
23
24  void mexFunction(int nlhs, mxArray *plhs[], int nrhs, mxArray
    *prhs[])
25  {
26      if (nrhs ! = 2)
27          mexErrMsgTxt("Invaid number of input arguments");
28
29      if (nlhs ! = 1)
30          mexErrMsgTxt("Invalid number of outputs");
31
32      if (!mxIsSingle(prhs[0]) && !mxIsSingle(prhs[1]))
33          mexErrMsgTxt("input image and mask type must be single");
34
35      float* image = (float*)mxGetData(prhs[0]);
36      float* mask = (float*)mxGetData(prhs[1]);
37
38      int numRows = (int)mxGetM(prhs[0]);
39      int numCols = (int)mxGetN(prhs[0]);
40      int numKRows = (int)mxGetM(prhs[1]);
41      int numKCols = (int)mxGetN(prhs[1]);
42
43      if (numKRows ! = 3 || numKCols ! = 3)
44          mexErrMsgTxt("Invalid mask size. It must be 3 × 3");
45
46      plhs[0] = mxCreateNumericMatrix(numRows, numCols,
        mxSINGLE_CLASS, mxREAL);
47      float* out = (float*)mxGetData(plhs[0]);
48
49      conv2Mex(image, out, numRows, numCols, mask);
50  }
```

In mexFunction, we first check the number of inputs and outputs. In this example, there must be two inputs, image and mask, and one output, the convolution result. We then make sure that the input data type is *single*. We find out the size of the input image and the mask and make sure mask is of 3×3. In line 46, we prepare the output array in which we will put our result and pass it back to MATLAB. Then, we call our custom convolution function, conv2Mex to do the number crunching.

Step 2. We compile our mex function and call from the MATLAB command window. Compiling is very simple:

```
>> mex conv2Mex.cpp
```

If compiled successfully, mex creates a binary file, conv2Mex.mexw64 in Windows 64 bit.

Step 3. We can call this function anywhere in our MATLAB and display the result:

```
>> quaters = (single)imread('eight.tif');
>> mask = single([1 2 1; 0 0 0; -1 -2 -1]);
>> H2 = conv2Mex(quarters, mask);
>> imagesc(H2);
>> colormap(gray);
```

You can run this whole process using `convol_mex.m` as follows:

```
% convol_mex.m

mex conv2Mex.cpp

quarters = single(imread('eight.tif'));
mask = single([1 2 1; 0 0 0; -1 -2 -1]);
imagesc(quarters);
colormap(gray);

H2 = conv2Mex(quarters, mask);
imagesc(H2);
colormap(gray);
```

2.6.3 Convolution in Custom c-mex with CUDA

In this example, we use a CUDA function to do convolution operations. This CUDA function is functionally same as the c-mex function in previous section except for the CUDA implementation.

Step 1. First, we define the function prototype we call in our CUDA function. Create a new file and save it as `conv2Mex.h`:

```
1   #ifndef __CONV2MEXCUDA_H__
2   #define __CONV2MEXCUDA_H__
3
4   extern void conv2Mex(float* in,
5                        float* out,
6                        int numRows,
7                        int numCols,
8                        float* mask);
9
10  #endif // __CONV2MEXCUDA_H__
```

Step 2. We implement our `conv2Mex` function in CUDA. Create `conv2Mex.cu` and add the following code:

```
1   #include "conv2Mex.h"
2
3   __global__ void conv2MexCuda(float* src,
4                                float* dst,
```

```
5                                         int numRows,
6                                         int numCols,
7                                         float* mask)
8   {
9       int row = blockIdx.x;
10      if (row < 1 || row > numRows - 1)
11          return;
12
13      int col = blockIdx.y;
14      if (col < 1 || col > numCols - 1)
15          return;
16
17      int dstIndex = col * numRows + row;
18      dst[dstIndex] = 0;
19      int kerIndex = 3 * 3 - 1;
20      for (int kc = -1; kc < 2; kc++)
21      {
22          int srcIndex = (col + kc) * numRows + row;
23          for (int kr = -1; kr < 2; kr++)
24          {
25              dst[dstIndex] + = mask[kerIndex--] * src
                [srcIndex + kr];
26          }
27      }
28  }
29
30  void conv2Mex(float* src, float* dst, int numRows, int numCols,
    float* ker)
31  {
32      int totalPixels = numRows * numCols;
33      float *deviceSrc, *deviceKer, *deviceDst;
34
35      cudaMalloc(&deviceSrc, sizeof(float) * totalPixels);
36      cudaMalloc(&deviceDst, sizeof(float) * totalPixels);
37      cudaMalloc(&deviceKer, sizeof(float) * 3 * 3);
38
39      cudaMemcpy(deviceSrc,
40                  src,
41                  sizeof(float) * totalPixels,
42                  cudaMemcpyHostToDevice);
43
44      cudaMemcpy(deviceKer,
45                  ker,
46                  sizeof(float) * 3 * 3,
47                  cudaMemcpyHostToDevice);
48
49      cudaMemset(deviceDst, 0, sizeof(float) * totalPixels);
50
51      dim3 gridSize(numRows, numCols);
52
53      conv2MexCuda << <gridSize, 1>> >(deviceSrc,
54                                        deviceDst,
55                                        numRows,
56                                        numCols,
57                                        deviceKer);
```

```
58
59      cudaMemcpy(dst,
60                  deviceDst,
61                  sizeof(float) * totalPixels,
62                  cudaMemcpyDeviceToHost);
63
64      cudaFree(deviceSrc);
65      cudaFree(deviceDst);
66      cudaFree(deviceKer);
67  }
```

We use cudaMalloc to allocate memory on our CUDA device. The function cudaMemcpy copies data from host to device or from device to host, based on the fourth parameter. On the CUDA device, we allocated memory for input and output images and a mask. Then, we copied the input and mask data from host to our CUDA device. Using cudaMemset, we initialized the output data to zero. Our CUDA call is made with conv2MexCuda. Here, we simply assigned the grid size to be same as the image size. Each CUDA grid calculates the final value for each output pixel by applying a 3×3 mask in conv2MexCuda. We explain about the grid size more in detail in Chapter 4.

Step 3. Compile our CUDA codes to an object file, which we link to our c-mex function in a later step. To compile in MATLAB, enter the following in MATLAB command window:

```
>> system('nvcc -c conv2Mex.cu')
```

If you encounter any compilation error, please refer to Section 2.5, "Example: Simple Vector Addition using CUDA." On success, this generates a conv2Mex.obj file.

Step 4. We then create the mex function in which we call our CUDA-based convolution function. Create a new file, enter the code that follows, and save it as conv2MexCuda.cpp:

```
1   #include "mex.h"
2   #include "conv2Mex.h"
3
4   void mexFunction(int nlhs, mxArray *plhs[], int nrhs, mxArray
    *prhs[])
5   {
6       if (nrhs != 2)
7           mexErrMsgTxt("Invaid number of input arguments");
8
9       if (nlhs != 1)
10          mexErrMsgTxt("Invalid number of outputs");
11
12      if (!mxIsSingle(prhs[0]) && !mxIsSingle(prhs[1]))
13          mexErrMsgTxt("input image and mask type must be single");
14
```

```
15    float* image = (float*)mxGetData(prhs[0]);
16    float* mask = (float*)mxGetData(prhs[1]);
17
18    int numRows = (int)mxGetM(prhs[0]);
19    int numCols = (int)mxGetN(prhs[0]);
20    int numKRows = (int)mxGetM(prhs[1]);
21    int numKCols = (int)mxGetN(prhs[1]);
22
23    if (numKRows != 3 || numKCols != 3)
24        mexErrMsgTxt("Invalid mask size. It must be 3×3");
25
26    plhs[0] = mxCreateNumericMatrix(numRows, numCols,
      mxSINGLE_CLASS, mxREAL);
27    float* out = (float*)mxGetData(plhs[0]);
28
29    conv2Mex(image, out, numRows, numCols, mask);
30  }
```

Our new mex function is almost the same as we had in a previous section. The only difference is #include "conv2Mex.h" on line 1. Here, we define our conv2Mex function in conv2Mex.h and implemented it in conv2Mex.cu.

Step 5. We are ready to make our CUDA-based mex function. However, our conv2Mex function is in conv2Mex.obj, so we have to tell our linker where that function is. Also, we tell the linker that we will be using CUDA runtime libraries and where they are located. Enter the following in the MATLAB command window. For Windows 64 bit,

```
>> mex conv2MexCuda.cpp conv2Mex.obj -lcudart -L"C:\Program Files
\NVIDIA GPU Computing Toolkit\CUDA\v5.0\lib\x64"
```

For Windows 32 bit,

```
>> mex conv2MexCuda.cpp conv2Mex.obj -lcudart -L"C:\Program Files
\NVIDIA GPU Computing Toolkit\CUDA\v5.0\lib\Win32"
```

For Linux,

```
>> mex conv2MexCuda.cpp conv2Mex.obj -lcudart -L"/usr/local/cuda/
lib"
```

For MAC OSX,

```
>> mex conv2MexCuda.cpp conv2Mex.obj -lcudart -L"/Developer/
NVIDIA/CUDA-5.0/lib"
```

On success, MATLAB creates our mex function, convMexCuda.mexw64 for Windows 64 bit.

Step 6. Execute our CUDA-based convolution function in the MATLAB command
window:

```
>> quarters = single(imread('eight.tif'));
>> mask = single([1 2 1; 0 0 0; -1 -2 -1]);
>> H3 = conv2MexCuda(quarters, mask);
>> imagesc(H3);
>> colormap(gray);
```

We should now see the same output image in the MATLAB figure.

You can run this whole process using `convol_cuda.m` as follows:

```
% convol_cuda.m

system('nvcc -c conv2Mex.cu -ccbin "C:\Program Files (x86)\Microsoft
Visual Studio 10.0\VC\bin')
mex conv2MexCuda.cpp conv2Mex.obj -lcudart -L"C:\Program Files\NVIDIA
GPU Computing Toolkit\CUDA\v5.0\lib\x64"

quarters = single(imread('eight.tif'));
mask = single([1 2 1; 0 0 0; -1 -2 -1]);
imagesc(quarters);
colormap(gray);

H3 = conv2MexCuda(quarters, mask);
imagesc(H3);
colormap(gray);
```

2.6.4 Brief Time Performance Profiling

We did two-dimensional convolution operation in three ways, resulting in the same
output image. How each performs in terms of time is our main interest. More
detailed instructions and information are discussed in the next chapter. Here, we
briefly examine using `tic` and `toc` command in the MATLAB.

The following is the sample MATLAB session to see the time performance for
each case.

```
>> tic;  H1 = conv2(quaters, mask); toc;
Elapsed time is 0.001292 seconds.
>> tic;  H1 = conv2(quaters, mask); toc;
Elapsed time is 0.001225 seconds.
>> tic;  H2 = conv2Mex(quaters, mask); toc;
Elapsed time is 0.001244 seconds.
>> tic;  H2 = conv2Mex(quaters, mask); toc;
Elapsed time is 0.001118 seconds.
>> tic;  H3 = conv2MexCuda(quaters, mask); toc;
Elapsed time is 0.036286 seconds.
```

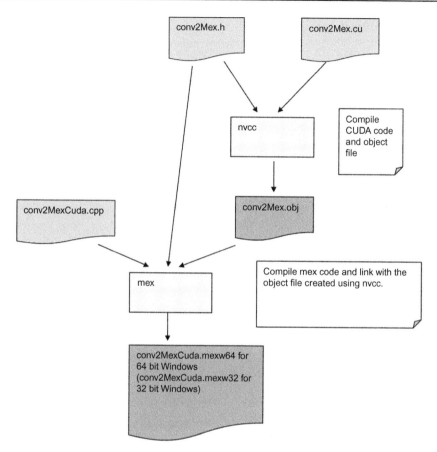

Figure 2.14 The summarized block diagram for the example (☐: input source files, ☐: commands, ■: generated files).

```
>> tic; H3 = conv2MexCuda(quaters, mask); toc;
Elapsed time is 0.035877 seconds.
```

Both the built-in `conv2` and our custom `conv2Mex` functions perform about the same. However, our CUDA-based convolution in this example is very slow compared to the former two functions, because the processing data size is small and our grid and block sizes are not taking advantage of GPU architecture.

	conv2	conv2Mex	Conv2MexCuda
Time in second	0.00123	0.00122	0.0358

In later chapters, we introduce how to get more detailed time profiling and how to optimize our simple CUDA functions to achieve our goal for acceleration.

2.7   Summary

As we did in AddVectors, we put CUDA-related functions in conv2Mex.cu
(Figure 2.14). The file conv2Mex.h contains the function definition that our mex
function, conv2MexCuda.cpp, calls within its gateway routine. Once we compile
CUDA code into an object file, we use the mex command to compile our mex code
and link it to the CUDA object file.

3 Optimization Planning through Profiling

3.1 Chapter Objectives

From profiling, we can find where our codes consume more running time and identify the bottlenecks in our codes. Since many big codes have multiple layers in practice, it is not straightforward to find functions that in turn, call other time-consuming functions. And, we might encounter this situation several layers down in the codes. Through the profiling process, we can efficiently determine which of our codes are responsible for such calls. This is an essential step for optimization planning. In this chapter, we examine the following:

- Employing the MATLAB built-in profiler to find the bottlenecks in m-files.
- Employing C/C++ profiling methods for c-mex codes.
- Employing CUDA code profiling methods using Visual Studio and NVIDIA Visual Profiler.
- Employing the environment setting for the c-mex debugger.

3.2 MATLAB Code Profiling to Find Bottlenecks

Fortunately, MATLAB provides a decent easy-to-use profiler. We are going to use the 2D convolution examples in the previous chapter again for profiling demonstrations.

You can invoke the MATLAB profiler in two ways. First, select Profiler in MATLAB Desktop as shown in Figure 3.1. Second, simply type profile viewer in the command window.

```
>> profile viewer
```

Then, we obtain a profiler window as in Figure 3.2.

To use the 2D convolution examples, change the current folder in the main MATLAB window before using the profiler window (Figure 3.3). Then, type the command you want to run at Run This Code:. We use convQuarterImage.m as an example here (Figure 3.4).

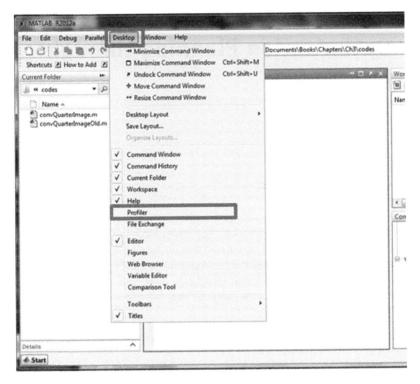

Figure 3.1 Select `Profiler` **from the MATLAB desktop menu.**

You can get the profile results as in Figure 3.5. In each column index, you can click on `Function Name`, `Calls`, `Total Time`, and `Self Time` to sort the results according to the index.

If you click `convQuarterImage` within the `Function Name` column, you get more specific information on every line within the `convQuarterImage` file (Figure 3.6).

When you scroll down this window, we can see the color highlighted code depending on each category (time, numcalls, coverage, etc.). According to this profiling result (Figure 3.7), we see that `imagesc()` and `imread()` take most of running time of `convQuarterImage`. Since `imread()` is a function to read an input image and the `imagesc()` is a function to scale or display the input image, we can focus on the pure computation part, which consumes more running time:

```
H = conv2(single(quarters), single(kernel));
```

In the next section, we see the profiling result when we replace this line with the `c-mex` version of it and the C/C++ profiling method in `c-mex`.

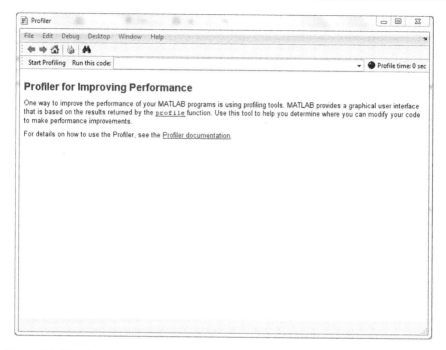

Figure 3.2 MATLAB profiler window.

Figure 3.3 Change the current folder in the main MATLAB window.

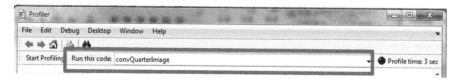

Figure 3.4 Run this code in the MATLAB profiler.

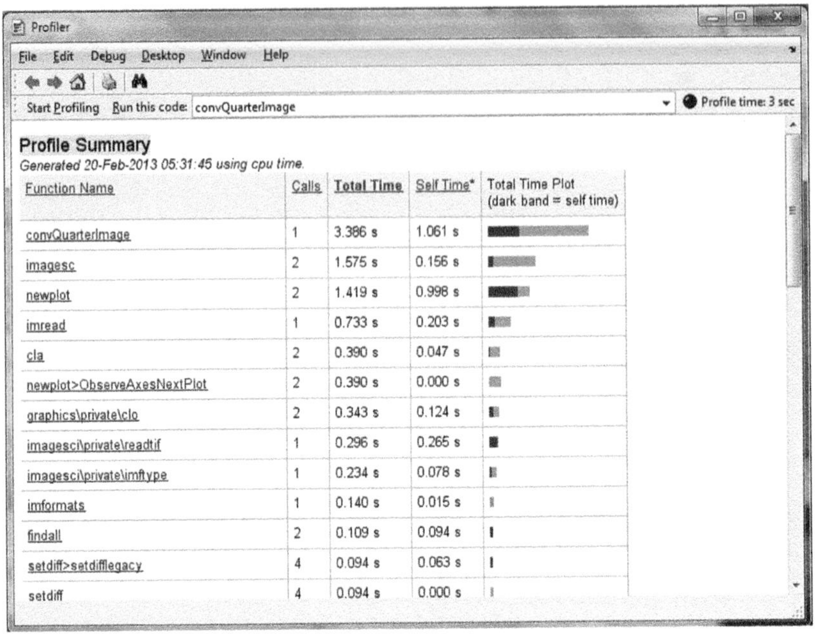

Figure 3.5 Profile Summary from the MATLAB profiler.

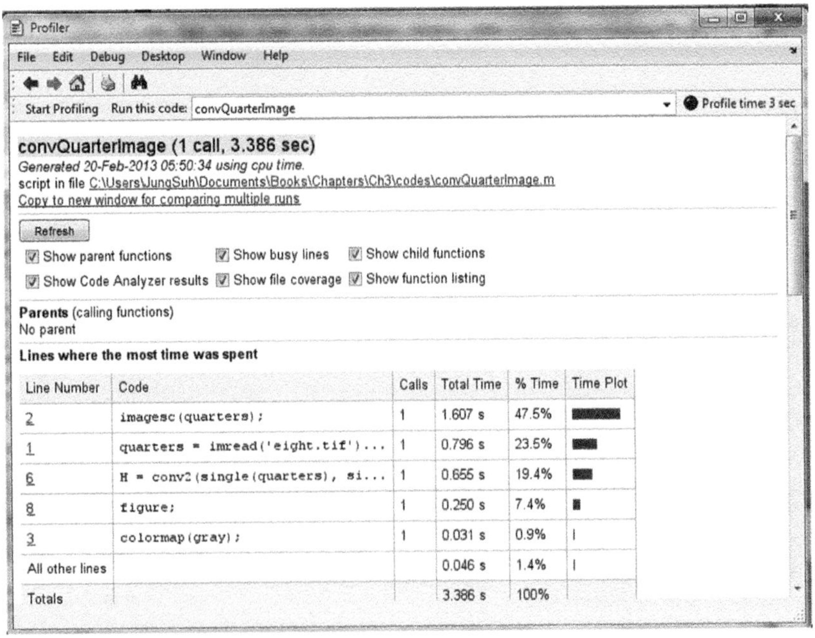

Figure 3.6 More detail in profiling results.

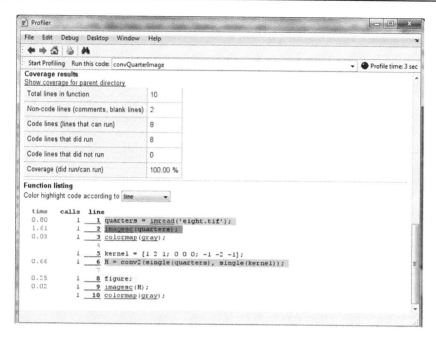

Figure 3.7 Execution timing information in each line of profiling results.

3.2.1 More Accurate Profiling with Multiple CPU Cores

Nowadays, multicore CPU machines are common, and the program running speed is directly related to the number of available cores and their usability. If we want to know the number of function calls and their consuming times in just ballpark figures without more precise information on the CPU's usage, the previous profiler setting would be enough. In some cases, however, we need more accurate analysis for program usage. To do that, we should manually set the number of cores to use outside of MATLAB and profile the codes we want to accurately measure. In the Windows system, it is easy to manipulate the number of CPU cores to use, as shown in Figure 3.8.

You get the Start Task Manager menu when you click the right button of mouse on the task bar. After clicking on the Start Task Manager, you get the Windows Task Manager window shown in Figure 3.9.

For the MATLAB process, select the Set Affinity... through clicking the right button of mouse. Then, you can access the selection window for each processor (Figure 3.10). You can select a specific processor to use for profiling your codes. After selecting one processor and turning off others for MATLAB.exe, you can profile your codes more accurately (Figure 3.11).

Click the right button
of mouse on the task bar

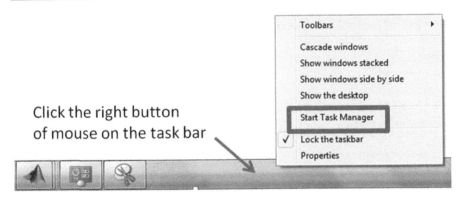

Figure 3.8 To manipulate the number of CPU cores to use, open the `Start Task Manager`.

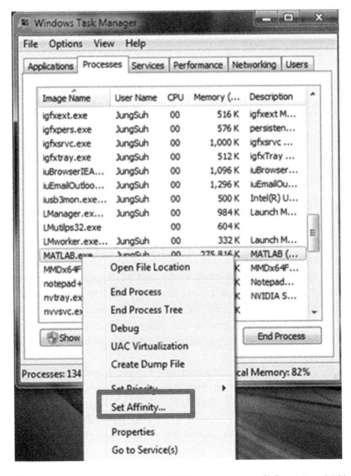

Figure 3.9 To manipulate the number of CPU cores to use, click on `Set Affinity`.

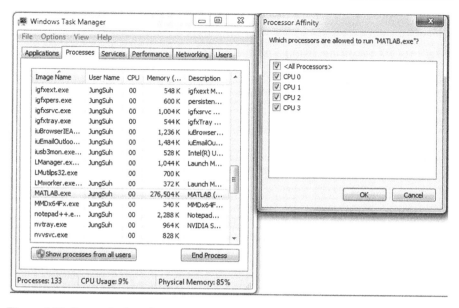

Figure 3.10 To manipulate the number of CPU cores to use, click on the `Processor Affinity` **window.**

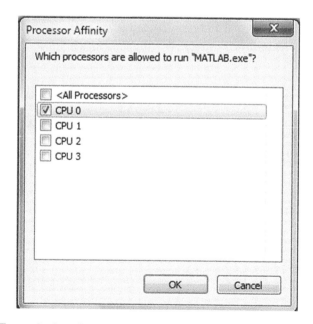

Figure 3.11 To manipulate the number of CPU cores to use, select processors we want to use.

3.3   c-mex **Code Profiling for CUDA**

3.3.1   CUDA Profiling Using Visual Studio

NVIDIA Nsight, Visual Studio Edition, is a free development environment for CUDA installed within Microsoft Visual Studio. NVIDIA Nsight, Visual Studio Edition, provides strong debugging and profiling functions, which are very efficient for CUDA code development. To download and install the NVIDIA Nsight, please refer to Appendix 2.

Let us revisit our convolution example using CUDA. In Chapter 2, we created a convolution function using CUDA functions and ran in the MATLAB command window as

```
>> quarters = single(imread('eight.tif'));
>> mask = single([1 2 1; 0 0 0; -1 -2 -1]);
>> H3 = conv2MexCuda(quarters, mask);
>> imagesc(H3);
>> colormap(gray);
```

Open Visual Studio as described in the previous section (Figure 3.12).

Go to Nsight in the menu and select Start Performance Analysis.... It may ask you to connect unsecurely (Figure 3.13). Selecting Connect unsecurely brings your Visual Studio to the screen shown in Figure 3.14.

In Application:, click on the folder browser button to select MATLAB executable. MATLAB executable can be found where your MATLAB is installed. You have to specifically select the one that is correct for your system architecture. For example, in Window 7, the 64-bit version of MATLAB can be found at the location shown in Figure 3.15.

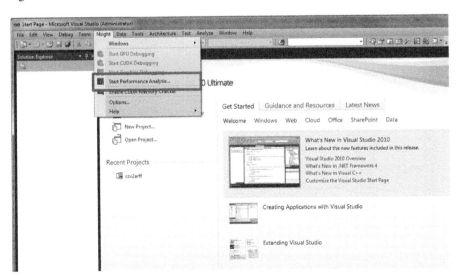

Figure 3.12 Nsight installed in Microsoft Visual Studio.

Select MATLAB.exe and click on Open to close the dialog. Now, scroll down a little bit to Activity Type. Select the Profile CUDA Application button (Figure 3.16). After you select this option, the Launch button in Application Control is enabled.

Click on Launch. After you click, you see that MATLAB starts running along Visual Studio (Figure 3.17).

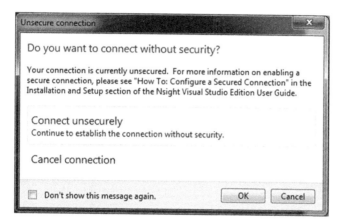

Figure 3.13 Unsecure connection window for connecting Nsight with MATLAB.

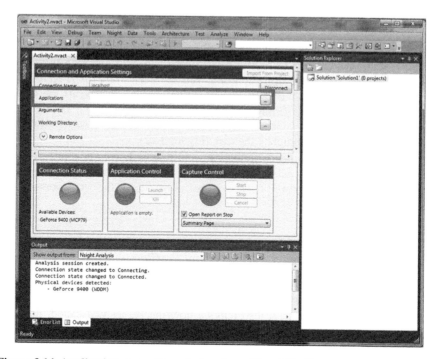

Figure 3.14 Application connection window from Visual Studio.

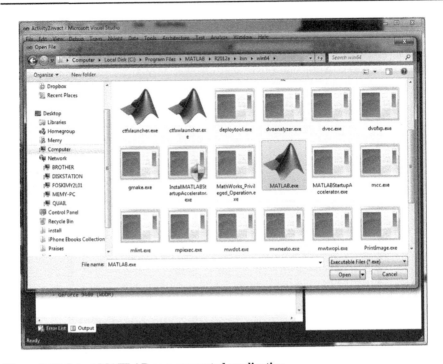

Figure 3.15 Select MATLAB as a connected application.

In the MATLAB command window, run the CUDA-based convolution as shown in Figure 3.18, and then go back to Visual Studio and click on Stop in Capture Control (Figure 3.19). After stop capturing, you see CUDA Overview (Figure 3.20). Select the link, Lauches in the CUDA Overview title bar. It now reveals the CUDA function and all the kernel details and time profiles (Figure 3.21). If you select conv2MexCuda [CUDA Kernel], you see what grid and block sizes we specified and how much time it took to complete the task (Figure 3.22).

You can repeat this profiling by going back to the activity tab and click on Start in Capture Control (Figure 3.23). Once you are done, clos thee MATLAB window or click on Kill in Application Control. That closes down the whole session for profiling in Visual Studio.

3.3.2 CUDA Profiling Using NVIDIA Visual Profiler

NVIDIA Visual Profiler provides a rich graphic user environment to give more insight into how CUDA works under the hood. In addition to giving us time profiles for each CUDA function call, it also tells us how the kernel was called, memory usage, and the like. It helps locate where possible bottlenecks are and explains how kernels were invoked in great detail.

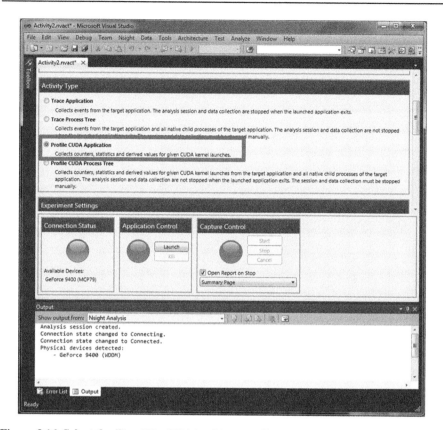

Figure 3.16 Select the "Profile CUDA Application" as an activity type.

In this section, we show how this wonderful tool can be used with MATLAB and CUDA. NVIDIA Visual Profiler can be found at where your CUDA is installed (Figure 3.24). For Windows, it can usually be found at C:\Program Files\NVIDIA GPU Computing Toolkit\CUDA\v5.0\libnvvp. For Mac OS X, see Figure 3.25. For Linux Distributions, go to /usr/local/cuda/libnvvp (Figure 3.26). Start nvvp; you will get an empty window at the beginning.

First, open NVIDIA Visual Profiler. Then, create a new session from the main menu, File -> New Session (Figure 3.27).

Click on the Browse... button and select your MATLAB executable (Figure 3.28) as we did previously. The actual MATLAB executable is found by going to the MATLAB installed bin directory. The actual binary depends on your system architecture:

For Windows 64, C:\Program Files\MATLAB\R2012a\bin\x64\MATLAB.exe.
For Windows 32, C:\Program Files\MATLAB\R2012a\bin\win32\MATLAB.exe.
For Mac OS X, /Applications/MATLAB_R2012a.app/bin/maci64/MATLAB.
For Linux, /usr/local/MATLAB/R2012a/bin/glnxa64/MATLAB.

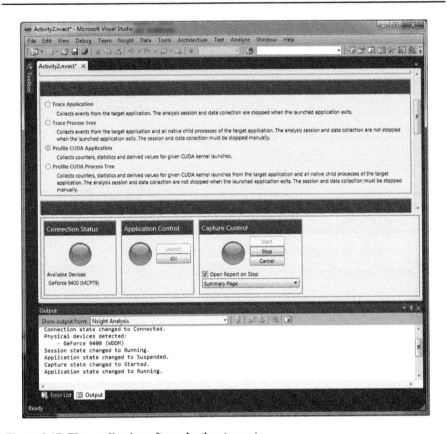

Figure 3.17 The application after selecting `Launch`.

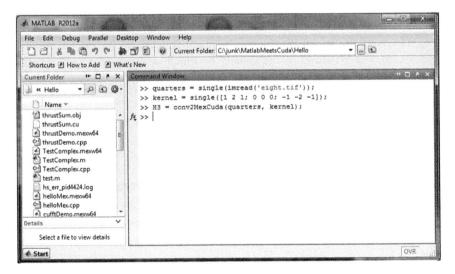

Figure 3.18 Running MATLAB as an application of profiling.

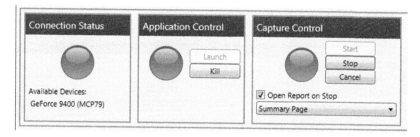

Figure 3.19 Finishing MATLAB profiling within Visual Studio.

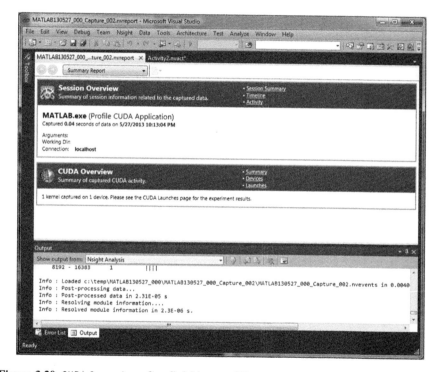

Figure 3.20 CUDA Overview **after finishing profiling.**

After selecting MATLAB executable for your architecture, click on Open in the file selection dialog box. This brings you back to the Create New Session dialog box (Figure 3.29). Click on Next in the Create New Session dialog box. Then, move on to the next step, where you can select executable properties (Figure 3.30). For now, leave all the default values as they are and click on Finish to complete creating a new session. As soon as this is done, NVIDIA

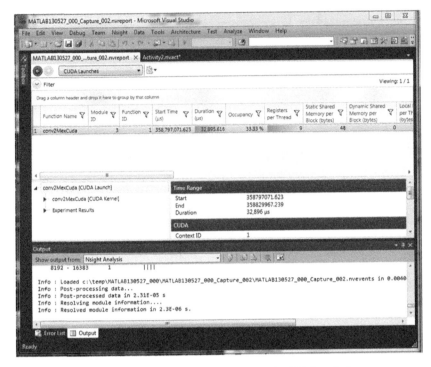

Figure 3.21 CUDA kernel details and time profiles in the Nsight window.

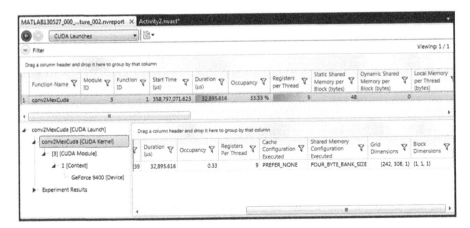

Figure 3.22 More detailed information on CUDA kernel and time profiles in the Nsight window.

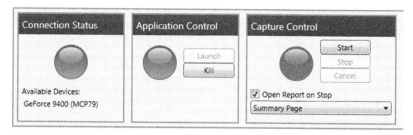

Figure 3.23 `Capture Control` **in Nsight.**

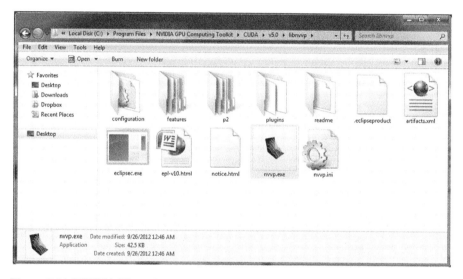

Figure 3.24 NVIDIA Visual Profiler is where CUDA is installed.

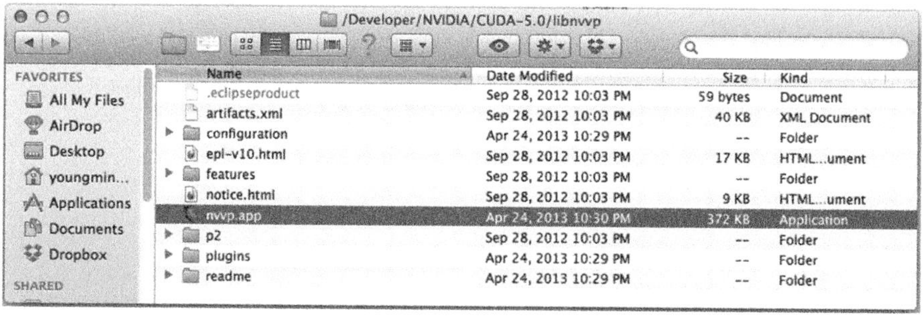

Figure 3.25 NVIDIA Visual Profiler for Mac OS X.

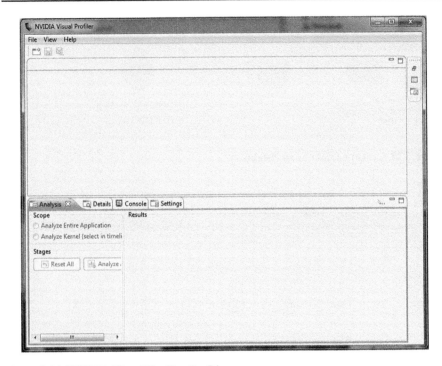

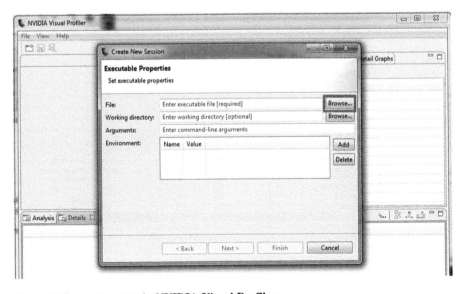

Figure 3.26 NVIDIA Visual Profiler for Linux.

Figure 3.27 New Session **in NVIDIA Visual Profiler.**

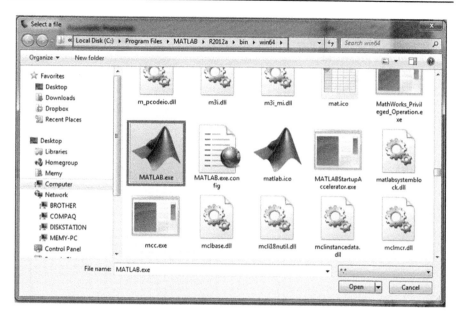

Figure 3.28 Selecting MATLAB executable for NVIDIA Visual Profiler.

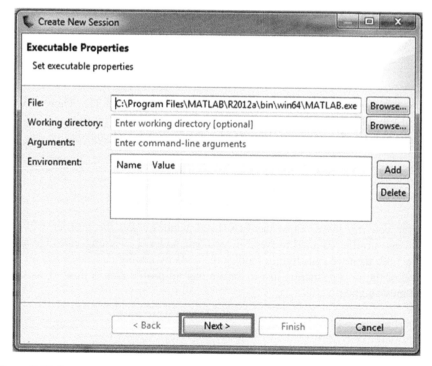

Figure 3.29 Create New Session dialog window.

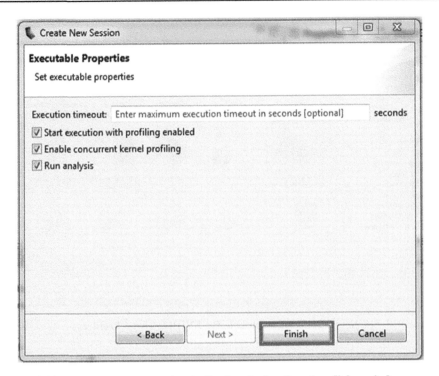

Figure 3.30 `Executable Properties` **in the** `Create New Session` **dialog window.**

Visual Profiler launches the MATLAB executable (Figure 3.31). Then, it waits until MATLAB is closed.

In the MATLAB command Window, run the CUDA-based convolution as

```
>> quaters = (single)imread('eight.tif');
>> mask = single([1 2 1; 0 0 0; −1 −2 −1]);
>> H3 = conv2MexCuda(quarters, mask);
```

After you run these, close the MATLAB window, and the profiler will start generating profile data. However, if you encounter a warning message as in Figure 3.32, then we can slightly modify the code by adding `cudaDeviceReset()` at the end of the `c-mex` function just to ensure that all profile data is flushed, as stated in the message box:

```
#include "mex.h"
#include "conv2Mex.h"
#include <cuda_runtime.h>
```

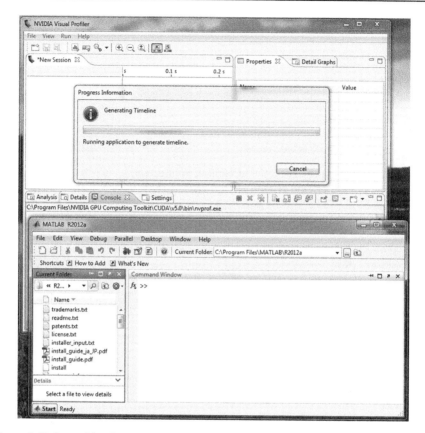

Figure 3.31 Launching MATLAB for profiling in NVIDIA Visual Profiler.

```
void mexFunction(int nlhs, mxArray *plhs[], int nrhs, mxArray *prhs[])
{

  float* out = (float*)mxGetData(plhs[0]);
  conv2Mex(image, out, numRows, numCols, kernel);
  cudaDeviceReset();

}
```

and recompile `c-mex` with an additional include option:

```
>> mex conv2MexCuda.cpp conv2Mex.obj -lcudart -L"C:\Program Files\NVIDIA
GPU Computing Toolkit\CUDA\v5.0\lib\x64" -I"C:\Program Files\NVIDIA GPU
Computing Toolkit\CUDA\v5.0\include"
```

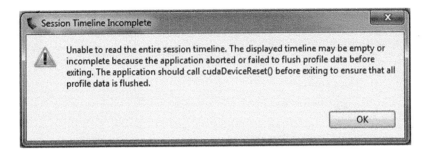

Figure 3.32 Warning message on the incomplete application.

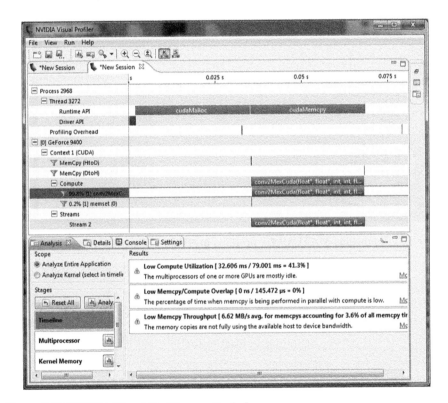

Figure 3.33 NVIDIA Visual Profiler result window.

Rerun the convolution and close the MATLAB window. Now NVIDIA Visual Profiler presents all the information as shown in Figure 3.33.

You will obtain a pretty good idea about how much time each CUDA function took, the utilization of GPUs, and so on. If you click on the Details tab at the bottom, it even shows you thread sizes in the grid and block (Figure 3.34).

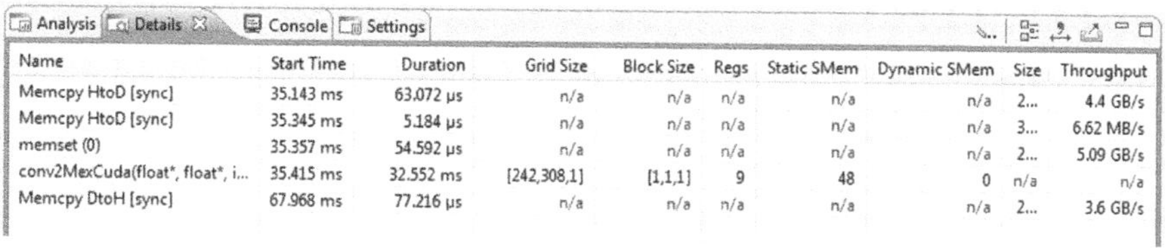

Name	Start Time	Duration	Grid Size	Block Size	Regs	Static SMem	Dynamic SMem	Size	Throughput
Memcpy HtoD [sync]	35.143 ms	63.072 µs	n/a	n/a	n/a	n/a	n/a	2...	4.4 GB/s
Memcpy HtoD [sync]	35.345 ms	5.184 µs	n/a	n/a	n/a	n/a	n/a	3...	6.62 MB/s
memset (0)	35.357 ms	54.592 µs	n/a	n/a	n/a	n/a	n/a	2...	5.09 GB/s
conv2MexCuda(float*, float*, i...	35.415 ms	32.552 ms	[242,308,1]	[1,1,1]	9	48	0	n/a	n/a
Memcpy DtoH [sync]	67.968 ms	77.216 µs	n/a	n/a	n/a	n/a	n/a	2...	3.6 GB/s

Figure 3.34 Timing information from the Details tab in the NVIDIA Visual Profiler.

3.4   Environment Setting for the c-mex Debugger

For debugging C/C++ codes within a c-mex file, we use a debugger other than MATLAB, because MATLAB provides only a m-file editor and m-file-related tools. Still, it is very easy to use other debugger for c-mex files associated with a MATLAB m-file. We used the conv2d3×3.cpp file in previous chapter. This C++ file is called by the convQuarterImageCmex.m file as follows:

The conv2d3×3.cpp File

```
#include "mex.h"
#include "conv2d3x3.h"

void conv2d3x3(float* src, float* dst, int numRows, int numCols, float* mask)
{
  int boundCol = numCols - 1;
  int boundRow = numRows - 1;

  for (int c = 1; c < boundCol; c++)
  {
    for (int r = 1; r < boundRow - 1; r++)
    {
      int dstIndex = c * numRows + r;
      int mskIndex = 8;
      for (int kc = -1; kc < 2; kc++)
      {
        int srcIndex = (c + kc) * numRows + r;
        for (int kr = -1; kr < 2; kr++)
          dst[dstIndex]+ = mask[mskIndex--] * src[srcIndex + kr];
      }
    }
  }
}
```

```
void mexFunction(int nlhs, mxArray *plhs[], int nrhs, mxArray *prhs[])
{
  if (nrhs != 2)
    mexErrMsgTxt("Invaid number of input arguments");

  if (nlhs != 1)
    mexErrMsgTxt("Invalid number of outputs");

  if (!mxIsSingle(prhs[0]) && !mxIsSingle(prhs[1]))
    mexErrMsgTxt("input image and mask type must be single");

  float* image = (float*)mxGetData(prhs[0]);
  float* mask = (float*)mxGetData(prhs[1]);

  int numRows = mxGetM(prhs[0]);
  int numCols = mxGetN(prhs[0]);
  int numKRows = mxGetM(prhs[1]);
  int numKCols = mxGetN(prhs[1]);

  if (numKRows != 3 || numKCols != 3)
    mexErrMsgTxt("Invalid mask size. It must be 3x3");

  plhs[0] = mxCreateNumericMatrix(numRows, numCols, mxSINGLE_CLASS,
  mxREAL);
  float* out = (float*)mxGetData(plhs[0]);

  conv2d3x3(image, out, numRows, numCols, mask);
}
```

The convQuarterImageCmex.m **File**

```
quarters = imread('eight.tif');
imagesc(quarters);
colormap(gray);

mask = [1 2 1; 0 0 0; -1 -2 -1];
single_q = single(quarters);
single_k = single(mask);

H = conv2d3x3(single_q, single_k);   % Call C-Mex file here

figure;
imagesc(H);
colormap(gray);
```

For debugging the `conv2d3×3.cppc-mex` file associated with the `convQuarterImageCmex.m` m-file, we compile the `conv2d3×3.cpp` file in the MATLAB command window with the `−g` option:

```
>> mex −g conv2d3×3.cpp
```

On success, this creates a new file, `conv2d3×3.mexw64` (or `conv2d3×3.mexw32`), in the same directory. Then, start your Visual Studio while maintaining your MATLAB session and select `Attach to Process...` on the `Tools` menu (Figure 3.35).

In the `Attach to Process` box, you see available processes working on your PC (Figure 3.36). If you turn off MATLAB, you cannot find the `MATLAB.exe` in the available process window. Select `MATLAB.exe` and click on `Attach`. Then, Visual Studio shows an empty window with `Solution1 (Running)` at its top, as in Figure 3.37. Open the source `conv2d3×3.cpp` C-Mex file through `File ...` under `Open` on the `File` menu in the Visual Studio (Figure 3.38). Next, set a breakpoint in a line, wherever you want, by clicking the right mouse button (Figure 3.39). Then, you can see the inactivated breakpoint and a warning message. But, you can ignore it (Figure 3.40). Once you correctly set the breakpoint, you can use all the functions on the `Debug` menu with no limitations (Figure 3.41).

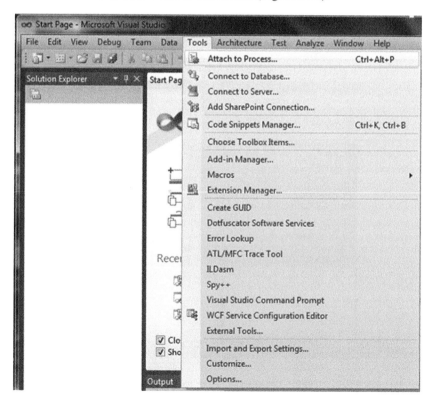

Figure 3.35 `Attach to Process...` **menu for the Microsoft Visual Studio debugger.**

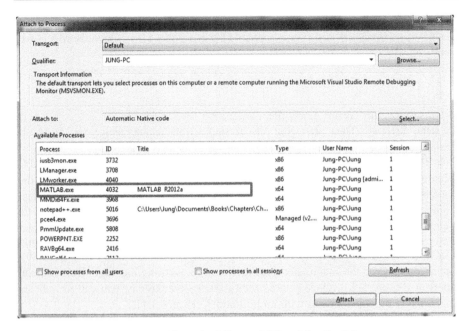

Figure 3.36 Attaching MATLAB to the Microsoft Visual Studio debugger.

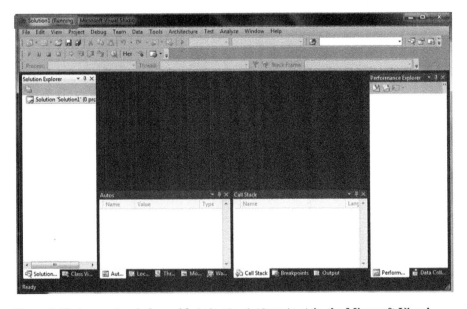

Figure 3.37 An empty window with `Solution1 (Running)` **in the Microsoft Visual Studio debugger.**

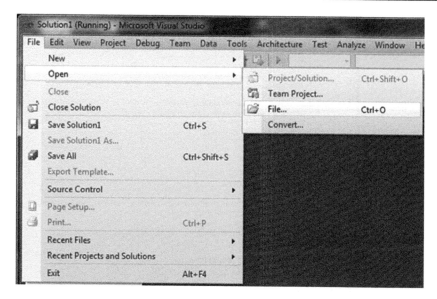

Figure 3.38 Open source code in the Microsoft Visual Studio debugger.

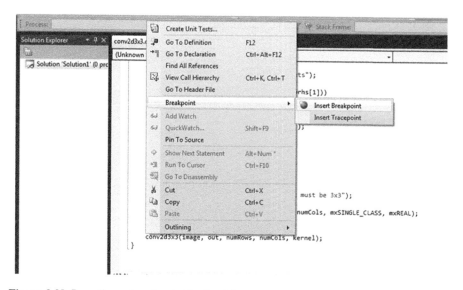

Figure 3.39 Inserting a breakpoint in the debugger.

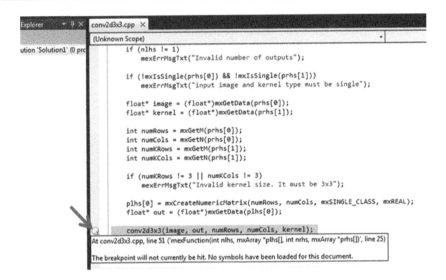

Figure 3.40 An inactivated breakpoint.

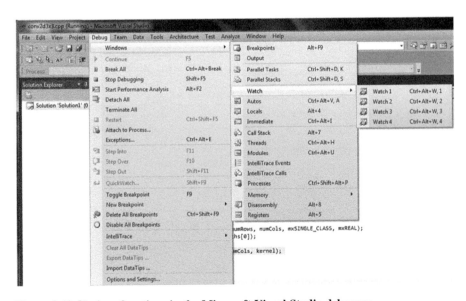

Figure 3.41 Various functions in the Microsoft Visual Studio debugger.

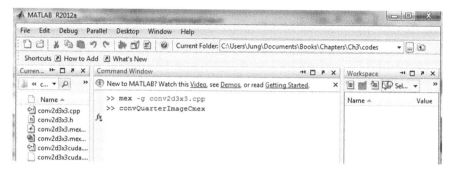

Figure 3.42 Running the MATLAB main module for debugging.

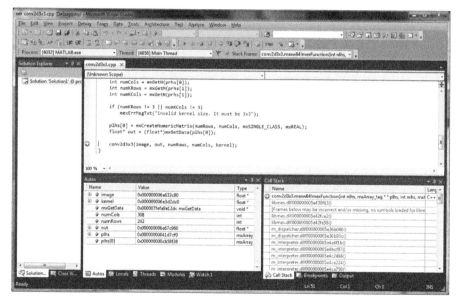

Figure 3.43 Automatically activated debugging mode after running the MATLAB main module.

Now, let us go back to MATLAB. Run the `convQuarterImageCmex.m` file that calls the `conv2d3×3.cpp c-mex` file in the MATLAB command window (Figure 3.42). Then, the debugging mode in Visual Studio is automatically activated, as in Figure 3.43, and the code running stops at the breakpoint you set.

Figure 3.44 Example of debugging tools in the Microsoft Visual Studio debugger with MATLAB.

From now on, you can freely use any debug menu in Visual Studio, such as Step into (F11) and Step over (F10), to track variables change. The boxed Autos in Figure 3.44 shows the example where we see the variable values through navigating by Step into (F11) and Step over (F10).

4 CUDA Coding with c-mex

4.1 Chapter Objectives

When we know the tools we use, we can better utilize them and maximize their usage. When programming c-mex, we must have firm understanding of how data is passed between MATLAB and c-mex functions. Without knowing exactly how this occurs, we most likely will spend our valuable time in vain. Likewise, in CUDA, if we are better equipped with the knowledge of GPU, we then can stretch out its capabilities to their maximum.

In this chapter, we examine the following:

- Memory layouts in c-mex.
- Some basics of GPU hardware.
- Thread grouping for CUDA.

4.2 Memory Layout for c-mex

Understanding the memory layout of input data is crucial to successful c-mex programming. When the input arrays are passed to the gateway routine, mexFunction, we receive an array of input arguments as a parameter, prhs. Each input argument is a pointer to an mxArray. Let us focus our attention on only a 2D numerical array for now, for simplicity. As an example, we use the following MATLAB preprocessor macros and APIs to find out the array information:

mxIsSingle	to determine whether mxArray data represents a single-precision, floating-point numbers.
mxGetM	to get number of rows.
mxGetN	to get number of columns.
mxGetData	to get pointer to data.

Once we get the pointer to our data, we use it as a regular C/C++ pointer for the rest of the part. For this reason, we must have a clear idea how MATLAB data are stored in memory space.

4.2.1 Column-Major Order

All MATLAB data are stored in column major order, following a FORTRAN language convention. In column-major order, each column is juxtaposed one after the other in contiguous memory locations. To have a better understanding of column-major order, consider the following 3×4 matrix:

$$A = \begin{bmatrix} 1 & 2 & 3 & 4 \\ 5 & 6 & 7 & 8 \\ 9 & 10 & 11 & 12 \end{bmatrix}$$

We have three rows and four columns. In our memory space, each element is stored as

Memory offset	0	1	2	3	4	5	6	7	8	9	10	11
Data	1	5	9	2	6	10	3	7	11	4	8	12

In the MATLAB command window, we write this as

```
A = [1 2 3 4; 5 6 7 8; 9 10 11 12]
```

In c-mex, this matrix is passed as one of the arguments in prhs. Assuming this is a first input element, we get this matrix as a single-precision piece of data in the gateway routine, then we obtain a pointer as

```
float* ptr = (float*)mxGetData(prhs[0]);
```

In C/C++, using a *zero-based index*,[1] we access each element using the pointer arithmetic. To get the value, 10, we write

```
ptr[5]
or
*(ptr + 5)
```

In general, to access a 2D matrix element at m-th row and n-th column of $M \times N$ matrix, we calculate the pointer offset and access it as

```
ptr[ (n * M) + m ]
     or
*(ptr + (n * M) + m)
```

For 3D arrays, $M \times N \times P$, we access the m-th row, n-th column, p-th depth as

```
ptr[ ( p * N + n) * M + m ]
     or
*(ptr + ((p * N + n) * M + m))
```

---

[1] Note that every matrix index in MATLAB starts with 1, while a C/C++ array index starts with 0.

As you can see, when accessing data sequentially in memory, the row index varies more quickly than the column index varies.

The following example shows memory locations of 2D array in c-mex. A simple array is passed to our c-mex function, and we just print out each array element and its corresponding memory address in our MATLAB command window for both single-precision and byte data types.

For single-precision data types,

```
// column_major_order_single.cpp

#include "mex.h"

void mexFunction(int nlhs, mxArray *plhs[], int nrhs, const mxArray
*prhs[])
{
    if (!mxIsSingle(prhs[0]))
        mexErrMsgTxt("input vector data type must be single");

    int rows = (int)mxGetM(prhs[0]);
    int cols = (int)mxGetN(prhs[0]);
    int totalElements = rows * cols;

    float* A = (float*)mxGetData(prhs[0]);

    for (int i = 0; i < totalElements; ++i)
        mexPrintf("%f at %p\n", A[i], A + i);
}

>> mex column_major_order_single.cpp
>> column_major_order_single(single([1 2 3 4; 5 6 7 8; 9 10 11 12]))
 1.000000 at 0x128406240
 5.000000 at 0x128406244
 9.000000 at 0x128406248
 2.000000 at 0x12840624c
 6.000000 at 0x128406250
10.000000 at 0x128406254
 3.000000 at 0x128406258
 7.000000 at 0x12840625c
11.000000 at 0x128406260
 4.000000 at 0x128406264
 8.000000 at 0x128406268
12.000000 at 0x12840626c
```

(You can test this with our example column_major_single.m.)

Note that each data element occupies 4 bytes, which is a typical byte size for single-precision data.

The next example demonstrates the single-byte data type, 8-bit unsigned integer:

```cpp
// column_major_order_unit8.cpp

#include "mex.h"

void mexFunction(int nlhs, mxArray *plhs[], int nrhs, const mxArray *prhs[])
{
    if (!mxIsUint8(prhs[0]))
        mexErrMsgTxt("input vector data type must be single");

    int rows = (int)mxGetM(prhs[0]);
    int cols = (int)mxGetN(prhs[0]);
    int totalElements = rows * cols;

    unsigned char* A = (unsigned char*)mxGetData(prhs[0]);

    for (int i = 0; i < totalElements; ++i)
        mexPrintf("%f at %p\n", A[i], A + i);
}
```

```
>> mex column_major_order_uint8.cpp
>> column_major_order_uint8(uint8([1 2 3 4;5 6 7 8; 9 10 11 12]))
 1 at 0x128408960
 5 at 0x128408961
 9 at 0x128408962
 2 at 0x128408963
 6 at 0x128408964
10 at 0x128408965
 3 at 0x128408966
 7 at 0x128408967
11 at 0x128408968
 4 at 0x128408969
 8 at 0x12840896a
12 at 0x12840896b
```

(You can test this with our example `column_major_uint8.m`.)

As you may notice, in the single-precision data type, the memory address jumps 4 bytes, whereas 8-bit unsigned integer increments jump by 1 byte.

4.2.2   *Row-Major Order*

Row-major order is exactly the opposite of column-major order. Consider the same example matrix:

```
a = [1 2 3 4; 5 6 7 8; 9 10 11 12]
```

Memory offset	0	1	2	3	4	5	6	7	8	9	10	11
Data		1	2	3	4	5	6	7	8	9	10	11	12

The value, 10, can be accessed as

```
ptr[9]
or
*(ptr + 9)
```

For 2D arrays, the element at m-th row and n-th column of an $M \times N$ matrix is accessed as

```
ptr[ ( m * N ) + n ]
or
*(ptr + (m * N) + n)
```

and for a 3D array, the element at m-th row, n-th column, and p-th depth of an $M \times N \times P$ array is accessed as

```
ptr[ ( p * M + m ) * N + n ]
or
*(ptr + (p * M + m) * N + n)
```

Here, the column index varies more quickly than the row index varies.

When we mingle C/C++ and MATLAB, we need to be very mindful about how input data are stored and indexed. For instance, many C/C++ image libraries store images in row-major order while data passed from MATLAB is in column-major order. In CUDA, threads are accessed based on row-major order. Another important thing we must keep in mind is the indexing scheme. C/C++ uses a zero-based index, while MATLAB accesses the array element using a one-based index.

4.2.3   Memory Layout for Complex Numbers in c-mex

Often, we face complex numbers in many aspects. Especially in image or signal processing, our data are either complex or real numbers or both. Through algorithms, they change from real to complex numbers or from complex to real numbers. Therefore, we want to make sure that we understand how MATLAB packs our complex number in memory space when we receive it from or pass it back to MATLAB in our c-mex function.

When storing a complex number in memory, we can put the real part first then the imaginary part or vice versa. Typically, a complex number is stored with real part first. For instance, a complex number, $C = 3 + 7i$, is stored as

Memory offset	0	1
Data	3	7

Let us quickly experiment to see how MATLAB stores our complex number:

```
// TestComplex1.cpp

#include "mex.h"

void mexFunction(int nlhs, mxArray *plhs[], int nrhs, const mxArray *prhs[])
{
    if (!mxIsComplex(prhs[0]))
        mexErrMsgTxt("input data must be complex");
    if (!mxIsSingle(prhs[0]))
        mexErrMsgTxt("input data must be single");

    float* pReal = (float*)mxGetPr(prhs[0]);
    float* pImag = (float*)mxGetPi(prhs[0]);

    mexPrintf("%p: %f\n", pReal, *pReal);
    mexPrintf("%p: %f\n", pImag, *pImag);
}
```

Compile this test c-mex code and run with a sample number.

```
>> mex TestComplex1.cpp
>> TestComplex1(single(4 + 5i))
000000006F2FBB80: 4.000000
000000006F2FC940: 5.000000
```

(You can test this with our example TestComplex_first.m.)

The real part of our sample number is stored at 0x6F2FBB80, while the imaginary part of the number is at 0x6F2FC940. As you can see, they are not next to each other. As a matter of fact, MATLAB stores complex numbers in two separate arrays. For this reason, it provides two functions to access these arrays. Using mxGetPr(...) gives us the pointer to the array for the real number, while mxGetPi(...) is for the imaginary number. We can modify a little bit our test program and see what happens when our data are an array of complex numbers:

```
#include "mex.h"

void mexFunction(int nlhs, mxArray *plhs[], int nrhs, const mxArray *prhs[])
{
    if (!mxIsComplex(prhs[0]))
        mexErrMsgTxt("input data must be complex");
    if (!mxIsSingle(prhs[0]))
        mexErrMsgTxt("input data must be single");

    float* pReal = (float*)mxGetPr(prhs[0]);
    float* pImag = (float*)mxGetPi(prhs[0]);
    int m = (int)mxGetM(prhs[0]);
```

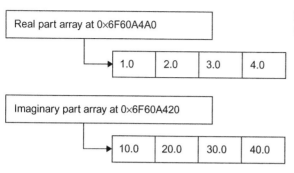

Figure 4.1 Complex arrays in C-MEX.

```
int n = (int)mxGetN(prhs[0]);
int numElems = (m >= n) ? m : n;

for (int i = 0; i < numElems; ++i, ++pReal, ++pImag)
{
    mexPrintf("Real = %f @%p\t", *pReal, pReal + i);
    mexPrintf("Imag = %f @%p\n", *pImag, pImag + i);
}
}
```

When compiled and run with a sample complex array, we get data as follows:

```
>> mex TestComplex.cpp
>> TestComplex(single([1 + 10i, 2 + 20i, 3 + 30i, 4 + 40i]))
Real = 1.000000 @000000006F60A4A0  Imag = 10.000000 @000000006F60A420
Real = 2.000000 @000000006F60A4A8  Imag = 20.000000 @000000006F60A428
Real = 3.000000 @000000006F60A4B0  Imag = 30.000000 @000000006F60A430
Real = 4.000000 @000000006F60A4B8  Imag = 40.000000 @000000006F60A438
```

(You can test this with our example TestComplex_second.m.)

We see clearly two different arrays for each part of complex number (Figure 4.1).

If our input data are two-dimensional complex numbers, we receive two 2D arrays for each part: a 2D array of the real part and a 2D array of the imaginary part. And remember that they are column-major ordered.

4.3   Logical Programming Model

When we write a CUDA program (.cu file), we use special syntax, $<<< \cdots >>>$, on functions that need to be run on the GPU. In Chapter 2, we had the example AddVectors.cu.

| | ```
// AddVectors.cu in Chapter 2 with C-mex
#include "AddVectors.h"
``` |
| Kernel | ```
__global__ void addVectorsKernel(float* A, float* B, float* C, int size)
{
    int i = blockIdx.x;
    if (i >= size)
        return;

    C[i] = A[i] + B[i];
}
``` |
| Code for the Host (CPU) | ```
void addVectors(float* A, float* B, float* C, int size)
{
    float *devPtrA = 0, *devPtrB = 0, *devPtrC = 0;

    cudaMalloc(&devPtrA, sizeof(float) * size);
    cudaMalloc(&devPtrB, sizeof(float) * size);
    cudaMalloc(&devPtrC, sizeof(float) * size);

    cudaMemcpy(devPtrA, A, sizeof(float) * size, cudaMemcpyHostToDevice);
    cudaMemcpy(devPtrB, B, sizeof(float) * size, cudaMemcpyHostToDevice);
``` |
| Calling kernel | ```
    addVectorsKernel <<< size, 1 >>> (devPtrA, devPtrB, devPtrC, size);
``` |
| | ```
    cudaMemcpy(C, devPtrC, sizeof(float) * size, cudaMemcpyDeviceToHost);

    cudaFree(devPtrA);
    cudaFree(devPtrB);
    cudaFree(devPtrC);
}
``` |

The section of code that runs on GPU is called a *kernel*. When we define a kernel, we have to explicitly specify the total number of threads in which that kernel will be run. Basically, the same kernel will be run in parallel in multiple threads. We tell the GPU how many threads we would like to run in parallel. Depending on how many parallel jobs we need, we figure out how many threads are needed. Those threads are then logically grouped into a block. A group of blocks composes a grid. This logical grouping information is passed to the GPU inside the $<<< \cdots >>>$:

```
Kernel_Function <<< gridSize, blockSize >>> (parameter1, parameter2,....)
```

A grid size is specified by its number of blocks. A block size is specified by its number of threads. For instance, if the grid size is 10, then there are 10 blocks in a grid. If the block size is 5, then there are 5 threads in a block. Therefore, if we say that a grid size is 10 and a block size is 5, then it means there are 50 threads in total.

Let us compare a CPU code and a GPU code. In the CPU code, the additions in operation_at_cpu(..) occur by iteration within a loop. The iteration conditions are explicitly set by the serial setting (i = 0; i < N; i++) in a for-loop. The
```

corresponding part in GPU code performs the additions by a number of threads in parallel. The parallelization conditions are set by the combination of CUDA's built-in device variables (blockDim, blockIdx and threadIdx). The device variables such as blockDim, blockIdx, and threadIdx are limited by the gridSize and blockSize inside the <<<...>>> when we call the kernel. The actual parallel running is automatically activated by the GPU device when it is called. We deal with the blockDim, blockIdx and threadIdx in Section 4.5:

CPU code	GPU code
``void operation_at_cpu(float *a,
float val,
int N)
{
for (int i = 0; i < N; i++){
a[i] = a[i] + val;
}
}```	```__global__ void operation_at_gpu(float *a,
float val,
int N)
{
int i = blockIdx.x * blockDim.x +
threadIdx.x;
if (i < N){
a[i] = a[i] + val;
}
}```
``void mexFunction(...)
{
...
operation_at_cpu(a, val, N);
}```	```void mexFunction(...)
{
...
dim3 blockSize (number_Of_Threads);
dim3 gridSize(ceil(N / (float)
number_Of_Threads));
operation_at_gpu<<<gridSize,
blockSize>>>(a, val, N);
}```

In CUDA, it is our responsibility to tell GPU how many threads we need to run in parallel and how they are logically grouped into blocks and grids.

Suppose we have a simple matrix addition of size 3×4:

$$A = \begin{bmatrix} a & b & c & d \\ e & f & g & h \\ i & j & k & l \end{bmatrix}, \quad B = \begin{bmatrix} m & n & o & p \\ q & r & s & t \\ u & v & w & x \end{bmatrix}$$

$$A + B = \begin{bmatrix} a+m & b+n & c+o & d+p \\ e+q & f+r & g+s & h+t \\ i+u & j+v & k+w & l+x \end{bmatrix}$$

We can easily identify 12 independent additions that can be run in parallel. We can tell GPU in various ways how to group these threads in terms of grids and blocks (Figure 4.2).

4.3.1 Logical Grouping 1

These 12 independent additions can be grouped individually so that there are 12 blocks in a grid and each block with one thread only (Figure 4.3).

4.3.2 Logical Grouping 2

Another way of grouping these threads would be 6 blocks in a grid and two threads per block (Figure 4.4).

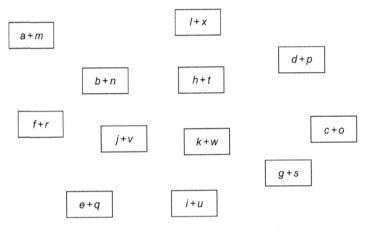

Figure 4.2 Twelve independent additions that can run in parallel.

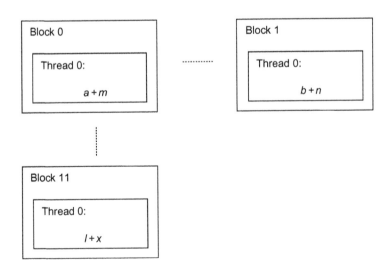

Figure 4.3 Logical grouping with a single thread per block.

4.3.3 Logical Grouping 3

CUDA also provides ways to specify the groupings in two or three dimensions. We could group these threads into 2×2 blocks per grid and 2×3 threads per block. This creates 24 threads in total, which is twice as many threads as we need (Figure 4.5).

Notice that some blocks have empty threads and do not need to do any calculation. We tell GPU that there are 24 threads but only 12 threads are the real ones. In our kernel, we skip these empty threads by checking its thread index.

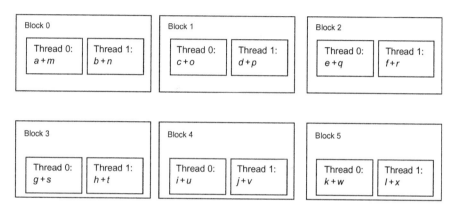

Figure 4.4 Logical grouping with two threads per block.

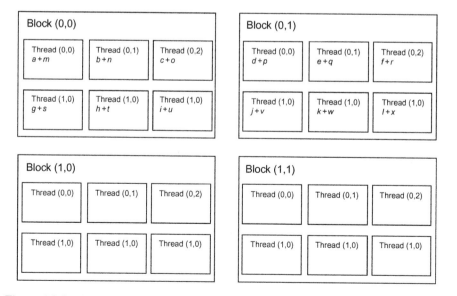

Figure 4.5 Logical grouping in two dimensions.

Naturally, you ask how we should group them. To answer this question, let us briefly take a look at some details of GPU hardware.

4.4   Tidbits of GPU

Based on the time performance profile we measured, the CUDA counterpart of the 2D convolution algorithm in Chapter 2 is very disappointing. Let us sit back and think a bit about what went wrong with our naïve approach to CUDA programming. As you might already know, the key to success in CUDA programming is very closely related to understanding GPU architecture. Let us briefly review how GPU is designed, so that we are better equipped with our tools.

4.4.1   Data Parallelism

Unlike CPU, GPU has been designed with the goal in mind for high throughput, so that it can process, for example, a same triangular mesh operation on millions of pixels for a given frame in graphics. As a matter of fact, GPU runs thousands of threads concurrently. This is a whole lot of threads compared to CPU, and it opens new ways for parallel processing number crunching activities. For this reason, when we can achieve *data parallelism*, GPU fits in naturally for its capability to run thousands of threads. Achieving data parallelism should be the foremost step. In our example of image convolution, each pixel could be independently processed in parallel with other pixels. If we have 10×10 size of image, we could assign each pixel to each thread and have all the 100 threads processed at the same time.

On hardware side, GPU uses a *single instruction, multiple data* (SIMD) model, where one single instruction can run on multiple different data. Compared to CPU, GPU has many more cores and registers to handle thousands of lightweight threads. GPU also schedules all those threads at the hardware level. Context switching requires almost zero overhead, whereas context switching in CPU is costly.

4.4.2   Streaming Processor

A fundamental unit of GPU is a *streaming processor* (SP). This provides the capability to fetch a single instruction from memory and carry it out on different data sets in parallel. Each GPU contains tens to hundreds of SPs in a single piece of hardware.

4.4.3   Steaming Multiprocessor

Each SP is then grouped as a *streaming multiprocessor* (SM). The SM provides thousands of registers, a thread scheduler, and shared memory for the group of SPs. Equipped with those components in its silicon backyard and a number of SPs, an SM manages thread scheduling, context switching, and data fetching and caching for the blocks of threads assigned to it.

4.4.4 Warp

The SM especially schedules threads in groups of 32 parallel threads called, *warp*. All threads in the same warp share a single instruction fetch from memory. All threads in each warp march at the same pace. A SM processes the next warp only when all the threads in the current warp finish their jobs. For instance, if one thread takes 10 seconds to finish its job while the rest of the threads take 1 second, the SM hase to wait 9 more seconds until it is ready to move to the next warp.

Overall, GPU receives a number of grids. Blocks from grids are then assigned to SMs. The SM assigns threads to SPs and manages them in a unit called a *warp*, as illustrated in Figures 4.6 and 4.7. Threads are processed in a group called a *warp*. The actual physical number of concurrent threads is limited by the number of SPs. The SM is responsible for scheduling the threads in warps.

4.4.5 Memory

Three major types of memory spaces are available. The first type of memory is *global* memory. This is the memory space accessible by both GPU and CPU. Usually, on CPU side, we first allocate on GPU using this global memory and copy our data from CPU side of memory to here. Also, this space is accessible to all grids and subsequently to all threads. Specifically, we use CUDA runtime API calls like `cudaMalloc` and `cudaMemcpy` to allocate and to copy data from GPU to CPU and vice versa.

The second type of memory is *shared* memory. Not all threads have access to this. Only the threads in the same block can access it. However, access time is much faster than that of global memory. We can allocate this type of memory using a keyword, `__shared__`. If values need to and can be shared within a block of threads, putting them for these threads in shared memory greatly reduces the memory access time overhead.

The third type is a memory space available only to each thread. It is the *per-thread local* memory using registers. Unlike CPU, GPU has thousands of registers per SM. They are dedicated for each thread and provide almost zero overhead thread context switching. Declaring data as a local variable in the kernel lets us use registers. However, the capacity of local memory in a kernel is very limited, and for this reason, we must ensure that we do not abuse it with excessive usage. When registers cannot accommodate the requested amount, it will place them at local memory that is local to the thread but does not give us as fast access time as registers.

Figure 4.8 shows an overview of memory in GPU.

4.5 Analyzing Our First Naïve Approach

Our first CUDA implementation of two-dimensional convolution turned out to be much slower than the native MATLAB function `conv2`. Equipped with knowledge

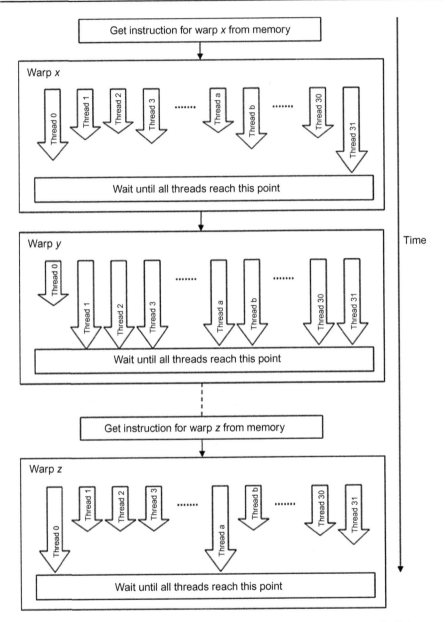

Figure 4.6 GPU gets one instruction for the threads in a warp. It waits until all the threads in the same warp complete the instruction, then moves on to the next warp.

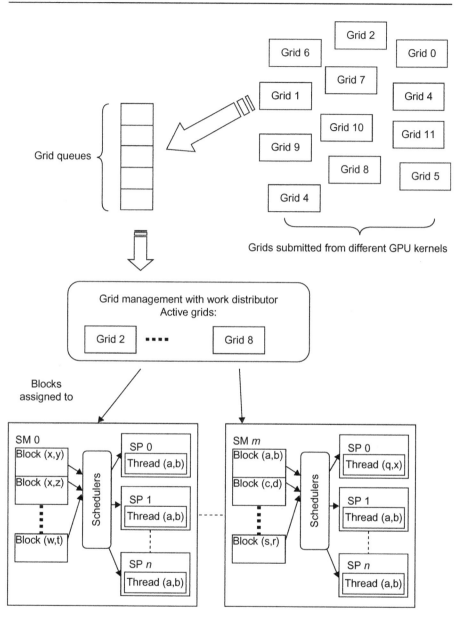

Figure 4.7 How grids, blocks and threads are routed in GPU.

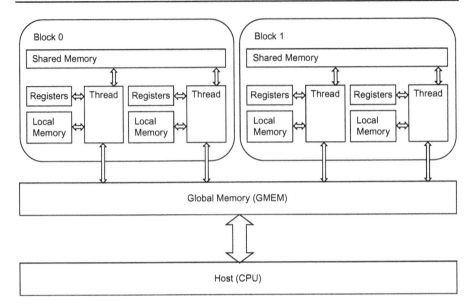

Figure 4.8 High-level overview of memory space.

of the inside of GPU, we are ready to tackle the problem. In our first approach, we mindlessly assigned a thread in each block and each block in one grid. This gave us the total number of threads we needed to run. We declared the kernel as

```
dim gridSize(numRows, numCols)
conv2MexCuda <<<gridSize, 1>>>
```

With this declaration, there are numRows × numCols blocks and each block contains one thread. Thus, we have the total of numRows × numCols threads. Remember, in MATLAB, data are passed to us in column-major order. So we assigned numRows first then numCols. In Figure 4.9, as we move horizontally, the first index of the block maps to the number of rows, while the second index maps to the number of columns. Each thread in a block handles each pixel in our input image.

Blocks of each grid are scheduled to SMs, and each SM schedules threads in the warp. When a SM processes threads, only one thread will run in each warp. But, a SM can handle 32 threads in a warp. Since there is only one thread in a warp, most of SPs in SMs sit idle. We heavily under-utilize GPU resources.

Let us run NVIDIA Visual Profiler once again to see how it performs when we assign each thread to each block (Figure 4.10).

As we can see in the Details tab, the kernel itself takes about 33 msec when our grid size is the same as the image size. Each thread handles each pixel. With the naïve approach, we even make our CUDA-based convolution worse than the MATLAB native function. Therefore, in this case, we gain no advantage from

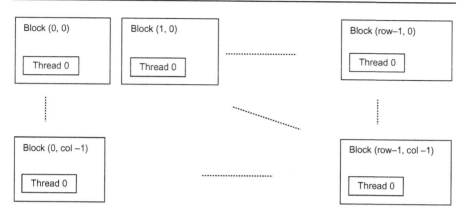

Figure 4.9 A single thread is assigned for each pixel per block.

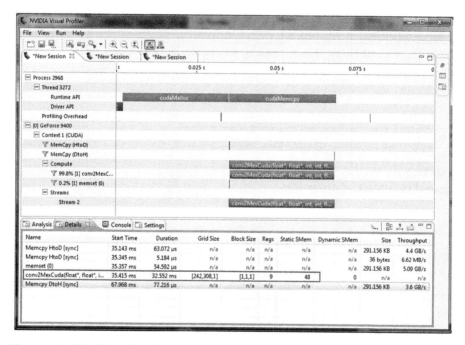

Figure 4.10 The Visual Profiler with the naïve approach.

GPU acceleration. In the next section, we try to resize our grids and blocks so that we can utilize rest of the threads in the warp in the SM.

4.5.1 Optimization A: Thread Blocks

In this optimization step, we try to optimize by resizing the grid and block. First, we decide a block size to be 16×16. This gives us a total of 256 threads in a block, and obviously, it is greater than the warp size. Based on this block size and the image size, we determine the grid size. By having more threads in a block, we can utilize rest of the threads in the block, whereas in the naïve approach, we utilize only one thread per block.

Each of our new blocks consists of 256 threads arranged two-dimensionally as Figure 4.11. Each thread in the block processes each pixel in the input image. Figure 4.12 shows the original input image from MATLAB.

For illustration purpose, let us first transpose the input image, since the input image coming from MATLAB is in column-major order and it is stored in row-major order in C/C++ and CUDA. Then, we put our blocks on top of it to see how the original image is divided into blocks and threads (Figure 4.13).

Given the size of the input image and the block size, we can determine how many blocks fit both horizontally and vertically. Note that the total area covered by the blocks is larger than the input image. This is because all the blocks should be

0,0	1,0	2,0	3,0	4,0	5,0	6,0	7,0	....	14,0	15,0
0,1	1,1	2,1	3,1	4,1	5,1	6,1	7,1	....	14,1	15,1
0,2	1,2	2,2	3,2	4,2	5,2	6,2	7,2	....	14,2	15,2

| 0,14 | 1,14 | 2,14 | 3,14 | 4,14 | 5,14 | 6,14 | 7,14 | .... | 14,14 | 15,14 |
| 0,15 | 1,15 | 2,15 | 3,15 | 4,15 | 5,15 | 6,15 | 7,15 | .... | 14,15 | 15,15 |

Figure 4.11 A block of size 16 × 16.

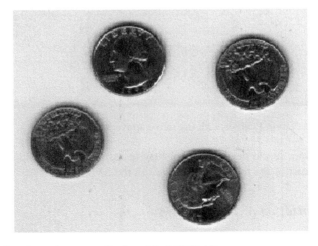

Figure 4.12 The input image as displayed in MATLAB.

the same size while the image size may not be in multiples of our block size. Therefore, we make the area covered by blocks larger than the image size.

```
dim3 blockSize(16, 16);
dim3 gridSize((numRows +15) / blockSize.x, (numCols +15) / blockSize.y);
```

This code snippet shows how we calculate the smallest number that is a multiple of 16 and equal to or greater than the image size. We introduce two variables, blockSize and gridSize, of dim3 type.

Now, the each pixel in the image can be accessed by the thread index and block sizes as we assign each pixel to each thread. When the CUDA kernel is called, we can access information about which thread and where in the block we are processing. Inside the kernel, we use the following global variables from CUDA to find out the exact pixel locations.

- blockDim: the block size (it is 16 × 16 in our case).
- blockIdx: the index of the block in a grid.
- threadIdx: thread index in a block.

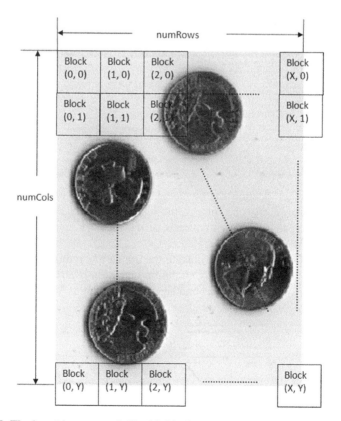

Figure 4.13 The input image overlaid with blocks.

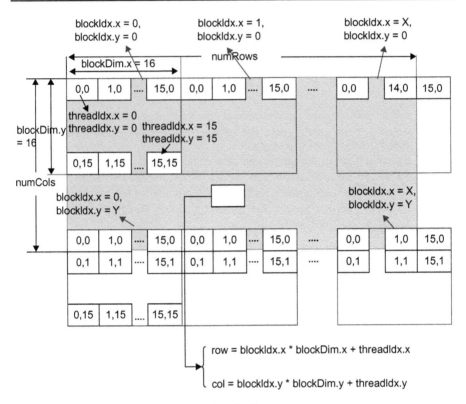

Figure 4.14 Blocks and threads assigned to the image.

Each specific pixel location can be calculated using these variables as shown in Figure 4.14. Note again that the rows of the image are presented horizontally while the columns are presented vertically, because the memory layout of our image in MATLAB is in column-major order.

Those threads assigned to pixels outside the image just return without doing any processing. The border area of our convolution operation is also ignored. Inside the kernel, we check if it is outside the boundary or the border as

```
int row = blockIdx.x * blockDim.x + threadIdx.x;
if (row < 1 || row > numRows − 1)
    return;

int col = blockIdx.y * blockDim.y + threadIdx.y;
if (col < 1 || col > numCols − 1)
    return;
```

Let us now create a new file and save it as conv2MexOptA.cu.

```
#include "conv2Mex.h"
__global__ void conv2MexCuda(float* src,
                             float* dst,
                             int numRows,
                             int numCols,
                             float* mask)
{
    int row = blockIdx.x * blockDim.x + threadIdx.x;
    if (row < 1 || row > numRows - 1)
        return;

    int col = blockIdx.y * blockDim.y + threadIdx.y;
    if (col < 1 || col > numCols - 1)
        return;

    int dstIndex = col * numRows + row;
    dst[dstIndex] = 0;
    int mskIndex = 3 * 3 - 1;
    for (int kc = -1; kc < 2; kc++)
    {
        int srcIndex = (col + kc) * numRows + row;
        for (int kr = -1; kr < 2; kr++)
        {
            dst[dstIndex] + = mask[mskIndex--] * src[srcIndex + kr];
        }
    }
}

void conv2Mex(float* src, float* dst, int numRows, int numCols, float* msk)
{
    int totalPixels = numRows * numCols;
    float *deviceSrc, *deviceMsk, *deviceDst;

    cudaMalloc(&deviceSrc, sizeof(float) * totalPixels);
    cudaMalloc(&deviceDst, sizeof(float) * totalPixels);
    cudaMalloc(&deviceMsk, sizeof(float) * 3 * 3);

    cudaMemcpy(deviceSrc, src, sizeof(float) * totalPixels,
    cudaMemcpyHostToDevice);
    cudaMemcpy(deviceMsk, msk, sizeof(float) * 3 * 3,
    cudaMemcpyHostToDevice);
    cudaMemset(deviceDst, 0, sizeof(float) * totalPixels);

    dim3 blockSize(16, 16);
    dim3 gridSize((numRows + 15) / blockSize.x, (numCols + 15) / blockSize.y);
    conv2MexCuda <<< gridSize, blockSize >>> (deviceSrc,
                                              deviceDst,
```

```
                                          numRows,
                                          numCols,
                                          deviceMsk);

    cudaMemcpy(dst, deviceDst, sizeof(float) * totalPixels,
    cudaMemcpyDeviceToHost);

    cudaFree(deviceSrc);
    cudaFree(deviceDst);
    cudaFree(deviceMsk);
}
```

In this example code, we create a new kernel and call it as folows:

```
conv2MexCuda <<< gridSize, blockSize >>> (deviceSrc,
                                          deviceDst,
                                          numRows,
                                          numCols,
                                          deviceMsk);
```

We passed new block and thread sizes to our kernel. Instead of processing each pixel at each block, we regrouped into 16 × 16 thread blocks. But, each thread performed 3 × 3 mask multiplication and addition as before.

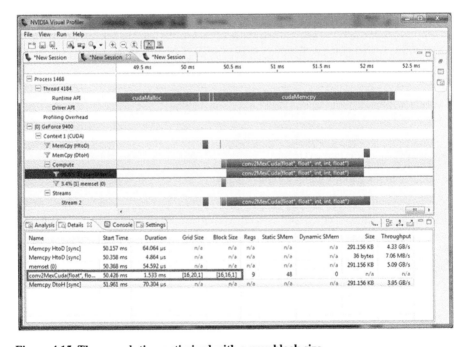

Figure 4.15 The convolution optimized with a new block size.

Then, we profiled this new approach with the NVIDIA Visual Profiler. We now see huge improvement over our first naïve approach. We achieved a time profile more than 30 times faster (Figure 4.15).

4.5.2 Optimization B

In this optimization step, we leave everything intact but introduce a shared memory in the CUDA kernel. When calculating convolution at each pixel, we use the same nine mask values over and over again. We query these values from the global memory every time we apply the mask. Getting these values from the GPU global memory is costly compared to getting them from a shared memory or registers. So, this motivates us to put the mask values in the shared memory and use them to minimize the global memory access overhead.

Inside our kernel, we declare

```
__shared__ float sharedMask[9];
```

This creates a shared memory in GPU, and it is shared by all the threads in a block. So, all 256 threads in a block use this shared memory. We then use the first nine threads to fill the shared memory with the mask values. After we prepare our shared memory with the convolution mask values, we process the actual calculation. To ensure that no other thread continues calculation before we fill in the shared memory, we call

```
__syncthreads();
```

Now, we create and save a new file, convMexOptB.cu, as follows:

```
#include "conv2Mex.h"

__global__ void conv2MexCuda(float* src,
                             float* dst,
                             int numRows,
                             int numCols,
                             float* mask)
{
    int row = blockIdx.x * blockDim.x + threadIdx.x;
    int col = blockIdx.y * blockDim.y + threadIdx.y;

    if (row < 1 || row > numRows - 1 || col < 1 || col > numCols - 1)
        return;

    __shared__ float sharedMask[9];
    if (threadIdx.x < 9)
    {
        sharedMask[threadIdx.x] = mask[threadIdx.x];
    }
```

```
    __syncthreads();

    int dstIndex = col * numRows + row;
    dst[dstIndex] = 0;
    int mskIndex = 8;
    for (int kc = -1; kc < 2; kc++)
    {
        int srcIndex = (col + kc) * numRows + row;
        for (int kr = -1; kr < 2; kr++)
        {
            dst[dstIndex] + = sharedMask[mskIndex--] * src[srcIndex + kr];
        }
    }
}

void conv2Mex(float* src, float* dst, int numRows, int numCols, float* msk)
{
    int totalPixels = numRows * numCols;
    float *deviceSrc, *deviceMsk, *deviceDst;

    cudaMalloc(&deviceSrc, sizeof(float) * totalPixels);
    cudaMalloc(&deviceDst, sizeof(float) * totalPixels);
    cudaMalloc(&deviceMsk, sizeof(float) * 3 * 3);

    cudaMemcpy(deviceSrc, src, sizeof(float) * totalPixels,
    cudaMemcpyHostToDevice);
    cudaMemcpy(deviceMsk, msk, sizeof(float) * 3 * 3,
    cudaMemcpyHostToDevice);
    cudaMemset(deviceDst, 0, sizeof(float) * totalPixels);

    const int size = 16;
    dim3 blockSize(size, size);
    dim3 gridSize((numRows + size - 1) / blockSize.x,
                  (numCols + size - 1) / blockSize.y);

    conv2MexCuda <<< gridSize, blockSize >>> (deviceSrc,
                                              deviceDst,
                                              numRows,
                                              numCols,
                                              deviceMsk);

    cudaMemcpy(dst, deviceDst, sizeof(float) * totalPixels,
    cudaMemcpyDeviceToHost);

    cudaFree(deviceSrc);
    cudaFree(deviceDst);
    cudaFree(deviceMsk);
}
```

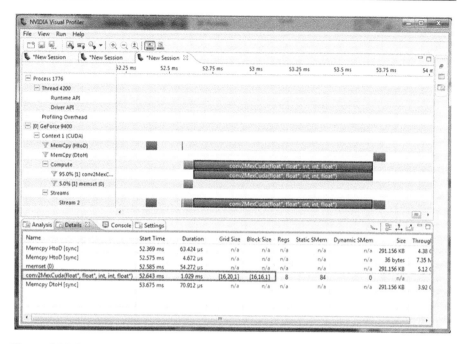

Figure 4.16 Optimization with shared memory.

We introduced the shared memory. Since values in the kernel are the same for all pixels, we put the kernel values in the shared memory, so that 16×16 threads can share the same kernel values from the L1 cache instead of fetching the values from the global memory.

We compile the preceding and run the code using the NVIDIA Visual Profiler. We now get the result shown in Figure 4.16. We achieved a little improvement over our first optimization step.

4.5.3 Conclusion

We see now that the overall performance did improve very much from our very first naïve method. But, we are still behind the native MATLAB function conv2 when considering the end-to-end function call. What makes us slower overall? Remember, we do cudaMemcpy whenever we call our function. We copy values to and from host memory to GPU device memory every time we invoke our method. This adds a lot of overhead, while the actual convolution inside GPU is much faster. So, we may want to do as much computation as possible inside GPU, minimizing data transfer between the host and the device.

5 MATLAB and Parallel Computing Toolbox

5.1 Chapter Objectives

MATLAB provides useful tools for parallel processing from the Parallel Computing Toolbox. The toolbox provides diverse methods for parallel processing, such as multiple computers working via a network, several cores in multicore machines, cluster computing as well as GPU parallel processing. Within the scope of this book, we focus more on GPU part of the Parallel Computing Toolbox. One of good things in the toolbox is that we can take advantage of GPUs without explicit CUDA programming or c-mex programming. However, this comes with a heavy price tag for us to install the Parallel Computing Toolbox. This chapter discusses

- GPU processing for built-in MATLAB functions.
- GPU processing for non-built-in MATLAB functions.
- Parallel task processing.
- Parallel data processing.
- The direct use of CUDA files without c-mex.

5.2 GPU Processing for Built-in MATLAB Functions

The MATLAB Parallel Computing Toolbox supports only a CUDA 1.3 version or later. To check your CUDA version and other GPU related information, use the gpuDevice command in the MATLAB command window, as in Figure 5.1.

In Figure 5.1, Name shows the hardware (H/W) GPU card installed in your computer, and ComputeCapability indicates the software (S/W) CUDA library version (CUDA version 3.0 in this example) installed in your system. If you cannot get information from the gpuDevice command, check your H/W GPU status or S/W CUDA installation before going to the next step.

Now, let us start to prepare data for the GPU in MATLAB. As mentioned in Chapter 3, when we use GPU for our computation, we always consider the data-transfer between the host (CPU and main memory) and the device (GPU and GPU

```
>> gpuDevice

ans =

CUDADevice with properties:

              Name: 'GeForce GT 640M LE'
             Index: 1
 ComputeCapability: '3.0'
     SupportsDouble: 1
     DriverVersion: 5
    ToolkitVersion: 5
 MaxThreadsPerBlock: 1024
  MaxShmemPerBlock: 49152
 MaxThreadBlockSize: [1024 1024 64]
       MaxGridSize: [2.1475e+09 65535 65535]
         SIMDWidth: 32
       TotalMemory: 1.0737e+09
        FreeMemory: 972619776
 MultiprocessorCount: 2
      ClockRateKHz: 570000
       ComputeMode: 'Default'
 GPUOverlapsTransfers: 1
 KernelExecutionTimeout: 1
   CanMapHostMemory: 1
    DeviceSupported: 1
     DeviceSelected: 1
```

Figure 5.1 GPU information brought by the gpuDevice command.

memory), because the GPU is attached to a CPU via the PCI bus. To transfer data from the MATLAB workspace (which is on the main memory) to the GPU device memory, we use the gpuArray command as follows:

```
%test_gpuArray.m

A = 1:0.01:50000;                     % About 5 million elements

A_gpu = gpuArray(A);                  % transfer data to GPU device memory

tic; B = fft(A); toc                  % FFT on CPU

tic; B_gpu = fft(A_gpu); toc          % FFT on GPU

B_from_gpu = gather(B_gpu);           % return data back to MATLAB workspace
```

In this example, the vector A is transferred to the GPU device memory through the gpuArray command. You can directly provide the data to the GPU like this:

```
>> A_gpu = gpuArray(1:0.01:50000);
```

Then, fft is computed on both the CPU and GPU. Note that we use the same fft function name for both the CPU version and GPU version, but because of different input data (A is data on the main memory while A_gpu is data on the GPU memory), the computations run on either the CPU or GPU. We can check this difference in the the MATLAB workspace window, as in Figure 5.2.

To return data back from the GPU device memory to the MATLAB workspace, we use the gather command. The results of the preceding code look as follows:

```
>> test_gpuArray
Elapsed time is 1.725417 seconds.
Elapsed time is 0.644574 seconds.
```

In this example, with about 5 million pieces of data, the elapsed time on the GPU is about one third of the elapsed time on the CPU, which makes us excited. But let us look at this code:

```
%test_gpuArray_small.m

A = 1:2:500;                         % data size = 250

A_gpu = gpuArray(A);                 % transfer to GPU device memory

tic;  B = fft(A);  toc

tic;  B_gpu = fft(A_gpu);  toc

B_from_gpu = gather(B_gpu);
```

```
>> test_gpuArray_small
Elapsed time is 0.000240 seconds.
Elapsed time is 0.000655 seconds.
```

In this example, with a small number of data, we get no speedup benefit from running the GPU. This corresponds to our previous mention (in Chapter 3) that the

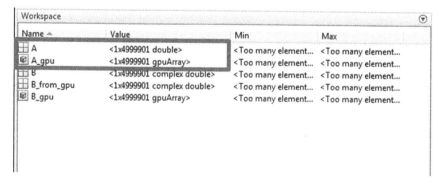

Figure 5.2 Data A on the main memory is represented as double, while data A_gpu on the GPU device memory is represented as gpuArray in the MATLAB Workspace.

speedup benefit from the GPU code conversion can be expected only from the computationally intensive case.

You can check the MATLAB built-in functions that support gpuArray through the methods('gpuArray') command:

```
>> methods('gpuArray')
```

Then, you can get the list of functions that support gpuArray. This means that all the MATLAB built-in functions are not fully supported for GPU processing yet, but the number of supported functions keeps growing in every new version release of the MATLAB Parallel Computing Toolbox. The following list is from MATLAB R2013a version, for example:

```
Methods for class gpuArray:

abs              ezsurfc          normest
acos             feather          not
acosh            fft              num2str
acot             fft2             numel
acoth            fftfilt          or
acsc             fftn             padarray
acsch            fill             pareto
all              fill3            pcolor
and              filter           permute
any              filter2          pie
applylut         find             pie3
area             fix              plot
arrayfun         floor            plot3
asec             fplot            plotmatrix
asech            fprintf          plotyy
asin             full             plus
asinh            gamma            polar
atan             gammaln          pow2
atan2            gather           power
atanh            ge               prod
bar              gpuArray         qr
bar3             gt               quiver
bar3h            hist             quiver3
barh             horzcat          rdivide
beta             hypot            real
betaln           ifft             reallog
bitand           ifft2            realpow
bitcmp           ifftn            realsqrt
bitget           imag             reducepatch
bitor            image            reducevolume
bitset           imagesc          rem
bitshift         imbothat         repmat
bitxor           imclose          reshape
bsxfun           imdilate         ribbon
```

bwlookup	imerode	rose
cast	imfilter	round
cat	imopen	scatter3
cconv	imrotate	sec
ceil	imshow	sech
chol	imtophat	semilogx
circshift	ind2sub	semilogy
clabel	int16	shiftdim
classUnderlying	int2str	shrinkfaces
comet	int32	sign
comet3	int64	sin
compass	int8	single
complex	interp1	sinh
cond	interpstreamspeed	size
coneplot	inv	slice
conj	ipermute	smooth3
contour	isa	sort
contour3	isempty	sprintf
contourc	isequal	spy
contourf	isequaln	sqrt
contourslice	isequalwithequalnans	stairs
conv	isfinite	stem
conv2	isfloat	stem3
convn	isinf	stream2
cos	isinteger	stream3
cosh	islogical	streamline
cot	ismember	streamparticles
coth	isnan	streamribbon
cov	isnumeric	streamslice
csc	isocaps	streamtube
csch	isocolors	sub2ind
ctranspose	isonormals	subsasgn
cumprod	isosurface	subsindex
cumsum	isreal	subsref
curl	issorted	subvolume
det	issparse	sum
diag	ldivide	surf
diff	le	surfc
disp	length	surfl
display	log	svd
divergence	log10	tan
dot	log1p	tanh
double	log2	times
eig	logical	transpose
end	loglog	tril
eps	lt	trimesh
eq	lu	trisurf
erf	mat2str	triu
erfc	max	uint16
erfcinv	mesh	uint32
erfcx	meshc	uint64
erfinv	meshgrid	uint8

```
errorbar              meshz                  uminus
existsOnGPU           min                    uplus
exp                   minus                  var
expm1                 mldivide               vertcat
ezcontour            mod                     vissuite
ezcontourf           mpower                  volumebounds
ezgraph3             mrdivide                voronoi
ezmesh               mtimes                  waterfall
ezmeshc              ndgrid                  xcorr
ezplot               ndims                   xor
ezplot3              ne
ezpolar              nnz
ezsurf               norm


Static methods:

colon                 logspace               randn
eye                   nan                    true
false                 ones                   zeros
inf                   rand
linspace              rand
```

5.2.1 Pitfalls in GPU Processing

When we use the GPU processing for large amount of data, we should do data verification. In the case of CPU processing, if we try to run data that exceed the current memory portion previously set by operating system, then the operating system automatically takes care of the memory shortage by swapping memory to and from the hard disk. Although the memory swapping makes computations slow, there is no need to worry about losing the data. In the case of GPU processing, however, memory swapping between the GPU device memory and the hard disk does not happen automatically, so the user should verify that the data on the GPU does not exceed GPU device memory limits.

Let us consider the following example:

```
%verify_gpuData.m

gpuDevice

A = rand(10000);        % 10000 × 10000 double on main memory
A_gpu = gpuArray(A);    % 10000 × 10000 double on GPU memory

gpuDevice

B = rand(10000);        % Another 10000 × 10000 double on main memory
B_gpu = gpuArray(B);    % Another 10000 × 10000 double on GPU memory
```

```
>> verify_gpuData

ans =
    CUDADevice with properties:

                        Name:  'GeForce GT 640M LE'
                       Index:  1
            ComputeCapability:  '3.0'
               SupportsDouble:  1
                DriverVersion:  5
               ToolkitVersion:  5
            MaxThreadsPerBlock:  1024
            MaxShmemPerBlock:  49152
           MaxThreadBlockSize:  [1024 1024 64]
                 MaxGridSize:  [2.1475e + 09 65535 65535]
                   SIMDWidth:  32
                 TotalMemory:  1.0737e + 09
                  FreeMemory:  973668352

           MultiprocessorCount:  2
                ClockRateKHz:  570000
                 ComputeMode:  'Default'
          GPUOverlapsTransfers:  1
        KernelExecutionTimeout:  1
            CanMapHostMemory:  1
              DeviceSupported:  1
               DeviceSelected:  1

ans =
    CUDADevice with properties:

                        Name:  'GeForce GT 640M LE'
                       Index:  1
            ComputeCapability:  '3.0'
               SupportsDouble:  1
                DriverVersion:  5
               ToolkitVersion:  5
            MaxThreadsPerBlock:  1024
            MaxShmemPerBlock:  49152
           MaxThreadBlockSize:  [1024 1024 64]
                 MaxGridSize:  [2.1475e + 09 65535 65535]
                   SIMDWidth:  32
                 TotalMemory:  1.0737e + 09
                  FreeMemory:  173604864

           MultiprocessorCount:  2
                ClockRateKHz:  570000
                 ComputeMode:  'Default'
          GPUOverlapsTransfers:  1
        KernelExecutionTimeout:  1
            CanMapHostMemory:  1
              DeviceSupported:  1
               DeviceSelected:  1

Error using gpuArray
```

```
Out of memory on device. To view more detail about
available memory on the GPU, use 'gpuDevice()'. If the
problem persists, reset the GPU by calling
'gpuDevice(1)'.

Error in verify_gpuData (line 11)
B_gpu = gpuArray(B); % Another 10000 × 10000 double on
GPU memory
```

From the first query using gpuDevice, before doing anything, the size of the free
GPU device memory was 973,668,352 bytes. After running A_gpu = gpuArray(A),
the size of the free GPU device memory was reduced to 173,604,864 bytes. From
the command B = rand(10000), the large matrix B was safely allocated on the main
memory in host, while we had an error message from the GPU side after running
B_gpu = gpuArray(B). In that case, we should clear some GPU data to make extra
room for a new GPU variable via the clear command or reset all GPU device
memory as follows:

```
>> clear A_gpu
```

or

```
>> g = gpuDevice(1);
>> reset(g);
```

5.3   GPU Processing for Non-Built-in MATLAB Functions

Now let us find a way to use GPU for our own MATLAB functions. To run our
own MATLAB code on a GPU, we can use arrayfun, which applies our own function to each data element by an elementwise operation. Actually, the arrayfun
function is not a GPU-dedicated function but a GPU-enabled function. So, we can
find the arrayfun function within the GPU-supporting function list in the
MATLAB Parallel Computing Toolbox in Section 5.2.

Using arrayfun means that we make a single call to a parallelized GPU operation that performs the whole calculation instead of making thousands of calls to
separate GPU-optimized operations. Therefore, the input function for arrayfun
should have only elementwise operations. For gpuArray data, which are stored in
the GPU device memory, our own MATLAB function is executed on the GPU
through arrayfun and the outputs are stored in the GPU device memory.

The format of using arrayfun follows:

```
result = arrayfun(@myFunction, arg1, arg2, ...);
```

The arg1 and arg2 are the input arguments for myFunction, and these input
arguments should be gpuArray data for GPU-processing purposes. The myFunction

should have scalar (i.e., elementwise) operations, so vector and matrix computations are not supported. The `result` is the output of `myFunction` and is stored in the GPU device memory as well.

Let us consider the following simple example:

```
% test_arrayfun.m

a = gpuArray(1:0.1:10);
b = gpuArray(2:0.1:11);
c = gpuArray(3:0.1:12);
d = gpuArray(4:0.1:13);

gpu_rlt = arrayfun(@myFunc,
a,b,c,d);

rlt = gather(gpu_rlt);
```

```
% my own element-wise MATLAB function
% myFunc.m

function out = myFunc(a, b, c, d)
out = b / (a * d * sin(c));
```

The code `myFunc.m` has four input arguments (a, b, c, d), which are all stored in the GPU device memory through `gpuArray` in `test_arrayfun.m`. The non-built-in function `myFunc` is composed of scalar operations only, which can be easily parallelized in GPU. Through the `arrayfun` function in `test_arrayfun.m`, we could run the `myFunc` function on GPU.

Although the input function for `arrayfun` should have only elementwise operations, this does not mean that only simple operations are allowed. Instead, the input function can be executed with any scalar operations and flow controls (such as `for-loop`, `while-loop`, `break`, `if`, etc.) on GPU through `arrayfun`:

```
% user's scalar MATLAB function

function [out, count] = myGoodFunc(a, b, maxIter)

    count = 0;
    out = 0;
    amp = abs(a^2 + b^2);
    while (count <= maxIter) & (amp < 1.5)

        out = (a^3 - b/a);
        count = count + 1;
    end
```

```
% scalar_arrayfun.m
A = gpuArray.rand(40,40);
B = gpuArray.rand(40,40);

max_Iter = 3000;

[gpu_rlt, gpu_count] = arrayfun(@myGoodFunc, A, B, max_Iter);

rlt = gather(gpu_rlt);
count = gather(gpu_count);
```

However, regular matrix and vector operations that require matrix-element indexing are not supported in GPU processing through arrayfun.

```
% test_arrayfun2.m                    % myFunc2.m

A = gpuArray.rand(2,5,4);            function out = myFunc2(A, B)
B = gpuArray.rand(2,5,4);

gpu_rlt = arrayfun(@myFunc2, A, B);   a1 = A(1,1,1);   % Matrix indexing

rlt = gather(gpu_rlt);               A(1,1,1) = a1 * B(1,2,1) - 3;
                                     out = B ./ A;
```

The test_arrayfun2.m causes an error message like the following because of the matrix indexing operation within myFunc2.m:

```
>> test_arrayfun2
Error using gpuArray/arrayfun
Indexing is not supported. error at line: 6

Error in test_arrayfun2 (line 6)
gpu_rlt = arrayfun(@myFunc2, A, B);
```

5.4   Parallel Task Processing

5.4.1   MATLAB Worker

The Parallel Computing Toolbox provides very efficient methods for both parallel "task" processing (parfor, with which we deal in the subsection 5.4.2.) and parallel "data" processing (spmd, with which we deal in the subsection 5.5.1.). Although both parallel task and data processing methods in the Parallel Computing Toolbox are related more to CPU than GPU, those methods become much stronger in speeding up when they are combined with GPU processing.

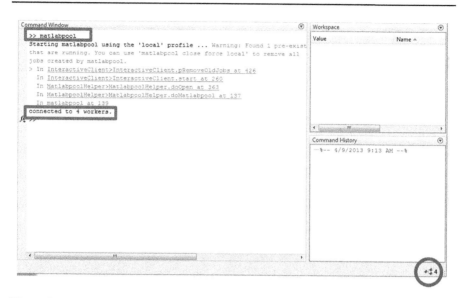

Figure 5.3 Preparing the available workers with the `matlabpool` command.

Each core of CPU can have an individual MATLAB session as a "worker."[1] The current version (2013a) of MATLAB can have up to 12 workers for a single machine, and the default number of workers is set to the number of available cores of the machine. To distinguish a main MATLAB session from the individual session on each worker, we call the main MATLAB session a "*client*". So, any main MATLAB session both before and after calling workers is the client. For the parallel processing, we should prepare the available worker by the command `matlabpool`, as in Figure 5.3.

In Figure 5.3, we can identify the default number of workers from the message containing `connected to 4 workers` in the MATLAB command window and the number 4 displayed in the right-bottom corner after executing the `matlabpool` command. You can change the number of default workers through the `Manage Cluster Profile` menu in Figures 5.4 and 5.5.

If you have only four cores and you ask for eight workers, MATLAB will create eight workers, but several of them have to share each core. Depending on your codes, sharing each core by multiple workers may or may not help running faster.

5.4.2 *parfor*

We can easily parallelize tasks using `parfor` instead of a `for-loop`. After reserving MATLAB workers with the `matlabpool` command, command lines between the

---

[1] Since the MATLAB-distributed computing server product can let users run extra workers on a remote computer clusters, we call the workers of multicores of single machine *local workers*. For simplicity, we deal with the parallel processing using only a single machine in this book, so *worker* means a "local worker" here.

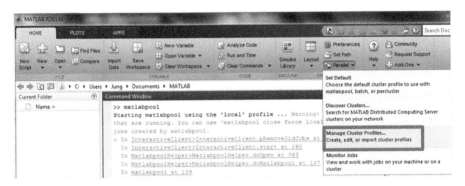

Figure 5.4 For changing the default number of workers, go to `Manage Cluster Profiles...` in the `Parallel` menu.

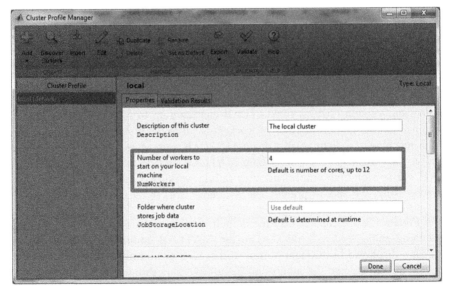

Figure 5.5 For changing the default number of workers, set the number of default workers in the `Cluster Profile Manager` window.

`for-loop` can be automatically distributed over the workers using `parfor`, as follows:

```
for i = 1:100
    command
        ...
end
```

matlabpool	If 4 workers are prepared by "matlabpool", then the left "parfor-loop" is implicitly divided into four "for-loop" commands and executed in parallel.			
parfor i = 1:100				
command ... end	for i = 1:25 command ... end	for i = 26:50 command ... end	for i = 51:75 command ... end	for i = 76:100 command ... end

To explain this concept, although the preceding example represents exact even distribution (1 ~ 25, 26 ~ 50, 51 ~ 75, and 76 ~ 100) over each for-loop iteration, the actual tasks are not always evenly distributed and it depends on the other programs running on CPU.

For the parfor loop, the same operations with different inputs can be executed in parallel in a task-independent and order-independent manner. In other words, the parfor loop offers a lot of benefits in parallel task processing when there is no interdependency between tasks. Since the parfor loop is used for parallel processing, it cannot contain a break or return statement within the loop. It also cannot contain another parfor loop as a nested loop while it allows a regular for-loop within itself.

We compare a regular for-loop command with a parfor-loop command by calculating the value of π using the Leibniz formula:

$$\pi = \cfrac{4}{1 + \cfrac{1^2}{2 + \cfrac{3^2}{2 + \frac{5^2}{2 + \dots}}}} = \sum_{n=0}^{\infty} \frac{4(-1)^n}{2n + 1}$$

```
% pi_Leib.m

tic
N = 10000000;
sum = 0;

for i = 1:(N-1)

    Denom = 2 * (i-1) + 1;
    Sign = (-1)^(i-1);
    sum = sum + 4 * Sign / Denom;
end
```

```
%pi_Leib_parfor.m

matlabpool
tic

N = 10000000;
sum = 0;

parfor i = 1:(N-1)

    Denom = 2 * (i-1) + 1;
    Sign = (-1)^(i-1);
```

sum toc	sum = sum + 4 * Sign / Denom; end sum toc

```
>> pi_Leib
sum =
    3.1416
Elapsed time is 25.535713 seconds.
>> pi_Leib_parfor
sum =
    3.1416
Elapsed time is 8.170260 seconds.
```

This example of `pi_Leib_parfor.m` uses four workers and the running time is almost one third that of `pi_Leib.m`, which uses the regular `for-loop`.

5.5 Parallel Data Processing

5.5.1 *spmd*

As a very efficient method of "data" parallel processing, the parallel computing toolbox provides `spmd` (single program, multiple data). Like the `parfor`, `spmd` uses MATLAB workers through a `matlabpool`. Here, *single program, multiple data* means that identical codes run simultaneously on the multiple MATLAB workers with different data, which leads to data parallel processing. The basic syntax of `spmd` has the following form:

```
spmd
    command
    ...
end
```

The difference between the `parfor` and the `spmd` starts with the fact that `spmd` divides data into multiple small pieces, while `parfor` divides a loop into smaller iterations. So `parfor` requires no dependencies or communication between workers, while `spmd` has a larger flexibility to allow communication and dependencies between operations (between different workers). In the case of `parfor`, a loop is automatically and implicitly divided onto each worker by MATLAB. In the case of `spmd`, however, each piece of data should be explicitly divided onto each worker by the user. Therefore, `spmd` requires more user control than the `parfor` command. Since both `parfor` and `spmd` use workers, the body of a `parfor`-loop cannot contain a `spmd` statement, and a `spmd` statement cannot contain a `parfor`-loop. However, a program can have multiple `spmd` blocks, as long as none is nested within the `spmd` block itself.

Unlike the `parfor`, the parallel data processing for commands within the `spmd` statement can be explicitly distributed by user using `labindex()` and `numlabs()`.

The command `labindex()` returns an unique index for the current worker, and `numlabs()`returns the number of available workers. Without the `labindex` function, the `spmd` statement is implicitly used on each worker, which means that the distribution of data processing is automatically assigned to each worker without user's intervention.

```
% spmd_index.m

matlabpool

A = 1:10;
B = 11:20;

spmd

    index = labindex();
    if index = = 1
        D = A .* B;
    else
        D = A + B;
    end

end

matlabpool close
```

The preceding code runs different operations on different workers, depending on the return values from `labindex()`. The variables (here A and B) in the client, i.e., all the command lines outside the `spmd` block, can be referenced by each worker within the `spmd` block. In the older version of MATLAB, the variables in the client cannot be modified within the `spmd` block, unlike later version of MATLAB. The result of the preceding code looks like this:

```
>> spdm_index
>> D
```

```
D =
   Lab 1: class = double, size = [1  10]
   Lab 2: class = double, size = [1  10]

>> D{1}

ans =
     11   24   39   56   75   96   119   144   171   200

>> D{2}

ans =
     12   14   16   18   20   22   24   26   28   30
```

The result D coming from the spmd block has a slightly different form from a
regular matrix or vector. MATLAB calls this form in a client as a *composite* object,
which references the variables on the assigned workers. Therefore, D has a following form, which indicates the separate data on each worker:

```
D =
   Lab 1: class = double, size = [1  10]
   Lab 2: class = double, size = [1  10]
```

To access the individual result on each worker, we use the cell-array indexing
method, using the curly braces as D{1} and D{2}. Thus, D{1} is the value of D computed by worker 1. The variables on each worker can be modified in the client
using this curly braces.

Table 5.1 shows a spmd example that has separate workspaces for the client and
two workers. Here, the bold numbers represent the newly updated variables in all
workspaces. From this table, we can see that all commands in the client and all the
spmd blocks themselves are executed serially, but the commands *within* the spmd
block are executed simultaneously in each worker.

Let us look the spmd_value_modification.m code in the Table 5.1. First, a composite object for each worker can be created using the Composite() function and
initialized in the client workspace from line 3 to line 5. The composite object can
also be directly created within the spmd block, like D in spmd_index.m example.
Second, the variables i, k, z in the first spmd block have different values for different workers, depending on the labindex(), and were processed independently but
in parallel. Third, the value of a composite variable k, which was created in
the spmd block, was changed in the client workspace (line 13) and the changed
value was used in the following spmd block with no problem.

Please note the second spmd block, from line15 to line 18. All variables previously used in the first spmd block (from line 7 to line 11) store the same values
except k{2}. The variable k{2} was modified in the client workspace in line 13,
even though the first spmd block was completely finished at line 11 and some client
program was executed after that. However, if a MATLAB function that is called by
another function uses a spmd block within the function, the variables in the spmd
block lose their values when the function is completed, like the regular MATLAB
function data.

Table 5.1 Separate Workspaces for Client and spmd Workers

Line #	Code	Client		Worker 1					Worker 2				
	spmd_value_modification.m	x	y	i	k	z	j	m	i	k	z	j	m
1	x = 5;	5	—	—	—	—	—	—	—	—	—	—	—
2	y = 6;	5	6	—	—	—	—	—	—	—	—	—	—
3	z = Composite();	5	6	—	—	—	—	—	—	—	—	—	—
4	z{1} = 1;	5	6	—	—	1	—	—	—	—	—	—	—
5	z{2} = 2;	5	6	—	—	1	—	—	—	—	2	—	—
6		5	6	—	—	—	—	—	—	—	—	—	—
7	spmd												
8	i = labindex();	5	6	1	—	1	—	—	2	—	2	—	—
9	k = x+i;	5	6	1	6	1	—	—	2	7	2	—	—
10	z = 10*i;	5	6	1	6	10	—	—	2	7	20	—	—
11	end	5	6	1	6	10	—	—	2	7	20	—	—
12													
13	k{2} = 10;	5	6	1	6	10	—	—	2	10	20	—	—
14													
15	spmd												
16	j = labindex();	5	6	1	6	10	1	—	2	10	20	2	—
17	m = k*j;	5	6	1	6	10	1	6	2	10	20	2	20
18	end												
final		5	6	1	6	10	1	6	2	10	20	2	20

5.5.2 Distributed and Codistributed Arrays

The distributed array is one of the most efficient methods for parallel data processing using spmd. The basic concept for the distributed array is simple but strong. When we need to deal with a huge matrix, we can partition the matrix into smaller submatrixes and process them on multiple workers in parallel. Since the calculation for a huge matrix requires a large memory and longer processing time, distributing a big array practically helps a lot. The first distributed example that follows shows its basic operation. (We assume that the matlabpool is already activated in this subsection.)

```
% dist_first.m

A = rand(2,8);
dA = distributed (A);

spmd
    localPart = getLocalPart(dA);
end
```

Matrix A is 2×8 in size. The distributed(A) distributes the element of A to each worker in 2×2 form as below (four workers are used):

	Worker1		Worker2		Worker3		Worker4	
	localPart{1}		localPart{2}		localPart{3}		localPart{4}	
Col:	Col1	Col2	Col3	Col4	Col5	Col6	Col7	Col8
Row1	0.3804	0.0759	0.5308	0.9340	0.5688	0.0119	0.1622	0.3112
Row2	0.5678	0.0540	0.7792	0.1299	0.4694	0.3371	0.7943	0.5285

Here, the elements of matrix A are distributed by column as a default. In a higher dimensional matrix, the last dimension is used for the base of distribution. From the getLocalPart() function, we can get the each part of distributed matrix from workers. The result of the example is as follow:

```
>> dist_first
>> A

A =
    0.3804   0.0759   0.5308   0.9340   0.5688   0.0119   0.1622   0.3112
    0.5678   0.0540   0.7792   0.1299   0.4694   0.3371   0.7943   0.5285

>> localPart{1}

ans =
    0.3804   0.0759
    0.5678   0.0540
```

```
>> localPart{2}
ans =
     0.5308   0.9340
     0.7792   0.1299
```

The distributed()function distributes a matrix as evenly as possible, which means that, in the case of an odd numbered column size, the last worker has the odd number of column data, as follows:

```
% dist_second.m

A = rand(2,7)                      % odd number of column
dA = distributed(A);

spmd

    localPart = getLocalPart(dA);
    localPart(1,1)

end
```

```
>> dist_second

A =
    0.6555   0.7060   0.2769   0.0971   0.6948   0.9502   0.4387
    0.1712   0.0318   0.0462   0.8235   0.3171   0.0344   0.3816

Lab 1:

  ans =
        0.6555

Lab 2:

  ans =
        0.2769

Lab 3:

  ans =
        0.6948

Lab 4:
  ans =
        0.4387

>> localPart

localPart =
   Lab 1:  class = double, size = [2  2]
   Lab 2:  class = double, size = [2  2]
   Lab 3:  class = double, size = [2  2]
   Lab 4:  class = double, size = [2  1]
```

```
>> localPart{3}

ans =
     0.6948   0.9502
     0.3171   0.0344

>> localPart{4}

ans =
     0.4387
     0.3816
```

Please note that the distributed matrix localPart has its own local index, which is different from the original non-distributed matrix A.

There are two ways to distribute a matrix to multiple workers: distributed() and codistributed(). The distributed() partitions a matrix *before* it enters spmd block, while codistributed() partitions a matrix *within* the spmd block. Since the main purpose of matrix distribution is to handle a huge matrix that is too large to be processed on a single core, the creation of a big matrix on the client and distribution to multiple workers (using distributed()) is less efficient. In many cases, it would be better to directly construct a distributed matrix on multiple workers using codistributed(). The previous dist_first.m example, which uses a distributed function, can be changed into the following using codistributed function. The result is same as with the dist_first.m example, although the method of distribution is changed.

```
% codist_first.m

spmd
     A = rand(2,8);
     dA = codistributed (A);
     localPart = getLocalPart(dA);
end
```

This example still constructs matrix A first and then distributes to workers within spmd block. In this case, each worker has its own replication of matrix A, which is worse than the the dist_first.m example. In order to fully utilize the benefit of codistritbuted function, we can initialize the matrix A with codistritbuted. rand() function without constructing a regular matrix in the client.

```
% codist_rand.m

spmd
     dA = codistributed.rand(2,8);
     localPart = getLocalPart(dA);
end
```

The command `codist_rand.m` directly constructs a matrix in a distributed form on each worker using the `codistributed.rand()` function. In addition to the `codistributed.rand()` function, MATLAB provides abundant functions that enable distribution on workers at the time of matrix construction, as follows:

```
codistributed.cell        Create codistributed cell array
codistributed.colon       Distributed colon operation
codistributed.eye         Create codistributed identity matrix
codistributed.false       Create codistributed false array
codistributed.Inf         Create codistributed array of Inf values
codistributed.NaN         Create codistributed array of Not-a-Number values
codistributed.ones        Create codistributed array of ones
codistributed.rand        Create codistributed array of uniformly
                              distributed pseudo-random numbers
codistributed.randn       Create codistributed array of normally
                              distributed random values
codistributed.spalloc     Allocate space for sparse codistributed matrix
codistributed.speye       Create codistributed sparse identity matrix
codistributed.sprand      Create codistributed sparse array of uniformly
                              distributed pseudo-random values
codistributed.sprandn     Create codistributed sparse array of uniformly
                              distributed pseudo-random values
codistributed.true        Create codistributed true array
codistributed.zeros       Create codistributed array of zeros
```

When you need to restore the codistributed matrixes into a undistributed large matrix after calculation by each worker, you can use the `gather()` function to restore them:

```
% codist_gather.m

spmd
    dA = codistributed.ones(500,500);
    localPart = getLocalPart(dA);
end

A = gather(dA);
```

When we run the `codist_gather.m` with four workers, each 500×125 partitioned matrix is combined into a 500×500 large matrix on the client using the `gather()` function:

```
>> codist_gather
>> localPart

localPart =
    Lab 1: class = double, size = [500  125]
    Lab 2: class = double, size = [500  125]
```

```
Lab 3: class = double, size = [500 125]
Lab 4: class = double, size = [500 125]
```

```
>> size(A)
```

```
ans =
    500   500
```

5.5.3   Workers with Multiple GPUs

As mentioned earlier, the workers in the parallel computing toolbox share CPU cores by default. So, if the user's machine has a single GPU and multiple workers try to access that single GPU, then we cannot expect any speedup benefit. In many cases, this would make whole process much slower than when we use the multiple workers without using the single GPU, because the parallel processing by workers (CPU cores) should be serialized in transferring data to a single GPU device. However, if the user's machine has multiple GPUs corresponding to the number of CPU cores, then it works well with multiple workers. In that case, we explicitly designate the GPU device for each worker by a GPU device ID. Since a multicore machine installed with multiple GPUs is not currently the general situation, we are not going to deal with multiple GPUs for multiple workers in this book.

5.6   Direct use of CUDA Files without c-mex

When you lack the Parallel Computing Toolbox in your computer, you can employ the c-mex file to use a CUDA file (.cu file) for GPU, which was explained in Chapter 2. When you have the Parallel Computing Toolbox, you can directly use the CUDA file for GPU, without c-mex file. In this case, we do not need to compile the c-mex file but need only the nvcc compilation for the CUDA files.

We are going to tweak the AddVectors.cu example, which was used in Chapter 2 for c-mex. Here is the AddVectors_noCmex.cu file. First of all, the AddVectors_noCmex.cu file has only the CUDA kernel part (__global__ void AddVectors_noCmex()), unlike the AddVectors.cu in Chapter 2 that has CUDA memory allocation and memory copy related to the c-mex interface.

```
// AddVectors_noCmex.cu with Parallel Computing Toolbox

__global__ void AddVectors_noCmex(double* A, double* B)
{
        int i = threadIdx.x;

        A[i]+= B[i];
}
```

The basic process to direct use of the `cu` file in MATLAB is as follows:

```
1) nvcc —ptx AddVectors_noCmex.cu
```

In the shell (DOS or Linux shell), we should compile the `cu` file with `nvcc` in the NVIDIA CUDA Toolkit with the `—ptx` option to generate the `ptx` file. We can also run this shell command within the MATLAB command window using the `system` command as:

```
system('nvcc -ptx AddVectors_noCmex.cu -ccbin
"C:\ProgramFiles(x86)\Microsoft Visual Studio 10.0\VC\bin"');
```

Although we do not compile the `c-mex` file, we still need the C/C++ compiler to compile the `cu` file with `nvcc`, because the `cu` file has a C/C++ format and `nvcc` forwards all non-CUDA compilation steps to the C/C++ compiler. If your system does not set the path to the C/C++ compiler (e.g. `cl.exe`), then we can explicitly set the path using the `—ccbin` option. For the installation of `nvcc` from the NVIDIA website, refer to Chapter 2. Usually, the successful installation of the NVIDIA CUDA toolkit automatically sets the path to the `nvcc.exe` location (`C:\Program Files\NVIDIA GPU Computing Toolkit\CUDA\v5.0\bin`). However, if you do not set path to the location for some reason, then you need to add the `addpath('C:\Program Files\NVIDIA GPU Computing Toolkit\CUDA\v5.0\bin')` command before running.

```
2) myCu = parallel.gpu.CUDAKernel('AddVectors_noCmex.ptx','AddVectors_
noCmex.cu');
```

We generate a CUDA kernel object using both the `ptx` and `cu` files with same file name from the `parallel.gpu.CUDAKernel()` function. When your `cu` file is composed of several functions, you can specify the entry point name as follows:

```
myCu = parallel.gpu.CUDAKernel('AddVectors_noCmex.ptx', 'AddVectors_
noCmex','AddVectors_noCmex.cu');

3) CuOut = feval(myCu, A, B)
```

With the function handle `myCu` for the CUDA object `AddVectors_noCmex`, the `feval` function runs with two input arguments, matrixes A and B. The `nvcc_noCmex.m` file below shows the full codes that compile the `cu` file, generate the CUDA object, and run it with test inputs.

```
% nvcc_noCmex.m

% Use the following when MS Visual Studio 2010 or later
system('nvcc -ptx AddVectors_noCmex.cu -ccbin "C:\Program Files (x86)
\Microsoft Visual Studio 10.0\VC\bin"');
```

```
myCu = parallel.gpu.CUDAKernel('AddVectors_noCmex.ptx','AddVectors_
noCmex.cu');

A = single([1 2 3 4 5 6 7 8 9 10]);
B = single([10 9 8 7 6 5 4 3 2 1]);

N = length(A)
myCu.ThreadBlockSize = N

CuOut = feval(myCu, A, B)
```

When we run this code, we have the following results:

```
>> nvcc_noCmex
AddVectors_noCmex.cu
tmpxft_00001328_00000000-5_AddVectors_noCmex.cudafe1.gpu
tmpxft_00001328_00000000-10_AddVectors_noCmex.cudafe2.gpu

N =
    10

myCu =
        parallel.gpu.CUDAKernel handle
        Package: parallel.gpu

        Properties:
            ThreadBlockSize:     [10 1 1]
         MaxThreadsPerBlock:     1024
                   GridSize:     [1 1]
          SharedMemorySize:     0
                 EntryPoint:     '_Z17AddVectors_noCmexPdS_'
         MaxNumLHSArguments:     2
            NumRHSArguments:     2
              ArgumentTypes:     {'inout double vector' 'inout double
                                  vector'}

Methods, Events, Superclasses

CuOut =
     11   11   11   11   11   11   11   11   11   11
```

By the MATLAB command myCu.ThreadBlockSize = N (Here N = 10 which is
the length of vector A), the ThreadBlockSize sets as [10 1 1]. This
ThreadBlockSize controls i = threadIdx.x in AddVectors_noCmex.cu to add 10
elements of data in parallel within the GPU, which results in all 11s of 10 data elements. If we change the value of myCu.ThreadBlockSize to 8, as shown next, the
last two elements are not correctly added:

```
% nvcc_noCmex2.m

system('nvcc -ptx AddVectors_noCmex.cu -ccbin "C:\Program Files (x86)
\Microsoft Visual Studio 10.0\VC\bin"');
```

```
myCu = parallel.gpu.CUDAKernel('AddVectors_noCmex.ptx', 'AddVectors_
noCmex.cu');

A = single([1 2 3 4 5 6 7 8 9 10]);
B = single([10 9 8 7 6 5 4 3 2 1]);

N = length(A)
myCu.ThreadBlockSize = N-2

CuOut = feval(myCu, A, B)
```

```
>> nvcc_noCmex2
N =
   10

myCu =
       parallel.gpu.CUDAKernel handle
       Package: parallel.gpu

       Properties:
             ThreadBlockSize:  [8 1 1]
          MaxThreadsPerBlock:  1024
                    GridSize:  [1 1]
           SharedMemorySize:  0
                  EntryPoint:  '_Z17AddVectors_noCmexPdS_'
          MaxNumLHSArguments:  2
             NumRHSArguments:  2
               ArgumentTypes:  {'inout double vector' 'inout double
                                 vector'}

Methods, Events, Superclasses

CuOut =
        11   11   11   11   11   11   11   11    9   10
```

The main difference between `AddVectors.cu` and `AddVectors_noCmex.cu` is the number of arguments of the CUDA kernel in addition to the use of the c-mex interface:

```
// AddVectors_noCmex.cu with Parallel Computing Toolbox

__global__ void AddVectors_noCmex(double* A, double* B)
{
        int i = threadIdx.x;

        A[i] + = B[i];
}
```

```
// AddVectors.cu in Chapter 2 with C-mex

__global__ void addVectorsKernel(float* A, float* B, float* C, int size)
```

```
{
      int i = blockIdx.x;
      if (i >= size)
          return;

      C[i] = A[i] + B[i];
}
```

In the case of AddVectors.cu in Chapter 2, the CUDA kernel function
(addVectorsKernel()) for c-mex was called by other functions after the c-mex
function, so the number and order of arguments can be freely decided by the user.
However, the CUDA kernel function (AddVectors_noCmex()), which was directly
used by the MATLAB function feval() through parallel.gpu.CUDAKernel should
follow the strict rule. When we call [output1, output2] = feval(CUDA_Kernel,
input1, input2, input3), the input1, input2, and input3 should be the same as
the input arguments for the CUDA_Kernel function. If we have more than two input
arguments, then first two input arguments are used as output arguments. If we have
two or fewer input arguments, then only the first input argument is used as an output argument. We can check this in the CUDA kernel properties brought by the
CUDA kernel handle.

```
>> myCu

myCu =
      parallel.gpu.CUDAKernel handle
      Package: parallel.gpu

      Properties:
            ThreadBlockSize:   [10 1 1]
         MaxThreadsPerBlock:   1024
                   GridSize:   [1 1]
          SharedMemorySize:   0
                 EntryPoint:   '_Z17AddVectors_noCmexPdS_'
         MaxNumLHSArguments:   2
            NumRHSArguments:   2
             ArgumentTypes:   {'inout double vector' 'inout double
                              vector'}

Methods, Events, Superclasses
```

Here, we see two inout descriptions in Argument Types. This inout indicates
that those two arguments are used as both input and output arguments. Let us see a
very simple case:

```
// Simple_noCmex.cu with Parallel Computing Toolbox

__global__ void Simple_noCmex(double* A, double val)
{
      int i = threadIdx.x;
```

```
        A[i] + = val;
}
```

```
% simple_noCmex.m

system('nvcc -ptx Simple_noCmex.cu -ccbin "C:\Program Files (x86)
\Microsoft Visual Studio 10.0\VC\bin"');

handleCu = parallel.gpu.CUDAKernel('Simple_noCmex.ptx',
'Simple_noCmex.cu');

A = single([1 2 3 4 5 6 7 8 9 10]);
handleCu.ThreadBlockSize = length(A);

CuOut = feval(handleCu, A, 5.0)
```

```
>> simple_noCmex
Simple_noCmex.cu
tmpxft_00001bdc_00000000-5_Simple_noCmex.cudafe1.gpu
tmpxft_00001bdc_00000000-10_Simple_noCmex.cudafe2.gpu

CuOut =
        6   7   8   9   10   11   12   13   14   15
>> handleCu

handleCu =
            parallel.gpu.CUDAKernel handle
            Package: parallel.gpu

            Properties:
                  ThreadBlockSize:    [10 1 1]
                MaxThreadsPerBlock:    1024
                         GridSize:    [1 1]
                 SharedMemorySize:    0
                       EntryPoint:    '_Z13Simple_noCmexPdd'
                MaxNumLHSArguments:    1
                  NumRHSArguments:    2
                    ArgumentTypes:    {'inout double vector' 'in double
                                       scalar'}

Methods, Events, Superclasses
```

In this simple CUDA kernel (Simple_noCmex.cu), the property by the kernel handle (handleCu) shows one inout argument and one in argument. The bottom line is that the return type of the kernel function always should be of the void type and the output values should be stored back into the first or second input argument.

6 Using CUDA-Accelerated Libraries

6.1 Chapter Objectives

The c-mex configuration opens many possibilities for what we can do with our MATLAB programs. By using CUDA-accelerated libraries available off the shelf, we can even push the limits far beyond what MATLAB can do. Using other third-party libraries in c-mex is no different from using them in regular C/C++ programs. In this chapter, we learn how to use

- CUDA Basic Linear Algebra Subroutines (CUBLAS) for MATLAB through c-mex.
- CUDA FFT library (CUFFT) for MATLAB through c-mex.
- Thrust, a C++ template library for CUDA based on the Standard Template Library (STL).

6.2 CUBLAS

CUBLAS is a BLAS (basic linear algebra subroutines) library provided by NVIDIA with GPU acceleration. It hides the details of CUDA, so that we can use it at a higher API level in our c-mex with almost no exposure to the explicit CUDA function calls. This section guides us through how to use CUBLAS library in our c-mex function by an example.

Let us start with some helpful information before writing our c-mex with CUBLAS. CUBLAS is distributed with NVIDIA CUDA. Its library and the header file can be found at the CUDA-installed directory as follows. Note that the exact path for your system may differ from these if it were not installed using defaults. Unlike examples presented in the previous chapters, we do not call a CUDA compiler, nvcc, this time, since we just use CUDA and CUBLAS runtime libraries in our functions.

- Header file required for compiling:
    ```
    cublas_v2.h
    cuda_runtime.h
    ```

- Libraries required for linking:
    ```
    cublas.lib, cudart.lib              Windows
    libculas.dylib, libcudart.dylib     Mac OS X
    libculas.so, libcudart.so           Linux
    ```

- Typical locations where you can find these files:

  Windows 64-bit:
  ```
  C:\Program Files\NVIDIA GPU Computing
  Toolkit\CUDA\v5.0\lib\x64\cublas.lib
  C:\Program Fiels\NVIDIA GPU Computing
  Toolkit\CUDA\v5.0\include\cublas_v2.h
  ```

  Windows 32-bit:
  ```
  C:\Program Files\NVIDIA GPU Computing
  Toolkit\CUDA\v5.0\lib\Win32\cublas.lib
  C:\Program Files\NVIDIA GPU Computing
  Toolkit\CUDA\v5.0\include\cublas_v2.h
  ```

  Mac OS X:
  ```
  /Developer/NVIDIA/CUDA-5.0/lib/libcublas.dylib
  /Developer/NVIDIA/CUDA-5.0/include/cublas_v2.h
  ```

  Linux 32-bit:
  ```
  /usr/local/cuda-5.0/lib/libcublas.so
  /usr/local/cuda-5.0/include/cublas_v2.h
  ```

  Linux 64-bit:
  ```
  /usr/local/cuda-5.0/lib64/libcublas.so
  /usr/local/cuda-5.0/include/cublas_v2.h
  ```

We use these files in our `c-mex` function. So, make sure that you find and verify where these files are located in your system before we move on to the next subsection.

6.2.1   CUBLAS Functions

Like MATLAB, data layout in a CUBLAS library is in column-major order. This is a huge advantage, especially when programming `c-mex`, since we need not consider the differences in data layout between `c-mex` and the library of our interest. Also, since this library provides a set of essential and useful linear algebra functions, we can easily identify the counterparts in the original MATLAB program. When we are dealing with a big data set in MATLAB programs, we find that CUBLAS can be used in many places for acceleration.

CUBLAS functions can be grouped into four different classes: helper functions, level-1 functions, level-2 functions, and level-3 functions. The helper functions basically provide ways to handle GPU and memory resources including data copies. These calls eliminate the need to call explicit CUDA runtime functions. Some of these functions are listed in Table 6.1. Tables 6.2 through 6.4 list some level-1 through level-3 functions.

6.2.2   CUBLAS Matrix-by-Matrix Multiplication

In our example, we simply do a matrix-by-matrix multiplication:

$$C = A \times B$$

Table 6.1 CUBLAS Helper Functions Providing Ways to Handle Hardware Resources

Function Name	Function Detail
cublasCreate	Initializes the CUBLAS library. Must be called before any CUBLAS library calls.
cublasDestroy	Releases hardware resources used by the CUBLAS library.
cublasSetVector	Copies elements from a vector in host memory space to a vector in GPU memory space.
cublasGetVector	Copies elements from a GPU memory space to a vector in host memory space.
cublasSetMatrix	Copies elements from a matrix in host memory space to a matrix in GPU memory space.
cublasGetMatrix	Copies elements from a matrix in GPU memory space to a matrix in host memory space.

Table 6.2 CUBLAS Level-1 Functions Performing Scalar and Vector Based Operations

Function Name	Function Detail
cublasIsamax	Finds the index of the element of the maximum magnitude in a vector of the single precision type.
cublasIdamax	Same as the preceding but for a double precision type.
cublasSaxpy	Multiples a vector by a scalar and adds it to another vector of a single precision type.
cublasDdot	Computes a dot product of two vectors of the double precision type.
cublasScrm2	Computes a Euclidean norm of the input vector of complex numbers of the single precision type.

Table 6.3 CUBLAS Level-2 Functions Performing Matrix-Vector Operations

Function Name	Function Detail
cublasSgemv	Performs the matrix-vector multiplication of the single precision type.
cublasDsbmv	Performs the symmetric banded matrix-vector multiplication of the double precision type.
cublasCsymv	Performs the symmetric matrix-vector multiplication of complex numbers of the single precision type.
cublasZhemv	Performs the Hermitian matrix-vector multiplication of the complex double precision type.
cublasCher2	Performs the Hermitian rank-2 update of complex numbers of the single precision type.

Table 6.4 CUBLAS Level-3 Functions Performing Matrix-Matrix Operations

Function Name	Function Detail
cublasSgemm	Performs the matrix-matrix multiplication of the single precision type.
cublasZgemm	Performs the matrix-matrix multiplication of complex numbers of the double precision type.
cublasDtrmm	Performs the triangular matrix-matrix multiplication of complex numbers of the double precision type.
cublasChemm	Performs the Hermitian matrix-matrix multiplication of complex the single precision type.
cublasCher2k	Performs the Hermitian rank-2 k update of complex numbers of the single precision type.

where **A**'s dimension is $M \times N$ and **B**'s dimension is $N \times P$, and the resulting **C**'s dimension is $M \times P$.

6.2.2.1 Step 1

Open MATLAB command window, create a new file, and save it as cublasDemo. cpp.

6.2.2.2 Step 2

In the empty cublasDemo.cpp file, enter the following code:

```
#include "mex.h"

Void mexFunction(int nlhs, mxArray *plhs[], int nrhs, const mxArray
*prhs[])
{
}
```

As you may remember, this is just an empty gateway routine, where we start our c-mex program.

6.2.2.3 Step 3

Next, we check if the input data type is single precision or float. Then, we obtain pointers to both inputs **A** and **B** and their sizes. Again, for simplicity, we just assume the input data type to be single precision. Otherwise, we exit our program.

```
#include "mex.h"

void mexFunction(int nlhs, mxArray *plhs[], int nrhs, const mxArray
*prhs[])
```

```
{
     if (nrhs != 2)
        mexErrMsgTxt("Invaid number of input arguments");

     if (!mxIsSingle(prhs[0]) && !mxIsSingle(prhs[1]))
        mexErrMsgTxt("input matrices must be single ");

      float* A = (float*)mxGetData(prhs[0]);
      float* B = (float*)mxGetData(prhs[1]);

      int numARows = mxGetM(prhs[0]);
      int numACols = mxGetN(prhs[0]);
      int numBRows = mxGetM(prhs[1]);
      int numBCols = mxGetN(prhs[1]);

      If (numACols != numBRows)
         mexErrMsgTxt("Invalid matrix dimension");
}
```

6.2.2.4 Step 4

In this step, we create the output matrix, **C**, whose dimension is determined by the number of rows of **A** and the number of columns of **B**:

```
#include "mex.h"

void mexFunction(int nlhs, mxArray *plhs[], int nrhs, const mxArray
*prhs[])
{
     if (nrhs != 2)
        mexErrMsgTxt("Invaid number of input arguments");

     if (!mxIsSingle(prhs[0]) && !mxIsSingle(prhs[1]))
        mexErrMsgTxt("input matrices must be single ");

     float* A = (float*)mxGetData(prhs[0]);
     float* B = (float*)mxGetData(prhs[1]);

     int numARows = mxGetM(prhs[0]);
     int numACols = mxGetN(prhs[0]);
     int numBRows = mxGetM(prhs[1]);
     int numBCols = mxGetN(prhs[1]);
     int numCRows = numARows;
     int numCCols = numBCols;

     plhs[0] = mxCreateNumericMatrix(numCRows, numCCols, mxSINGLE_
     CLASS, mxREAL);
```

```
        float* C = (float*)mxGetData(plhs[0]);
}
```

6.2.2.5 Step 5

We now create memory in the GPU device where we copy our matrix data. We use
cudaMalloc and cudaFree to allocate and deallocate memory, respectively. These
functions are defined in cuda_runtime.h. So, we include this header file at the very
beginning:

```
#include "mex.h"
#include <cuda_runtime.h>

void mexFunction(int nlhs, mxArray *plhs[], int nrhs, const mxArray
*prhs[])
{
        if (nrhs != 2)
            mexErrMsgTxt("Invaid number of input arguments");

        if (!mxIsSingle(prhs[0]) && !mxIsSingle(prhs[1]))
            mexErrMsgTxt("input matrices must be single ");

        float* A = (float*)mxGetData(prhs[0]);
        float* B = (float*)mxGetData(prhs[1]);

        int numARows = mxGetM(prhs[0]);
        int numACols = mxGetN(prhs[0]);
        int numBRows = mxGetM(prhs[1]);
        int numBCols = mxGetN(prhs[1]);
        int numCRows = numARows;
        int numCCols = numBCols;

        plhs[0] = mxCreateNumericMatrix(numCRows, numCCols, mxSINGLE_
        CLASS, mxREAL);
        float* C = (float*)mxGetData(plhs[0]);

        float *deviceA, *deviceB, *deviceC;
        cudaMalloc(&deviceA, sizeof(float) * numARows * numACols);
        cudaMalloc(&deviceB, sizeof(float) * numBRows * numBCols);
        cudaMalloc(&deviceC, sizeof(float) * numCRows * numCCols);

        // insert cuBLAS function(s) here

        cudaFree(deviceA);
        cudaFree(deviceB);
        cudaFree(deviceC);
}
```

Note that we are just allocating and deallocating the memory in GPU. We insert the CUBLAS codes in between.

6.2.2.6 Step 6

Now, it is time to add CUBLAS codes. We start by adding another header file, `cublas_v2.h`, at the beginning:

```
#include "mex.h"
#include <cuda_runtime.h>
#include <cublas_v2.h>

void mexFunction(int nlhs, mxArray *plhs[], int nrhs, const mxArray
*prhs[])
{
    if (nrhs != 2)
        mexErrMsgTxt("Invaid number of input arguments");

    if (!mxIsSingle(prhs[0]) && !mxIsSingle(prhs[1]))
        mexErrMsgTxt("input matrices must be single ");

    float* A = (float*)mxGetData(prhs[0]);
    float* B = (float*)mxGetData(prhs[1]);

    int numARows = mxGetM(prhs[0]);
    int numACols = mxGetN(prhs[0]);
    int numBRows = mxGetM(prhs[1]);
    int numBCols = mxGetN(prhs[1]);
    int numCRows = numARows;
    int numCCols = numBCols;

    plhs[0] = mxCreateNumericMatrix(numCRows, numCCols, mxSINGLE_
    CLASS, mxREAL);
    float* C = (float*)mxGetData(plhs[0]);

    float *deviceA, *deviceB, *deviceC;
    cudaMalloc(&deviceA, sizeof(float) * numARows * numACols);
    cudaMalloc(&deviceB, sizeof(float) * numBRows * numBCols);
    cudaMalloc(&deviceC, sizeof(float) * numCRows * numCCols);

    cublasHandle_t handle;
    cublasCreate(&handle);
    cublasSetMatrix(numARows,
                    numACols,
                    sizeof(float),
                    A,
                    numARows,
```

```
                              deviceA,
                              numARows);
              cublasSetMatrix(numBRows,
                              numBCols,
                              sizeof(float),
                              B,
                              numBRows,
                              deviceB,
                              numBRows);

      cublasDestroy(handle);
      cudaFree(deviceA);
      cudaFree(deviceB);
      cudaFree(deviceC);
  }
```

The header file, cublas_v2.h, contains the function prototypes for CUBLAS library. We start by creating a handle for CUBLAS, which we destroy at the end by calling cublasDestroy(...). This is the very first thing we do before we call any CUBLAS functions. Next, we prepare our matrix by calling cublasSetMatrix(...). This copies our matrix data from the host memory to the device memory we allocated. Note that we do not call cudaMemcpy(...) explicitly to move our data to GPU device. The file cublasSetMatrix(...) does the job under the hood for us.

6.2.2.7 Step 7

In this step, we simply call one of the matrix-matrix multiplication function, cublasSgemm(...), which does the actual computation on GPU. This is a matrix-matrix multiplication function for single precision data type as you can tell from its function name.

```
#include "mex.h"
#include <cuda_runtime.h>
#include <cublas_v2.h>

void mexFunction(int nlhs, mxArray *plhs[], int nrhs, const mxArray
*prhs[])
{
      if (nrhs != 2)
          mexErrMsgTxt("Invaid number of input arguments");

      if (!mxIsSingle(prhs[0]) && !mxIsSingle(prhs[1]))
          mexErrMsgTxt("input matrices must be single");

      float* A = (float*)mxGetData(prhs[0]);
      float* B = (float*)mxGetData(prhs[1]);
```

```
int numARows = mxGetM(prhs[0]);
int numACols = mxGetN(prhs[0]);
int numBRows = mxGetM(prhs[1]);
int numBCols = mxGetN(prhs[1]);
int numCRows = numARows;
int numCCols = numBCols;

plhs[0] = mxCreateNumericMatrix(numCRows, numCCols, mxSINGLE_
CLASS, mxREAL);
float* C = (float*)mxGetData(plhs[0]);

float *deviceA, *deviceB, *deviceC;
cudaMalloc(&deviceA, sizeof(float) * numARows * numACols);
cudaMalloc(&deviceB, sizeof(float) * numBRows * numBCols);
cudaMalloc(&deviceC, sizeof(float) * numCRows * numCCols);

cublasHandle_t handle;
cublasCreate(&handle);
cublasSetMatrix(numARows,
                numACols,
                sizeof(float),
                A,
                numARows,
                deviceA,
                numARows);
cublasSetMatrix(numBRows,
                numBCols,
                sizeof(float),
                B,
                numBRows,
                deviceB,
                numBRows);

float alpha = 1.0f;
float beta = 0.0f;
cublasSgemm(handle,
            CUBLAS_OP_N,
            CUBLAS_OP_N,
            numARows,
            numBCols,
            numACols,
            &alpha,
            deviceA,
            numARows,
            deviceB,
            numBRows,
            &beta,
            deviceC,
```

```
            numCRows);

    cublasGetMatrix(numCRows,
                    numCCols,
                    sizeof(float),
                    deviceC,
                    numCRows,
                    C,
                    numCRows);

    cublasDestroy(handle);
    cudaFree(deviceA);
    cudaFree(deviceB);
    cudaFree(deviceC);
}
```

The file `cublasSgemm(...)` does all the low-level CUDA tasks and returns the final values to the memory allocated on GPU for matrix **C**. The file `cublasGetMatrix(...)` then copies these results in the device memory to the host memory. We did not even bother to determine the block and thread sizes for our data set. CUBLAS automatically determines their dimension, launches the kernel, and returns the output values.

6.2.2.8 Step 8

Now we have our c-mex code ready. We go to the MATLAB command window and actually compile our code using mex command:

```
mex cublasDemo.cpp -lcudart -lcublas -L"C:\Program Files\NVIDIA GPU
Computing Toolkit\CUDA\v5.0\lib\x64" -v -I"C:\Program Files\NVIDIA GPU
Computing Toolkit\CUDA\v5.0\include"
```

Let us take a look at the options we specified here one by one:

- -lcudart   This indicates that we are using a CUDA runtime library. Specifically, we are calling two basic CUDA fuctions, cudaMalloc(...) and cudaFree(...).
- -lcublas   This indicates that we are using a CUBLAS library. Specifically, we care calling cublasXXX calls.
- -Ldir   dir is our library directory where CUDA and cuBLAS are located.
- -Idir   dir is our header file directory where CUDA and CUBLAS are located.

6.2.2.9 Step 9

The MATLAB command in Step 8 generates our c-mex code as cublasDemo1. mexw64 if compiled on Windows 64 bit, for instance. In the MATLAB command window, we are now ready to call our function to do the multiplication:

```
>> A = single(rand(200,300));
```

```
>> B = single(rand(300, 400));
>> C = cublasDemo(A, B);
```

You can test these codes with `cublasExample.m` in our sample code folder.

6.2.3   CUBLAS with Visual Profiler

Let us look a little deeper inside our CUBLAS function, `cublasSgemm(...)` using NVIDIA Visual Profiler. NVIDIA Visual Profiler gives us a better idea what happens under the hood in addition to a time profile.

First, open NVIDIA Visual Profiler. Then, launch MATLAB from this profiler as explained in Chapter 3. When the MATLAB window is open, set the current folder to where our compiled `c-mex` file is located. Then, run our `c-mex` function as, for example, in Figure 6.1.

After you run the `c-mex` function, exit the MATLAB executable by closing the MATLAB window. After MATLAB is closed, go back to the NVIDIA Visual Profiler. At this time, the NVIDIA Visual Profiler will finish collecting information from MATLAB and generate the results in its window (Figure 6.2).

Let us zoom in to where the CUBLAS function was invoked. As we zoom in, the screen reveals details in addition to the time profile (Figure 6.3).

In this example, you see the actual CUDA calls made with a timeline. We see that, for our matrix-to-matrix calculation, the kernel, `gen_sgemmNN_val(...)`, was called (Figure 6.4).

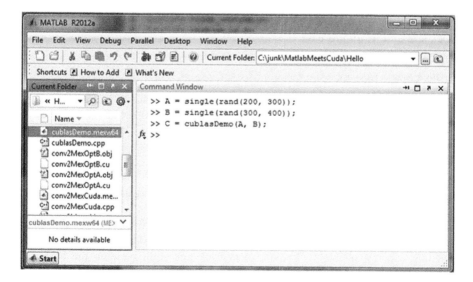

Figure 6.1 Running `cublasDemo` **in MATLAB.**

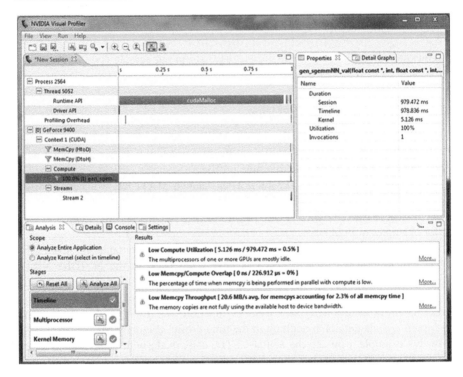

Figure 6.2 Running `cublasDemo` **with Visuaithe Visual Profiler.**

Let us look at the `Details` tab. In this tab, you see the actual times it took for the calculation of each CUDA call. Especially, you can get more information about the kernel calls in terms of grid size and block size. CUBLAS determined grid and block sizes for us. In this case,

Grid Size : [4, 25, 1]
Block Size: [16, 4, 1]

From this information, we now know that CUBLAS set a total of 6400 ($16 \times 4 \times 4 \times 25$) threads for our result matrix **C** of size 200×400.

6.2.3.1 CUBLAS Summary

In summary, we included two header files in our `c-mex` function (Figure 6.5). When we compiled our code using `mex` in MATLAB, we also specified as an option what libraries we use and where they are located. In this way, we expand our `c-mex` function to include the CUBLAS library. We utilize CUDA runtime functions for allocating and deallocating memory for input and output data. The `cublas` functions are responsible for moving data back and forth between the host and device in addition to carrying out our core matrix-matrix multiplication.

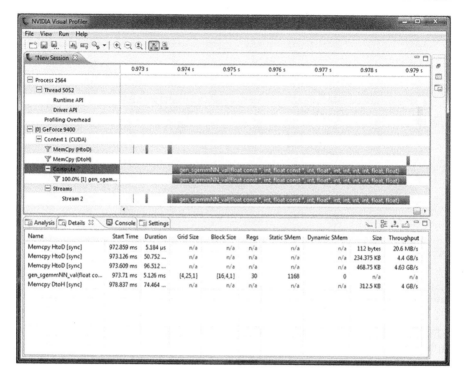

Figure 6.3 Running `cublasDemo` with Visual Profiler, zoomed in on GPU computing.

Name	Start Time	Duration	Grid Size	Block Size	Regs	Static SMem	Dynamic SMem	Size	Throughput
Memcpy HtoD [sync]	972.859 ms	5.184 µs	n/a	n/a	n/a	n/a	n/a	112 bytes	20.6 MB/s
Memcpy HtoD [sync]	973.126 ms	50.752 µs	n/a	n/a	n/a	n/a	n/a	234.375 KB	4.4 GB/s
Memcpy HtoD [sync]	973.609 ms	96.512 µs	n/a	n/a	n/a	n/a	n/a	468.75 KB	4.63 GB/s
gen_sgemmNN_val(float co...	973.71 ms	5.126 ms	[4,25,1]	[16,4,1]	30	1168	0	n/a	n/a
Memcpy DtoH [sync]	978.837 ms	74.464 µs	n/a	n/a	n/a	n/a	n/a	312.5 KB	4 GB/s

Figure 6.4 Running `cublasDemo` with Visual Profiler, with details on the `cublas` function.

6.3   CUFFT

CUFFT is a FFT library provided by NVIDIA with GPU acceleration. Like CUBLAS, it hides the details of CUDA, so we can take advantage of NVIDIA GPU power with a simple interface. This library supports FFTW-compatible data layouts, so we can seamlessly integrate existing FFTW codes.

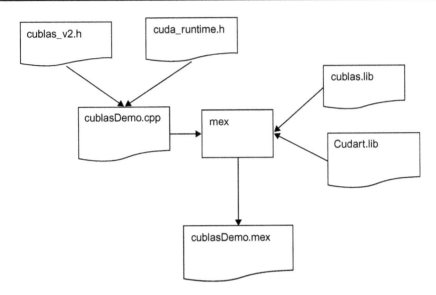

Figure 6.5 The cublasDemo c-mex **build process.**

Like CUBLAS, CUFFT requires both a C header file and the library. These files can be located in the directory where CUBLAS header and library files are located:

- Header file required for compiling:
  ```
  cufft.h
  cuda_runtime.h
  ```

- Libraries required for linking:
  ```
  cufft.lib, cudart.lib                    Windows
  libcufft.dylib, libcudart.dylib          Mac OS X
  libcufft.so, libcudart.so                Linux
  ```

  Windows 64-bit:
  ```
  C:\Program Files\NVIDIA GPU Computing
  Toolkit\CUDA\v5.0\lib\x64\cufft.lib
  C:\Program Fiels\NVIDIA GPU Computing
  Toolkit\CUDA\v5.0\include\cufft.h
  ```

  Windows 32-bit:
  ```
  C:\Program Files\NVIDIA GPU Computing
  Toolkit\CUDA\v5.0\lib\Win32\cufft.lib
  C:\Program Files\NVIDIA GPU Computing
  Toolkit\CUDA\v5.0\include\cufft.h
  ```

  Mac OS X:
  ```
  /Developer/NVIDIA/CUDA-5.0/lib/libcufft.dylib
  /Developer/NVIDIA/CUDA-5.0/include/cufft.h
  ```

  Linux 32-bit:
  ```
  /usr/local/cuda-5.0/lib/libcufft.so
  /usr/local/cuda-5.0/include/cufft.h
  ```

Linux 64-bit:
```
/usr/local/cuda-5.0/lib64/libcufft.so
/usr/local/cuda-5.0/include/cufft.h
```

6.3.1   2D FFT with CUFFT

We again go through a simple example to show how to use CUFFT library in the c-mex function. In this example, we will generate a random 2-D real data, perform 2D FFT, and return its complex output value back to MATLAB.

6.3.1.1   Step 1

Open MATLAB command window, create a new file, and save it as cufftDemo. cpp.

6.3.1.2   Step 2

In our empty cufftDemo.cpp file, type the following:

```
#include "mex.h"

Void mexFunction(int nlhs, mxArray *plhs[], int nrhs, const mxArray
*prhs[])
{
}
```

As in the CUBLAS example, this is our empty gateway routine.

6.3.1.3   Step 3

In this step, we check the input data type is single precision or float.

```
#include "mex.h"

void mexFunction(int nlhs, mxArray *plhs[], int nrhs, const mxArray
*prhs[])
{
    if (nrhs != 1)
        mexErrMsgTxt("Invaid number of input arguments");

    if (!mxIsSingle(prhs[0]) && !mxIsSingle(prhs[1]))
        mexErrMsgTxt("input data type must be single");

    float* A = (float*)mxGetData(prhs[0]);

    int numARows = mxGetM(prhs[0]);
    int numACols = mxGetN(prhs[0]);

}
```

6.3.1.4 Step 4

In this step, we create memory on the device for our input matrix, **A**, and copy data
to the device.

```
#include "mex.h"

void mexFunction(int nlhs, mxArray *plhs[], int nrhs, const mxArray
*prhs[])
{
    if (nrhs != 1)
        mexErrMsgTxt("Invaid number of input arguments");

    if (!mxIsSingle(prhs[0]) && !mxIsSingle(prhs[1]))
        mexErrMsgTxt("input data type must be single");

    float* A = (float*)mxGetData(prhs[0]);

    int numARows = mxGetM(prhs[0]);
    int numACols = mxGetN(prhs[0]);

    float *deviceA;

    cudaMalloc(&deviceA, sizeof(float) * numARows * numACols);
    cudaMemcpy(deviceA, A, numARows * numACols * sizeof(float),
            cudaMemcpyHostToDevice);
}
```

6.3.1.5 Step 5

Now, we create memory in GPU to hold our output FFT data in complex data type.

```
#include "mex.h"

void mexFunction(int nlhs, mxArray *plhs[], int nrhs, const mxArray
*prhs[])
{
    if (nrhs != 1)
        mexErrMsgTxt("Invaid number of input arguments");

    if (!mxIsSingle(prhs[0]) && !mxIsSingle(prhs[1]))
        mexErrMsgTxt("input data type must be single");

    float* A = (float*)mxGetData(prhs[0]);

    int numARows = mxGetM(prhs[0]);
    int numACols = mxGetN(prhs[0]);
```

```
float* deviceA;

cudaMalloc(&deviceA, sizeof(float) * numARows * numACols);
cudaMemcpy(deviceA, A, numARows * numACols * sizeof(float),
           cudaMemcpyHostToDevice);

int outRows = numARows /2 + 1;
int outCols = numACols;
cufftComplex* deviceOut;
cudaMalloc(&deviceOut, sizeof(cufftComplex) * outRows * outCols);

}
```

We have to pay particular attention here. Remember that MATLAB data layout is in column-major order, meaning elements in columns are put contiguously in memory space. However, CUFFT data layout assumes a row-major order. CUFFT expects our data to be contiguous, row by row, unlike our MATLAB data type.

Let us look at the input and output data size summary table from the CUFFT API reference (Table 6.5).

Here, 2D and R2C (real-to-complex) are the dimension and type of our interest. N_2 is the one that runs through in column; it varies most as we move along the contiguous memory regions. So in MATLAB data type case, N_1 is the row dimension and N_2 is the column dimension. The column and row dimensions in MATLAB correspond to N_1 and N_2 in CUFFT. If we pay no attention to its dimension and data layout, the result would be transposed.

- A row dimension, **M**, in MATLAB maps to N_2 in CUFFT.
- A column dimension, **N**, in MATLAB maps to N_1 in CUFFT.

Therefore, the output row size is half of the row plus 1. Take a look at the function definition of cufftPlan2d(...) from its reference. This is the function we call in the next step.

The `cufftResult cufftPlan2d(cufftHandle *plan, int nx, int ny, cufftType type)` creates a 2D FFT plan configuration according to specified signal sizes and data types. For example, the inputs are as follows:

plan	Pointer to a `cufftHandle` object.
nx	The transform size in the x dimension (number of rows).
ny	The transform size in the y dimension (number of columns.)
type	The transform data type (e.g., `CUFFT_C2R` for a single precision complex to real).

For the input parameters, nx and ny, we pass numACols and numARows, respectively.

Table 6.5 Input and Output Data Sizes (from CUFFT API Reference)

Dims	FFT Type	Input Data Size	Output Data Size
1D	C2C (complex-to-complex)	$\mathbf{N_1}$ `cufftComplex`	$\mathbf{N_1}$ `cufftComplex`
	C2R (complex-to-real)	$\left[\dfrac{\mathbf{N_1}}{2}\right] + 1$ `cufftComplex`	$\mathbf{N_1}$ `cufftReal`
	R2C (real-to-complex)	$\mathbf{N_1}$ `cufftReal`	$\left[\dfrac{\mathbf{N_1}}{2}\right] + 1$ `cufftComplex`
2D	C2C (complex-to-complex)	$\mathbf{N_1N_2}$ `cufftComplex`	$\mathbf{N_1N_2}$ `cufftComplex`
	C2R (complex-to-real)	$\mathbf{N_1}\left(\left[\dfrac{\mathbf{N_1}}{2}\right] + 1\right)$ `cufftComplex`	$\mathbf{N_1N_2}$ `cufftReal`
	R2C (real-to-complex)	$\mathbf{N_1N_2}$ `cufftReal`	$\mathbf{N_1}\left(\left[\dfrac{\mathbf{N_2}}{2}\right] + 1\right)$ `cufftComplex`
3D	C2C (complex-to-complex) C2R (complex-to-real)	$\mathbf{N_1N_2N_3}$ `cufftComplex` $\mathbf{N_1N_2}\left(\left[\dfrac{\mathbf{N_3}}{2}\right] + 1\right)$ `cufftComplex`	$\mathbf{N_1N_2N_3}$ `cufftComplex` $\mathbf{N_1N_2N_3}$ `cufftReal`
	R2C (real-to-complex)	$\mathbf{N_1N_2N_3}$ `cufftReal`	$\mathbf{N_1N_2}\left(\left[\dfrac{\mathbf{N_3}}{2}\right] + 1\right)$ `cufftComplex`

6.3.1.6 Step 6

Having prepared inputs and output data arrays, we are ready to call the CUFFT function. First, we create its handle as we similarly did in CUBLAS example:

```
#include "mex.h"
#include <cuda_runtime.h>
#include <cufft.h>

void mexFunction(int nlhs, mxArray *plhs[], int nrhs, mxArray *prhs[])
{
    if (nrhs != 1)
        mexErrMsgTxt("Invaid number of input arguments");
```

```
if (!mxIsSingle(prhs[0]) && !mxIsSingle(prhs[1]))
    mexErrMsgTxt("input data type must be single");

float* A = (float*)mxGetData(prhs[0]);

int numARows = mxGetM(prhs[0]);
int numACols = mxGetN(prhs[0]);

float *deviceA;

cudaMalloc(&deviceA, sizeof(float) * numARows * numACols);
cudaMemcpy(deviceA, A, numARows * numACols * sizeof(float),
            cudaMemcpyHostToDevice);

int outRows = numARows /2 + 1;
int outCols = numACols;
cufftComplex* deviceOut;
cudaMalloc(&deviceOut, sizeof(cufftComplex) * outRows * outCols);

cufftHandle plan;
cufftPlan2d(&plan, numACols, numARow, CUFFT_R2C);
cufftExecR2C(plan, deviceA, deviceOut);

cufftDestroy(plan);
cudaFree(deviceA);
}
```

In cufftPlan2d(...), we indicate what the size of input data array and what operation we want to do. Once we create this plan, we can reuse it later in the program if needed, when you no longer need it, clean it out by calling cufftDestroy (...). The actual computation happens inside cufftExecR2C(...) and the output result becomes available in the output array, deviceOut.

6.3.1.7 Step 7

The resulting data is available in GPU memory. We bring this result back into the host memory so that we can use it in the MATLAB environment.

```
#include "mex.h"
#include <cuda_runtime.h>
#include <cufft.h>

void mexFunction(int nlhs, mxArray *plhs[], int nrhs, mxArray *prhs[])
{
    if (nrhs != 1)
        mexErrMsgTxt("Invaid number of input arguments");

    if (!mxIsSingle(prhs[0]) && !mxIsSingle(prhs[1]))
        mexErrMsgTxt("input data type must be single");
```

```
float* A = (float*)mxGetData(prhs[0]);

int numARows = mxGetM(prhs[0]);
int numACols = mxGetN(prhs[0]);

float *deviceA;

cudaMalloc(&deviceA, sizeof(float) * numARows * numACols);
cudaMemcpy(deviceA, A, numARows * numACols * sizeof(float),
            cudaMemcpyHostToDevice);

int outRows = numARows /2 + 1;
int outCols = numACols;
cufftComplex* deviceOut;
cudaMalloc(&deviceOut, sizeof(cufftComplex) * outRows * outCols);

cufftHandle plan;
cufftPlan2d(&plan, numACols, numARows, CUFFT_R2C);
cufftExecR2C(plan, deviceA, deviceOut);

float* out = (float*)mxMalloc(sizeof(cufftComplex) * outRows *
                outCols);
cudaMemcpy(out, deviceOut, outRows * outCols * sizeof(cufftComplex),
            cudaMemcpyDeviceToHost);

plhs[0] = mxCreateNumericMatrix(outRows, outCols, mxSINGLE_CLASS,
                                mxCOMPLEX);
float* real = (float*)mxGetPr(plhs[0]);
float* imag = (float*)mxGetPi(plhs[0]);
float* complex = out;
for (int c = 0; c < outCols; ++c)
{
    for (int r = 0; r < outRows; ++r)
    {
        *real++ = *complex++;
        *imag++ = *complex++;
    }
}

mxFree(out);
cufftDestroy(plan);
cudaFree(deviceA);
}
```

Unlike CUBLAS, we use CUDA functions to allocate, deallocate, and copy data back and forth between GPU and c-mex. But, other than these three CUDA functions, we do not need to define our own kernel and decide the block and thread sizes. As discussed in Chapter 4, MATLAB stores complex data in two separate arrays: one for real and the other for imaginary. CUFFT stores them in one chunk of memory space with the complex numbers stored next to each other. So, in this step, we create a complex array for MATLAB and copy real and imaginary components to each corresponding array.

6.3.1.8 Step 8

Now we have our c-mex code ready. Go to the MATLAB command window and let us compile our code.

```
mex cufftDemo.cpp -lcudart -lcufft -L"C:\Program Files\NVIDIA GPU Computing
Toolkit\CUDA\v5.0\lib\x64" -v -I"C:\Program Files\NVIDIA GPU Computing
Toolkit\CUDA\v5.0\include"
```

Let's take a look at the options we specified one by one.

- -lcudart   This indicates that we are using a CUDA runtime library. Specifically, we are calling two basic CUDA fuctions, cudaMalloc(...) and cudaFree(...).
- -lcufft   This indicates that we are using a CUFFT library. Specifically, we are calling cufftXXX calls.
- -L*dir*   dir is our library directory where CUDA and CUFFT are located.
- -I*dir*   dir is our header file directory where CUDA and CUFFT are located.

6.3.1.9 Step 9

The preceding generates our c-mex code as cublasDemo.mexw64, if compiled on Windows 64 bit, for instance. In the MATLAB command window, we call our function to do the multiplication:

```
>> A = single(rand(4, 4));
>> B = fft2(A)

B =
    9.7001             0.5174 - 0.9100i   1.6219            0.5174 + 0.9100i
   -0.6788 + 0.4372i   0.7316 + 0.5521i  -0.1909 - 1.0807i -1.3437 + 0.2664i
    1.3043            -0.9332 + 0.6233i  -2.0830            -0.9332 - 0.6233i
   -0.6788 - 0.4372i  -1.3437 - 0.2664i  -0.1909 + 1.0807i  0.7316 - 0.5521i

>> C = cufftDemo(A)

C =
    9.7001 - 0.0000i  0.5174 - 0.9100i   1.6219 - 0.0000i   0.5174 + 0.9100i
   -0.6788 + 0.4372i  0.7316 + 0.5521i  -0.1909 - 1.0807i  -1.3437 + 0.2664i
    1.3043 + 0.0000i -0.9332 + 0.6233i  -2.0830 + 0.0000i  -0.9332 - 0.6233i
```

We compare two results: one using MATLAB fft2 and the other using the CUFFT c-mex function. Note that the cufftDemo(A) returns one row short. This output is as per its API specification (see Table 6.5).

FFT Type	Input Data Size	Output Data Size
R2C (real-to-complex)	$N_1 N_2$ cufftReal	$N_1 \left(\left[\dfrac{N_2}{2} \right] + 1 \right)$ cufftComplex

In our case, $N_1 = 4$ and $N_2 = 4$. This gives us the final three rows as output.

This missing row, in this particular example, can be calculated using the complex conjugate of the second row as

```
>> D = [C; conj([fliplud([C(2:2,1), fliplr(C(2:2, 2:4))])])]

D =
    9.7001 − 0.0000i    0.5174 − 0.9100i    1.6219 − 0.0000i    0.5174 + 0.9100i
   −0.6788 + 0.4372i    0.7316 + 0.5521i   −0.1909 − 1.0807i   −1.3437 + 0.2664i
    1.3043 + 0.0000i   −0.9332 + 0.6233i   −2.0830 + 0.0000i   −0.9332 − 0.6233i
   −0.6788 − 0.4372i   −1.3437 − 0.2664i   −0.1909 + 1.0807i    0.7316 − 0.5521i
```

6.3.2 CUFFT with Visual Profiler

As with the CUBLAS example, we look a little deeper inside our cufft functions, using NVIDIA Visual Profiler.

Open NVIDIA Visual Profiler, create a new session. In our MATLAB window, set the current folder to where our compiled c-mex file is located. Then, run our c-mex function as in Figure 6.6, for example.

After running the c-mex function, exit MATLAB executable by closing the MATLAB window. After MATLAB is closed, go back to NVIDIA Visual Profiler. At this time NVIDIA Visual Profiler finishes collecting information from MATLAB and generates the results in its window. If NVIDIA Visual Profiler complains as shown in Figure 6.7, then, we temporarily add the cudaDeviceReset() function at the end of our c-mex function to make sure that CUDA profile data is flushed.

```
    mxFree(out);
    cufftDestroy(plan);
    cudaFree(deviceA);
    cudaFree(deviceB);

    cudaDeviceReset();
}
```

After MATLAB closes, we see the detailed analysis on how CUFFT performed (Figure 6.8).

Let us zoom in where the cufft function was invoked. As we zoom in, the screen reveals details in addition to the time profile. We have a better look under the hood of this specific cufft function. Notice that it creates multiple kernels with various thread sizes, as shown in Figure 6.9.

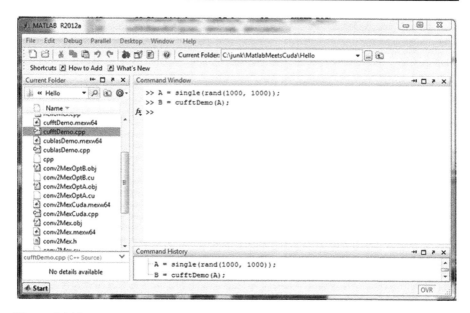

Figure 6.6 The `cufftDemo` **running on MATLAB.**

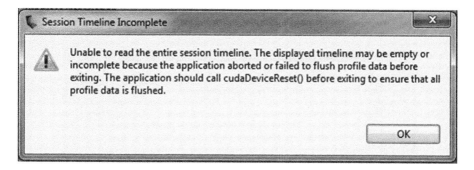

Figure 6.7 NVIDIA Visual Profiler Session Timeline Incomplete message.

6.3.2.1   CUFFT Summary

In summary, as in the CUBLAS example, we include two header files in our `c-mex` function. When we compile code using `mex` in MATLAB, we also specifiy, as an option, what libraries we use and where they are located. The `cuda` runtime functions we used were for allocating and deallocating memory and copying input and output data between the host and the device. When calling `cufft` functions, we have to consider whether the data layout from MATLAB is compatible with CUFFT. CUFFT is expecting data input to be in row-major order, while MATLAB passes data in column-major order. We have to pay particular attention as to how rows and columns in MATLAB map to `nx` and `ny` in CUFFT (Figure 6.10).

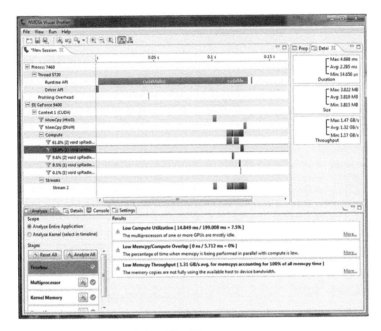

Figure 6.8 The `cufftDemo` with **Visual Profiler.**

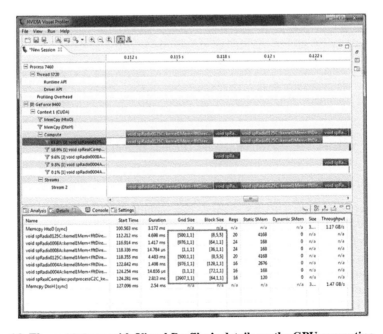

Figure 6.9 The `cufftDemo` with **Visual Profiler's details on the GPU computing.**

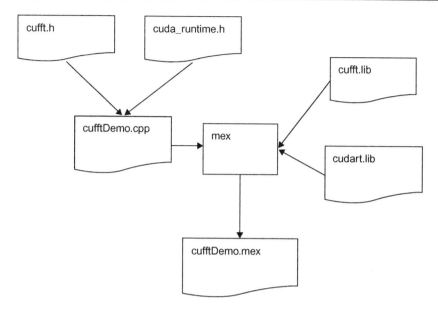

Figure 6.10 The cufftDemo c-mex **build process.**

6.4 Thrust

Thrust is a C++ template library that allows you to implement high performance parallel applications using CUDA. It provides a rich collection of data parallel primitives, such as scan, sort, and reduce. We can write more concise and more readable programs using these algorithms implemented in Thrust. Since Thrust is a template library, it does not require links to any libraries. All we need is to include its header files in the c-mex functions.

Thrust should have been already installed in your system if you are using CUDA 4.0 or better. The required include files are located at: Header file directory:

Windows 32-bit and 64-bit:
C:\Program Fiels\NVIDIA GPU Computing Toolkit\CUDA\v5.0\include

Mac OS X:
/Developer/NVIDIA/CUDA-5.0/include

Linux 32-bit and 64-bit:
/usr/local/cuda-5.0/include

6.4.1 *Sorting with Thrust*

6.4.1.1 *Step 1*

Open MATLAB command window, create a new file, and save it as thrustDemo. cpp.

6.4.1.2 Step 2

In the empty `thrustDemo.cpp` file, type the following:

```
#include "mex.h"

void mexFunction(int nlhs, mxArray *plhs[], int nrhs, const mxArray
*prhs[])
{

}
```

Again, this is the empty gateway routine.

6.4.1.3 Step 3

In this step, we check that the input data type is single precision or float. Also, at this step, we prepare the output data, which is just a float value. Then, we call `getSum(...)`, in which we invoke the `thrust` function. Line 3 in the following example tells the compiler that we will use the `getSum(...)` function, which is implemented outside this file.

```
#include "mex.h"

extern float getSum(float* A, int size);
void mexFunction(int nlhs, mxArray *plhs[], int nrhs, const mxArray
*prhs[])
{
    if (nrhs != 1)
        mexErrMsgTxt("Invaid number of input arguments");

    if (!mxIsSingle(prhs[0]) && !mxIsSingle(prhs[1]))
        mexErrMsgTxt("input data type must be single");

    float* A = (float*)mxGetData(prhs[0]);
    int numARows = mxGetM(prhs[0]);
    int numACols = mxGetN(prhs[0]);
    int numElem = (numARows > numACols) ? numARows: numACols;

    plhs[0] = mxCreateNumericMatrix(1, 1, mxSINGLE_CLASS, mxCOMPLEX);
    float* B = (float*)mxGetData(plhs[0]);

    *B = getSum(A, numElem);
}
```

6.4.1.4 Step 4

We now create the `thrustSum.cu` file, where all the `thrust` functions are compiled. We are compiling thrust codes with the nvcc compiler, which generates binaries for the CUDA backend. Create `thrustSum.cu` and type in the code that follows

```
#include <thrust/reduce.h>
#include <thrust/device_vector.h>

float getSum(float* A, int size)
{
      thrust::device_vector<float> deviceA(A, A+size);
      return thrust::reduce(deviceA.begin(),
                            deviceA.end(),
                            (float)0.0f,
                            thrust::plus<float>());
}
```

6.4.1.5   Step 5

We compile and create an object file, thrustSum.obj, to which we link our main c-mex file.

```
>> system('nvcc -c thrustSum.cu');
```

6.4.1.6   Step 6

Let us compile the main c-mex function and link it with the thrustSum.obj:

```
>> mex thrustDemo.cpp thrustSum.obj -lcudart -L"C:\Program Files\NVIDIA
GPU Computing Toolkit\CUDA\v5.0\lib\x64" -v -I"C:\Program Files\NVIDIA
GPU Computing Toolkit\CUDA\v5.0\include"
```

6.4.1.7   Step 7

We now have a c-mex function that we can call in MATLAB. We can run our function in MATLAB command window as

```
>> thrustDemo(single([1 2 3 4]))
ans =
    10
>> thrustDemo(single(rand(1, 10000)))
ans =
    4.9986e+03
```

6.4.2   Thrust with Visual Profiler

Having the c-mex function using Thrust, we can use NVIDIA Visual Profiler again to examine details as to what kind of kernels were executed and how the program performed. As we did with CUBLAS and CUFFT, run NVIDIA Visual

Profiler with MATLAB. Then, run in the MATLAB command window
as follows:

```
>> thrustDemo(single(rand(1, 12345)))

ans =
    6.1485e + 03
```

When MATLAB was stops and NVIDIA Visual Profiler shows an error requir-
ing cudaDeviceReset(), we can include this function at the end of the c-mex function, as

```
    *B = getSum(A, numElem);

    cudaDeviceReset();
}
```

Two kernels are defined in the reduce algorithm. Each kernel has an one-
dimensional grid and block size (Figure 6.11).

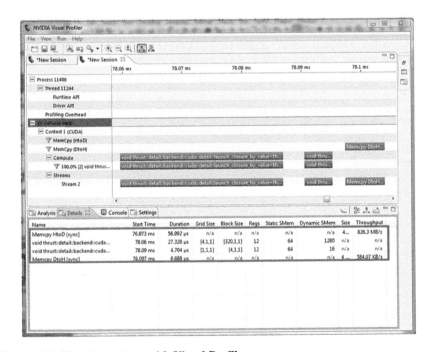

Figure 6.11 The thrustDemo **with Visual Profiler.**

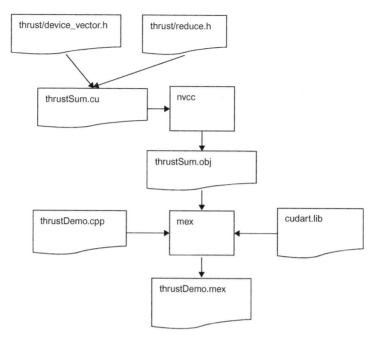

Figure 6.12 The `thrustDemo` c-mex **build process.**

6.4.2.1 Thrust Summary

Thrust is a C++ template library. When we use it (Figure 6.12), we have two steps of compilation using `nvcc` then `mex`. We create the `thrustSum.cu` file, in which we put all the Thrust stuff. Then, we compiled and generate the object file using the `nvcc` compiler. We had to declare only header files that contain the function or class of interest. Then, we compile our main `c-mex` function and link it with the object file for the final `c-mex` file generation.

7 Example in Computer Graphics

7.1 Chapter Objectives

In this chapter, we introduce a simple computer graphics algorithm called *marching cubes*. The algorithm is a simple but very data-intensive operation depending on the data set. In this chapter, we

- Introduce the marching cubes algorithm.
- Implement it in plain MATLAB.
- Improve speed performance in MATLAB.
- Accelerate the speed using c-mex and CUDA.

7.2 Marching Cubes

Marching cubes is a simple yet very powerful computer graphics algorithm that can be used in various applications, especially in 3D visualizations. Given a stack of images, this algorithm extracts a 3D isosurface in the form of triangles, where each point on the surface has the same constant value. Input data can come from various sources, such as CT and MRI scans. They usually come in a stack of 2D images as shown in Figure 7.1. In volume data, each data point is referred to as a *voxel*. The eight voxels in Figure 7.2 form a cube.

With $M \times N \times P$ volume data, we have $(M - 1) \times (N - 1) \times (P - 1)$ cubes in the whole data set. Each vertex of a cube is assigned a voxel value. The value at each vertex could be higher or lower than an isosurface value. The basic idea of the algorithm is to find the points where the isosurface intersect on the cube edges, then construct triangles from those points at intersections. Consider the cube in Figure 7.2 and let us label each vertex and edge. There are eight vertices and 12 edges. We label them as in Figure 7.3. Since each vertex in a cube can be higher or lower than the isosurface value, there are 256 (2^8) possible cases with 15 unique cases due to symmetry (Figure 7.4).

For simplicity, let us assume our vertex V0 is above the isosurface value and the rest are below it, so that our V0 is an inside object, as shown in Figure 7.5. This falls into the second case on the top in Figure 7.4. In this case, the isosurface crosses three edges: E0, E8 and E3. The intersection points on those edges can be linearly interpolated.

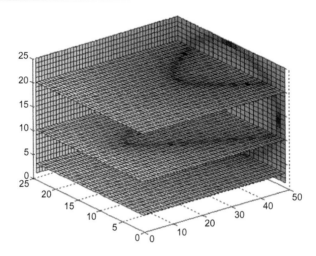

Figure 7.1 Sample volume data shown in slices.

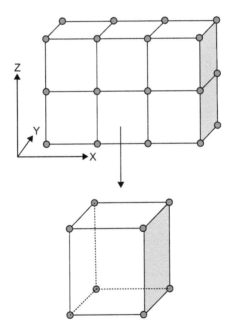

Figure 7.2 Volume data, voxels, and a grid of cubes.

The isosurface in this cube is then approximated with a triangle with three points. We define the normal vector for this triangle so that it points toward the lower isosurface side. We can work out all other 255 cases and determine all the triangles in each case. This has been worked out already and we can use the predetermined lookup tables for each case.

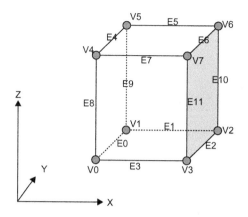

Figure 7.3 A cube with vertex and edge labels.

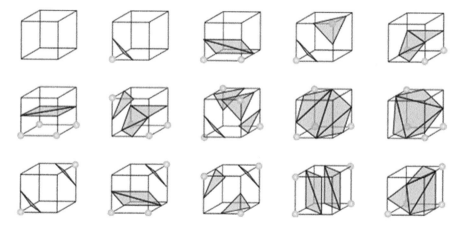

Figure 7.4 Fifteen unique cases.

The algorithm provides two main tables: edge table and triangle table. First, using eight vertexes as 8-bit binary numbers, we determine the cube number:

$$N\text{th bit} = \begin{cases} 0 \text{ if the value at } Vi < \text{isosurface value} \\ 1 \text{ if the value at } Vi \geq \text{isosurface value} \end{cases}$$

In our case, the cube number is 1:

8th bit	7th bit	6th bit	5th bit	4th bit	3rd bit	2nd bit	1st bit
V7	V6	V5	V4	V3	V2	V1	V0
0	0	0	0	0	0	0	1

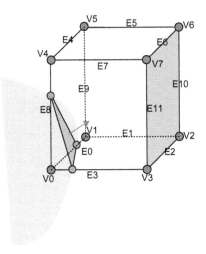

Figure 7.5 The vertex V0 is above the isosurface value. This results in one triangle with a normal vector.

Using this value, we look at the edge table. From the edge table, we get the value, 265. If we convert this to a 12-bit binary number, each bit represents the edge number. It is set to 1 if the isosurface intersects with this edge. In our case,

12th bit	11th bit	10th bit	9th bit	8th bit	7th bit	6th bit	5th bit	4th bit	3rd bit	2nd bit	1st bit
E11	E10	E9	E8	E7	E6	E5	E4	E3	E2	E1	E0
0	0	0	1	0	0	0	0	1	0	0	1

From the binary values, we now know that the edge, E0, E3, and E8 are the ones that intersect with the isosurface. We can linearly interpolate where on those edges the surface intersects. For instance, the intersection point on E3 can be estimated as

$$P3 = \frac{\text{isovalue} - I0}{I3 - I0} \times (V3 - V0) + V0$$

where $I0$ and $I3$ are intensity values at vertex V0 and V3, respectively.

Then, the second table gives indexes of a triangle in order. This enables us to determine in which direction the normal vector goes or which side faces outward. For our cube, the triangle table gives

```
0, 8, 3, -1, -1, -1, -1, -1, -1, -1, -1, -1, -1, -1, -1, -1
```

```
edgeTable = [
        0,   265,   515,    778, 1030, 1295, 1541, 1804,  ...
     2060,  2309,  2575,  2822, 3082, 3331, 3593, 3840,  ...
      400,   153,   915,   666, 1430, 1183, 1941, 1692,  ...
     2460,  2197,  2975,  2710, 3482, 3219, 3993, 3728,  ...
      560,   825,    51,   314, 1590, 1855, 1077, 1340,  ...
    ...
    ...
     1804,  1541,  1295,  1030,  778,  515,  265,    0];


triTable = [
   -1,  -1,  -1,  -1,  -1,  -1,  -1,  -1,  -1,  -1,  -1,  -1,  -1,  -1,  -1,  -1;
    0,   8,   3,  -1,  -1,  -1,  -1,  -1,  -1,  -1,  -1,  -1,  -1,  -1,  -1,  -1;
    0,   1,   9,  -1,  -1,  -1,  -1,  -1,  -1,  -1,  -1,  -1,  -1,  -1,  -1,  -1;
    1,   8,   3,   9,   8,  -1,  -1,  -1,  -1,  -1,  -1,  -1,  -1,  -1,  -1,  -1;
    1,   2,  10,  -1,  -1,  -1,  -1,  -1,  -1,  -1,  -1,  -1,  -1,  -1,  -1,  -1;
    0,   8,   3,   1,   2,  10,  -1,  -1,  -1,  -1,  -1,  -1,  -1,  -1,  -1,  -1;
    9,   2,  10,   0,   2,   9,  -1,  -1,  -1,  -1,  -1,  -1,  -1,  -1,  -1,  -1;
    2,   8,   3,   2,  10,   8,  10,   9,   8,  -1,  -1,  -1,  -1,  -1,  -1,  -1;
    3,  11,   2,  -1,  -1,  -1,  -1,  -1,  -1,  -1,  -1,  -1,  -1,  -1,  -1,  -1;
    ...
    ...
    1,  10,   2,  -1,  -1,  -1,  -1,  -1,  -1,  -1,  -1,  -1,  -1,  -1,  -1,  -1;
    1,   3,   8,   9,   1,   8,  -1,  -1,  -1,  -1,  -1,  -1,  -1,  -1,  -1,  -1;
    0,   9,   1,  -1,  -1,  -1,  -1,  -1,  -1,  -1,  -1,  -1,  -1,  -1,  -1,  -1;
    0,   3,   8,  -1,  -1,  -1,  -1,  -1,  -1,  -1,  -1,  -1,  -1,  -1,  -1,  -1;
   -1,  -1,  -1,  -1,  -1,  -1,  -1,  -1,  -1,  -1,  -1,  -1,  -1,  -1,  -1,  -1];
```

Figure 7.6 Edge and triangle lookup tables.

As per the table, the triangle is defined by points on E0, E8, and E3, in that order. The lookup tables in Figure 7.6 make it easy to find out all the possible triangles and their indexes.

7.3 Implementation in MATLAB

This section shows how to implement the marching cubes algorithm in MATLAB. We first do the straight implementation of the algorithm in MATLAB to demonstrate the algorithm itself. In this implementation, we visit each voxel and determine the triangles. The full implementation can be found in testSurfaceNoOpt.m and getSurfaceNoOpt.m or at the end of the steps.

7.3.1 Step 1

First, let us generate a small sample of volume data using the MATLAB command, flow. In the MATLAB command window, enter the following:

```
% generate sample volume data
[X, Y, Z, V] = flow;

% visualize volume data
figure
```

```
xmin = min(X(:));
ymin = min(Y(:));
zmin = min(Z(:));
xmax = max(X(:));
ymax = max(Y(:));
zmax = max(Z(:));
hslice = surf(linspace(xmin,xmax,100), linspace(ymin,ymax,100), zeros
(100));
rotate(hslice,[-1,0,0],-45)
xd = get(hslice,'XData');
yd = get(hslice,'YData');
zd = get(hslice,'ZData');
delete(hslice)
h = slice(X,Y,Z,V,xd,yd,zd);
set(h,'FaceColor','interp','EdgeColor','none','DiffuseStrength',0.8)
hold on
hx = slice(X,Y,Z,V,xmax,[],[]);
set(hx,'FaceColor','interp','EdgeColor','none')
hy = slice(X,Y,Z,V,[],ymax,[]);
set(hy,'FaceColor','interp','EdgeColor','none')
hz = slice(X,Y,Z,V,[],[],zmin);
set(hz,'FaceColor','interp','EdgeColor','none')
```

By default, this generates four variables: X, Y, Z, and V. They are $25 \times 50 \times 25$ matrices that contain the positions and intensities at voxels. The rest of the lines let you visualize data. If you execute the code now, this volume data will look like Figure 7.7.

If you wish, further explore visualization options from MATLAB Help in MATLAB>User's Guide>3-D Visualization>Volume Visualization Techniques>Exploring Volumes with Slice Planes. We later find the size of the volume data along X, Y, and Z and define our isovalue to be -3.

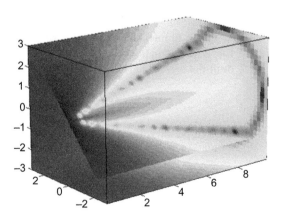

Figure 7.7 Sample volume data.

7.3.2 Step 2

We then define a function to perform the marching cubes algorithm and save it as getSurfaceNoOpt.m. This function gets five inputs and returns two outputs that contain all the vertexes and indexes of the triangles we find in the volume data. We show only partial table values. The full table values can be found in the provided getSurfaceNoOpt.m file.

```
function [Vertices, Indices] = getSurfaceNoOpt(X, Y, Z, V, isovalue)

edgeTable = uint16([
      0,  265,  515,  778,  1030,  1295,  1541,  1804,  ...
   2060,  2309,  2575,  2822,  3082,  3331,  3593,  3840,  ...
   ...
   ...
   1804, 1541, 1295, 1030, 778, 515, 265, 0]);

triTable = [
   -1, -1, -1, -1, -1, -1, -1, -1, -1, -1, -1, -1, -1, -1, -1, -1;
    0,  8,  3, -1, -1, -1, -1, -1, -1, -1, -1, -1, -1, -1, -1, -1;
   ...
   ...
   -1, -1, -1, -1, -1, -1, -1, -1, -1, -1, -1, -1, -1, -1, -1, -1];

sizeX = size(V, 1);
sizeY = size(V, 2);
sizeZ = size(V, 3);

MAX_VERTICES = 15;

% vertices and indices
VertexBin = single(zeros(sizeX, sizeY, sizeZ, MAX_VERTICES, 3));
TriCounter = zeros(sizeX, sizeY, sizeZ);
totalTriangles = 0;
```

We first create two precalculated lookup tables for the marching cubes algorithm. Next, we determine sizes of the volume in the x, y, and z directions. Then, we preallocate temporary variables for all of our vertex and index storages.

7.3.3 Step 3

In this step, we march through all the cubes in the volume data. We visit every cube in nested loops. If the volume data size is $M \times N \times P$, then there will be $(M - 1) \times (N - 1) \times (P - 1)$ cubes in all.

```
for k = 1:sizeZ - 1
    for j = 1:sizeY - 1
        for i = 1:sizeX - 1
            ...
```

```
        % algorithm goes in here
        ...
        end
      end
  end
```

7.3.4 Step 4

In the innermost loop, we read the intensity values and positions at eight vertexes of the cube we are processing. They are assigned according to the vertex labels in Figure 7.3.

```
% temp. vars for voxels and isopoints.
voxels = single(zeros(8,4));  %[v,x,y,z]
isoPos = single(zeros(12,3));  %[x,y,z]

%cube
voxels(1,:) = [V(i,     j,      k),     X(i,     j,      k),     Y(i,     j,      k),
              Z(i,     j,      k)];
voxels(2,:) = [V(i,     j+1,    k),     X(i,     j+1,    k),     Y(i,     j+1, k),
              Z(i,     j+1,    k)];
voxels(3,:) = [V(i+1,   j+1,    k),     X(i+1,   j+1,    k),     Y(i+1,   j+1, k),
              Z(i+1,   j+1,    k)];
voxels(4,:) = [V(i+1,   j,      k),     X(i+1,   j,      k),     Y(i+1,   j,      k),
              Z(i+1,   j,      k)];
voxels(5,:) = [V(i,     j,      k+1),   X(i,     j,      k+1),   Y(i,     j,      k+1),
              Z(i,     j,      k+1)];
voxels(6,:) = [V(i,     j+1,    k+1),   X(i,     j+1,    k+1),   Y(i,     j+1, k+1),
              Z(i,     j+1,    k+1)];
voxels(7,:) = [V(i+1,   j+1,    k+1),   X(i+1,   j+1,    k+1),   Y(i+1,   j+1, k+1),
              Z(i+1,   j+1,    k+1)];
voxels(8,:) = [V(i+1,   j,      k+1),   X(i+1,   j,      k+1),   Y(i+1,   j,      k+1),
              Z(i+1,   j,      k+1)];
```

7.3.5 Step 5

We check the intensity value at each vertex to see if it is above or below the isovalue. A bit position for a vertex is set if the value is above the isovalue. Since we have eight vertexes, there are 256 cases in total. After checking all the values at the eight vertexes, we determine the cube index. We use this cube index to get the edge values from the edge table.

```
% find the cube index
cubeIndex = uint16(0);
for n = 1:8
    if voxels(n,1) >= isovalue
        cubeIndex = bitset(cubeIndex, n);
    end
end
cubeIndex = cubeIndex + 1;
```

```
% get edges from edgeTable
edges = edgeTable(cubeIndex);
if edges == 0
    continue;
end
```

7.3.6 Step 6

After getting the edge values from the edge table, we locate the edges on which the isosurface intersects and find the intersection points on those edges. We first create a new function for the interpolation. This function receives two voxels and isovalues as input and outputs the interpolated position.

```
function [varargout] = interpolatePos(isovalue, voxel1, voxel2)
    scale = (isovalue - voxel1(:,1)) ./ (voxel2(:,1) - voxel1(:,1));
    interpolatedPos = voxel1(:,2:4) + [scale .* (voxel2(:,2) - voxel1(:,2)), ...
                                      scale .* (voxel2(:,3) - voxel1(:,3)), ...
                                      scale .* (voxel2(:,4) - voxel1(:,4))];

    if nargout == 1 || nargout == 0
        varargout{1} = interpolatedPos;
    elseif nargout == 3
        varargout{1} = interpolatedPos(:,1);
        varargout{2} = interpolatedPos(:,2);
        varargout{3} = interpolatedPos(:,3);
    end
```

Going back to our main function code, we continue checking the edges and call the interpolation function for each edge, if applicable:

```
% check 12 edges
if bitand(edges, 1)
    isoPos(1,:) = interpolatePos(isovalue, voxels(1,:), voxels(2,:));
end
if bitand(edges, 2)
    isoPos(2,:) = interpolatePos(isovalue, voxels(2,:), voxels(3,:));
end
if bitand(edges, 4)
    isoPos(3,:) = interpolatePos(isovalue, voxels(3,:), voxels(4,:));
end
if bitand(edges, 8)
    isoPos(4,:) = interpolatePos(isovalue, voxels(4,:), voxels(1,:));
end
if bitand(edges, 16)
    isoPos(5,:) = interpolatePos(isovalue, voxels(5,:), voxels(6,:));
end
if bitand(edges, 32)
    isoPos(6,:) = interpolatePos(isovalue, voxels(6,:), voxels(7,:));
```

```
end
if bitand(edges, 64)
    isoPos(7,:) = interpolatePos(isovalue, voxels(7,:), voxels(8,:));
end
if bitand(edges, 128)
    isoPos(8,:) = interpolatePos(isovalue, voxels(8,:), voxels(5,:));
end
if bitand(edges, 256)
    isoPos(9,:) = interpolatePos(isovalue, voxels(1,:), voxels(5,:));
end
if bitand(edges, 512)
    isoPos(10,:) = interpolatePos(isovalue, voxels(2,:), voxels(6,:));
end
if bitand(edges, 1024)
    isoPos(11,:) = interpolatePos(isovalue, voxels(3,:), voxels(7,:));
end
if bitand(edges, 2048)
    isoPos(12,:) = interpolatePos(isovalue, voxels(4,:), voxels(8,:));
end
```

7.3.7 Step 7

From the triangle table, we find out how many triangles there are and their indexes.
We go through the predetermined vertex order from the triangle table and register
all the triangles we identify. There can be five triangles at maximum.

```
%walk through the triTable and get the triangle(s) vertices
numTriangles = 0;
numVertices = 0;
for n = 1:3:16

    if triTable(cubeIndex, n) < 0
        break;
    end

    % first vertex
    numVertices = numVertices + 1;
    edgeIndex = triTable(cubeIndex, n) + 1;
    vertexBin(i, j, k, numVertices, :) = isoPos(edgeIndex, :);
    % second vertex
    numVertices = numVertices + 1;
    edgeIndex = triTable(cubeIndex, n + 1) + 1;
    vertexBin(i, j, k, numVertices, :) = isoPos(edgeIndex, :);
    % third vertex
    numVertices = numVertices + 1;
    edgeIndex = triTable(cubeIndex, n + 2) + 1;
    vertexBin(i, j, k, numVertices, :) = isoPos(edgeIndex, :);

    numTriangles = numTriangles + 1;
end
TriCounter(i, j, k) = numTriangles;
totalTriangels = totalTriangles + numTriangles;
```

7.3.8 Step 8

After we find all the triangles in a cube, we add them to our output storages for vertexes and indexes:

```
Vertices = single(zeros(totalTriangles * 3, 3));
Indices = uint32(zeros(totalTriangels, 3));
vIdx = 0;
tIdx = 0;
for k = 1:sizeZ - 1
    for j = 1:sizeY - 1
        for i = 1:sizeX - 1

            count = TriCounter(i, j, k);
            if count < 1
                continue;
            end

            for t = 0:count - 1
                vIdx = vIdx + 1;
                Vertices(vIdx, :) = vertexBin(i, j, k, 3*t + 1, :);
                vIdx = vIdx + 1;
                Vertices(vIdx, :) = vertexBin(i, j, k, 3*t + 2, :);
                vIdx = vIdx + 1;
                Vertices(vIdx, :) = vertexBin(i, j, k, 3*t + 3, :);

                tIdx = tIdx + 1;
                Indices(tIdx, :) = uint32([3 * tIdx - 2, 3 * tIdx - 1, 3 * tIdx]);
            end

        end
    end
end
```

7.3.9 Step 9

After we calculate all the vertexes and triangle indexes, we can visualize the triangles as follows. Back in `testSurfaceNoOpt.m`, append the following lines for triangle visualization:

```
% data type to single
X = single(X);
Y = single(Y);
Z = single(Z);
V = single(V);
isovalue = single(-3);

% Marching cubes
[Vertices1, Indices1] = getSurfaceNoOpt(X, Y, Z, V, isovalue);
```

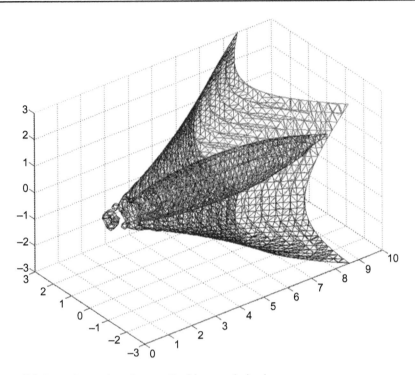

Figure 7.8 Isosurface at isovalue $= -3$ with no optimization.

```
% visualize triangles
figure
p = patch('Faces', Indices1, 'Vertices', Vertices1);
set(p, 'FaceColor', 'none', 'EdgeColor', 'red');
daspect([1,1,1])
view(3);
camlight
lighting gouraud
grid on
```

The triangles we found using marching cubes are now shown in Figure 7.8.

The following is the full implementation in MATLAB, including two lookup tables. Note that there are duplicate vertexes in our final vertex results. One go on to remove those duplicate vertexes, thus reducing our final storage size. However, we stop here without further reducing the duplicates for the purpose of demonstrating the algorithm.

Here are the full codes in three files. The table values shown are truncated. The full table values can be found in the provided getSurfaceNoOpt.m file.

```
getSurfaceNoOpt.m
function [Vertices, Indices] = getSurfaceNoOpt(X, Y, Z, V, isovalue)

edgeTable = uint16([
        0,  265,  515,  778, 1030, 1295, 1541, 1804, ...
     2060, 2309, 2575, 2822, 3082, 3331, 3593, 3840, ...
      400,  153,  915,  666, 1430, 1183, 1941, 1692, ...
     2460, 2197, 2975, 2710, 3482, 3219, 3993, 3728, ...
      560,  825,   51,  314, 1590, 1855, 1077, 1340, ...
    ...
    ...
    ...

     3728, 3993, 3219, 3482, 2710, 2975, 2197, 2460, ...
     1692, 1941, 1183, 1430,  666,  915,  153,  400, ...
     3840, 3593, 3331, 3082, 2822, 2575, 2309, 2060, ...
     1804, 1541, 1295, 1030,  778,  515,  265,    0]);

triTable = [
    -1, -1, -1, -1, -1, -1, -1, -1, -1, -1, -1, -1, -1, -1, -1, -1;
     0,  8,  3, -1, -1, -1, -1, -1, -1, -1, -1, -1, -1, -1, -1, -1;
     0,  1,  9, -1, -1, -1, -1, -1, -1, -1, -1, -1, -1, -1, -1, -1;
     1,  8,  3,  9,  8,  1, -1, -1, -1, -1, -1, -1, -1, -1, -1, -1;
    ...
    ...
    ...

     1,  3,  8,  9,  1,  8, -1, -1, -1, -1, -1, -1, -1, -1, -1, -1;
     0,  9,  1, -1, -1, -1, -1, -1, -1, -1, -1, -1, -1, -1, -1, -1;
     0,  3,  8, -1, -1, -1, -1, -1, -1, -1, -1, -1, -1, -1, -1, -1;
    -1, -1, -1, -1, -1, -1, -1, -1, -1, -1, -1, -1, -1, -1, -1, -1];

sizeX = size(V, 1);
sizeY = size(V, 2);
sizeZ = size(V, 3);

MAX_VERTICES = 15;

% vertices and indices
VertexBin = single(zeros(sizeX, sizeY, sizeZ, MAX_VERTICES, 3));
TriCounter = zeros(sizeX, sizeY, sizeZ);
totalTriangles = 0;

% marching through the cubes
for k = 1:sizeZ - 1
    for j = 1:sizeY - 1
        for i = 1:sizeX - 1

            % temp. vars for voxels and isopoints.
            voxels = single(zeros(8, 4)); %[v, x, y, z]
            isoPos = single(zeros(12, 3)); %[x, y, z]

            %cube
            voxels(1,:) = [V(i, j, k),  X(i, j, k), Y(i, j, k), Z(i, j, k)];
```

```
voxels(2,:) = [V(i, j + 1,k),   X(i, j + 1,k), Y(i, j + 1,k),
                Z(i, j + 1,k)];
voxels(3,:) = [V(i + 1,j + 1,k), X(i + 1,j + 1,k), Y(i + 1,j + 1,k),
                Z(i + 1,j + 1,k)];
voxels(4,:) = [V(i + 1,j, k), X(i + 1,j, k), Y(i + 1,j, k),
                Z(i + 1,j, k)];
voxels(5,:) = [V(i, j, k + 1),X(i, j, k + 1),Y(i, j, k + 1),
                Z(i, j, k + 1)];
voxels(6,:) = [V(i, j + 1,k + 1),X(i, j + 1,k + 1),Y(i, j + 1,
                k + 1),Z(i, j + 1,k + 1)];
voxels(7,:) = [V(i + 1,j + 1,k + 1),X(i + 1,j + 1,k + 1),Y(i + 1,
                j + 1,k + 1),Z(i + 1,j + 1,k + 1)];
voxels(8,:) = [V(i + 1,j, k + 1),X(i + 1,j, k + 1),Y(i + 1,j,
                k + 1),Z(i + 1,j, k + 1)];

% find the cube index
cubeIndex = uint16(0);
for n = 1:8
    if voxels(n, 1) > = isovalue
        cubeIndex = bitset(cubeIndex, n);
    end
end
cubeIndex = cubeIndex + 1;

% get edges from edgeTable
edges = edgeTable(cubeIndex);
if edges = = 0
    continue;
end

% check 12 edges
if bitand(edges, 1)
    isoPos(1,:) = interpolatePos(isovalue, voxels(1,:),
                voxels(2,:));
end
if bitand(edges, 2)
    isoPos(2,:) = interpolatePos(isovalue, voxels(2,:),
                voxels(3,:));
end
if bitand(edges, 4)
    isoPos(3,:) = interpolatePos(isovalue, voxels(3,:),
                voxels(4,:));
end
if bitand(edges, 8)
    isoPos(4,:) = interpolatePos(isovalue, voxels(4,:),
                voxels(1,:));
end
if bitand(edges, 16)
    isoPos(5,:) = interpolatePos(isovalue, voxels(5,:),
                voxels(6,:));
end
```

```
if bitand(edges, 32)
    isoPos(6,:) = interpolatePos(isovalue, voxels(6,:),
                 voxels(7,:));
end
if bitand(edges, 64)
    isoPos(7,:) = interpolatePos(isovalue, voxels(7,:),
                 voxels(8,:));
end
if bitand(edges, 128)
    isoPos(8,:) = interpolatePos(isovalue, voxels(8,:),
                 voxels(5,:));
end
if bitand(edges, 256)
    isoPos(9,:) = interpolatePos(isovalue, voxels(1,:),
                 voxels(5,:));
end
if bitand(edges, 512)
    isoPos(10,:) = interpolatePos(isovalue, voxels(2,:),
                 voxels(6,:));
end
if bitand(edges, 1024)
    isoPos(11,:) = interpolatePos(isovalue, voxels(3,:),
                 voxels(7,:));
end
if bitand(edges, 2048)
    isoPos(12,:) = interpolatePos(isovalue, voxels(4,:),
                 voxels(8,:));
end

%walk through the triTable and get the triangle(s) vertices
numTriangles = 0;
numVertices = 0;
for n = 1:3:16

    if triTable(cubeIndex, n) < 0
        break;
    end

    % first vertex
    numVertices = numVertices + 1;
    edgeIndex = triTable(cubeIndex, n) + 1;
    vertexBin(i, j, k, numVertices, :) = isoPos(edgeIndex, :);
    % second vertex
    numVertices = numVertices + 1;
    edgeIndex = triTable(cubeIndex, n + 1) + 1;
    vertexBin(i, j, k, numVertices, :) = isoPos(edgeIndex, :);
    % third vertex
    numVertices = numVertices + 1;
    edgeIndex = triTable(cubeIndex, n + 2) + 1;
    vertexBin(i, j, k, numVertices, :) = isoPos(edgeIndex, :);
```

```
                    numTriangles = numTriangles + 1;
                end
                TriCounter(i, j, k) = numTriangles;
                totalTriangels = totalTriangles + numTriangles;
            end
        end
end
Vertices = single(zeros(totalTriangles * 3, 3));
Indices = uint32(zeros(totalTriangels, 3));
vIdx = 0;
tIdx = 0;
for k = 1:sizeZ - 1
    for j = 1:sizeY - 1
        for i = 1:sizeX - 1

            count = TriCounter(i, j, k);
            if count < 1
                continue;
            end

            for t = 0:count - 1
                vIdx = vIdx + 1;
                Vertices(vIdx, :) = vertexBin(i, j, k, 3*t + 1, :);
                vIdx = vIdx + 1;
                Vertices(vIdx, :) = vertexBin(i, j, k, 3*t + 2, :);
                vIdx = vIdx + 1;
                Vertices(vIdx, :) = vertexBin(i, j, k, 3*t + 3, :);

                tIdx = tIdx + 1;
                Indices(tIdx, :) = uint32([3 * tIdx - 2, 3 * tIdx - 1, 3 * tIdx]);
            end
        end
    end
end


InterpolatePos.m
function [varargout] = interpolatePos(isovalue, voxel1, voxel2)
    scale = (isovalue - voxel1(:,1)) ./ (voxel2(:,1) - voxel1(:,1));
    interpolatedPos = voxel1(:,2:4) + [scale .* (voxel2(:,2) − voxel1(:,2)), ...
                                      scale .* (voxel2(:,3) − voxel1(:,3)), ...
                                      scale .* (voxel2(:,4) - voxel1(:,4))];

if nargout == 1 || nargout == 0
    varargout{1} = interpolatedPos;
elseif nargout == 3
    varargout{1} = interpolatedPos(:,1);
    varargout{2} = interpolatedPos(:,2);
    varargout{3} = interpolatedPos(:,3);
end
```

```
testSurfaceNoOpt.m
% generate sample volume data
[X, Y, Z, V] = flow;

% visualize volume data
figure
xmin = min(X(:));
ymin = min(Y(:));
zmin = min(Z(:));
xmax = max(X(:));
ymax = max(Y(:));
zmax = max(Z(:));
hslice = surf(linspace(xmin,xmax,100), linspace(ymin,ymax,100), zeros(100));
rotate(hslice,[-1,0,0],-45)
xd = get(hslice,'XData');
yd = get(hslice,'YData');
zd = get(hslice,'ZData');
delete(hslice)
h = slice(X,Y,Z,V,xd,yd,zd);
set(h,'FaceColor', 'interp', 'EdgeColor', 'none', 'DiffuseStrength', 0.8)
hold on
hx = slice(X,Y,Z,V,xmax,[],[]);
set(hx,'FaceColor', 'interp', 'EdgeColor', 'none')
hy = slice(X,Y,Z,V,[],ymax,[]);
set(hy,'FaceColor', 'interp', 'EdgeColor', 'none')
hz = slice(X,Y,Z,V,[],[],zmin);
set(hz,'FaceColor', 'interp', 'EdgeColor', 'none')

% data type to single
X = single(X);
Y = single(Y);
Z = single(Z);
V = single(V);
isovalue = single(-3);

% Marching cubes
[Vertices1, Indices1] = getSurfaceNoOpt(X, Y, Z, V, isovalue);

% visualize triangles
figure
p = patch('Faces', Indices1, 'Vertices', Vertices1);
set(p, 'FaceColor', 'none', 'EdgeColor', 'red');
daspect([1,1,1])
view(3);
camlight
lighting gouraud
grid on
```

Figure 7.9 Time profiling for MATLAB codes without optimization.

7.3.10 Time Profiling

Now, we can profile our implementation using `Profiler` in MATLAB. Open `Profiler` by pressing Ctrl + 5 or selecting `Windows > 5 Profiler` from the main MATLAB menu. Then, enter the MATLAB code file name and run it. We get the profile summary in Figure 7.9.

Overall, our performance took about 1.9 seconds in total. If we click on the `getSurfaceNoOpt` link in the summary, we see more detailed results (Figure 7.10).

According to our profiler results, we spent most of the time assigning empty voxels and finding out the cube index.

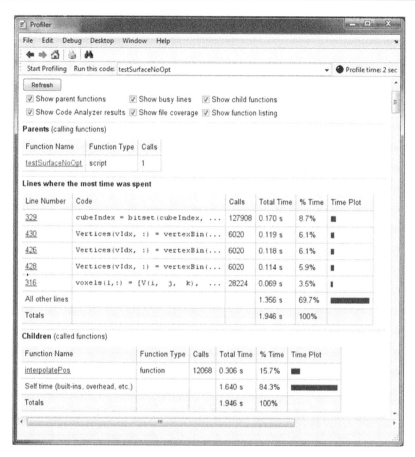

Figure 7.10 Time profiling details.

7.4 Implementation in `c-mex` with CUDA

With a straightforward implementation of the marching cubes algorithm, we got about 1.9 seconds of time performance. In this section, we will go show how we can improve our implementation using only MATLAB codes. We will use the concept of vectorization and preallocation introduced in Chapter 1. Our strategy will be, instead of visiting each and every voxel, we preallocate temporary storages for storing inter-mediate results and try to calculate the triangles without introducing triple for-loops.

7.4.1 Step 1

Create a new function, `getSurfaceWithOpt`, type in the code follows, and save it as `getSurfaceWithOpt.m`.

getSurfaceWithOpt.m

```matlab
function [Vertices, Indices] = getSurfaceWithOpt(X, Y, Z, V, isovalue)

edgeTable = uint16([
        0,   265,  515,  778, 1030, 1295, 1541, 1804, ...
     2060, 2309, 2575, 2822, 3082, 3331, 3593, 3840, ...
     ...
     ...
     1804, 1541, 1295, 1030, 778, 515, 265, 0]);

triTable = [
    -1, -1, -1, -1, -1, -1, -1, -1, -1, -1, -1, -1, -1, -1, -1, -1;
     0, 8, 3, -1, -1, -1, -1, -1, -1, -1, -1, -1, -1, -1, -1, -1;
     ...
     ...
    -1, -1, -1, -1, -1, -1, -1, -1, -1, -1, -1, -1, -1, -1, -1, -1];

sx = size(V, 1);
sy = size(V, 2);
sz = size(V, 3);

% Cube Index
CV = uint16(V > isovalue);
Cubes = zeros(sx-1, sy-1, sz-1, 'uint16');
Cubes = Cubes + CV(1:sx-1, 1:sy-1, 1:sz-1);
Cubes = Cubes + CV(1:sx-1, 2:sy, 1:sz-1) * 2;
Cubes = Cubes + CV(2:sx, 2:sy, 1:sz-1) * 4;
Cubes = Cubes + CV(2:sx, 1:sy-1, 1:sz-1) * 8;
Cubes = Cubes + CV(1:sx-1, 1:sy-1, 2:sz) * 16;
Cubes = Cubes + CV(1:sx-1, 2:sy, 2:sz) * 32;
Cubes = Cubes + CV(2:sx, 2:sy, 2:sz) * 64;
Cubes = Cubes + CV(2:sx, 1:sy-1, 2:sz) * 128;
Cubes = Cubes + 1;

% Edges
Edges = edgeTable(Cubes);
EdgeIdx = find(Edges > 0);
EdgeVal = Edges(EdgeIdx);

% Vertices with edges
[vdx, vdy, vdz] = ind2sub(size(Edges), EdgeIdx);
idx = sub2ind(size(X), vdx, vdy, vdz);
Vt1 = [V(idx), X(idx), Y(idx), Z(idx)];
idx = sub2ind(size(X), vdx, vdy + 1, vdz);
Vt2 = [V(idx), X(idx), Y(idx), Z(idx)];
idx = sub2ind(size(X), vdx + 1, vdy + 1, vdz);
Vt3 = [V(idx), X(idx), Y(idx), Z(idx)];
idx = sub2ind(size(X), vdx + 1, vdy, vdz);
Vt4 = [V(idx), X(idx), Y(idx), Z(idx)];
idx = sub2ind(size(X), vdx, vdy, vdz + 1);
Vt5 = [V(idx), X(idx), Y(idx), Z(idx)];
```

```
idx = sub2ind(size(X), vdx, vdy + 1, vdz + 1);
Vt6 = [V(idx), X(idx), Y(idx), Z(idx)];
idx = sub2ind(size(X), vdx + 1, vdy + 1, vdz + 1);
Vt7 = [V(idx), X(idx), Y(idx), Z(idx)];
idx = sub2ind(size(X), vdx + 1, vdy, vdz + 1);
Vt8 = [V(idx), X(idx), Y(idx), Z(idx)];

% EdgeNumber
PosX = zeros(size(EdgeVal,1), 12, 'single');
PosY = zeros(size(EdgeVal,1), 12, 'single');
PosZ = zeros(size(EdgeVal,1), 12, 'single');
idx = find(uint16(bitand(EdgeVal, 1)));
[PosX(idx,1), PosY(idx,1), PosZ(idx,1)] = interpolatePos(isovalue, Vt1
(idx,:), Vt2(idx,:));
idx = find(uint16(bitand(EdgeVal, 2)));
[PosX(idx,2), PosY(idx,2), PosZ(idx,2)] = interpolatePos(isovalue, Vt2
(idx,:), Vt3(idx,:));
idx = find(uint16(bitand(EdgeVal, 4)));
[PosX(idx,3), PosY(idx,3), PosZ(idx,3)] = interpolatePos(isovalue, Vt3
(idx,:), Vt4(idx,:));
idx = find(uint16(bitand(EdgeVal, 8)));
[PosX(idx,4), PosY(idx,4), PosZ(idx,4)] = interpolatePos(isovalue, Vt4
(idx,:), Vt1(idx,:));
idx = find(uint16(bitand(EdgeVal, 16)));
[PosX(idx,5), PosY(idx,5), PosZ(idx,5)] = interpolatePos(isovalue, Vt5
(idx,:), Vt6(idx,:));
idx = find(uint16(bitand(EdgeVal, 32)));
[PosX(idx,6), PosY(idx,6), PosZ(idx,6)] = interpolatePos(isovalue, Vt6
(idx,:), Vt7(idx,:));
idx = find(uint16(bitand(EdgeVal, 64)));
[PosX(idx,7), PosY(idx,7), PosZ(idx,7)] = interpolatePos(isovalue, Vt7
(idx,:), Vt8(idx,:));
idx = find(uint16(bitand(EdgeVal, 128)));
[PosX(idx,8), PosY(idx,8), PosZ(idx,8)] = interpolatePos(isovalue, Vt8
(idx,:), Vt5(idx,:));
idx = find(uint16(bitand(EdgeVal, 256)));
[PosX(idx,9), PosY(idx,9), PosZ(idx,9)] = interpolatePos(isovalue, Vt1
(idx,:), Vt5(idx,:));
idx = find(uint16(bitand(EdgeVal, 512)));
[PosX(idx,10), PosY(idx,10), PosZ(idx,10)] = interpolatePos(isovalue,
Vt2(idx,:), Vt6(idx,:));
idx = find(uint16(bitand(EdgeVal, 1024)));
[PosX(idx,11), PosY(idx,11), PosZ(idx,11)] = interpolatePos(isovalue,
Vt3(idx,:), Vt7(idx,:));
idx = find(uint16(bitand(EdgeVal, 2048)));
[PosX(idx,12), PosY(idx,12), PosZ(idx,12)] = interpolatePos(isovalue,
Vt4(idx,:), Vt8(idx,:));

% Triangles
Vertices = zeros(0, 3, 'single');
TriVal = triTable(Cubes(EdgeIdx),:) + 1;
```

```
for i = 1:3:15
    idx = find(TriVal(:,i) > 0);
    if isempty(idx)
        continue;
    end
    TriVtx = TriVal(idx, i:i+2);
    vx1 = PosX(sub2ind(size(PosX), idx, TriVtx(:,1)));
    vy1 = PosY(sub2ind(size(PosY), idx, TriVtx(:,1)));
    vz1 = PosZ(sub2ind(size(PosZ), idx, TriVtx(:,1)));
    vx2 = PosX(sub2ind(size(PosX), idx, TriVtx(:,2)));
    vy2 = PosY(sub2ind(size(PosY), idx, TriVtx(:,2)));
    vz2 = PosZ(sub2ind(size(PosZ), idx, TriVtx(:,2)));
    vx3 = PosX(sub2ind(size(PosX), idx, TriVtx(:,3)));
    vy3 = PosY(sub2ind(size(PosY), idx, TriVtx(:,3)));
    vz3 = PosZ(sub2ind(size(PosZ), idx, TriVtx(:,3)));
    vsz = 3 * size(vx1, 1);
    t1 = zeros(vsz, 3, 'single');
    t1(1:3:vsz,:) = [vx1 vy1 vz1];
    t1(2:3:vsz,:) = [vx2 vy2 vz2];
    t1(3:3:vsz,:) = [vx3 vy3 vz3];
    Vertices = [Vertices; t1];
end
Indices = reshape(1:size(Vertices,1), 3, size(Vertices,1)/3)';
```

In this code, we do have no nested for-loops. Instead, we calculate all the indexes and vertexes as a whole volume. This comes at the cost of more memory space for temporary variables. As the size of volume data grows, this technique might not become feasible. Anyway, if we execute this code, we will be surprised how much time we are able to save.

7.4.2 Step 2

Modify the testSurfaceNoOpt.m file, which follows, and save it as testSurfaceWithOpt.m:

```
testSurfaceWithOpt.m
% generate sample volume data
[X, Y, Z, V] = flow;
X = single(X);
Y = single(Y);
Z = single(Z);
V = single(V);
isovalue = single(-3);

[Vertices2, Indices2] = getSurfaceWithOpt(X, Y, Z, V, isovalue);

% visualize triangles
figure
```

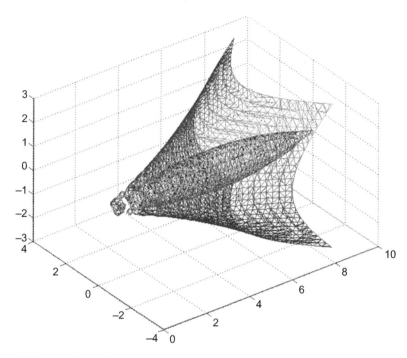

Figure 7.11 Isosurface at isovalue = −3 with optimization.

```
p = patch('Faces', Indices2, 'Vertices', Vertices2);
set(p, 'FaceColor', 'none', 'EdgeColor', 'green');
daspect([1,1,1])
view(3);
camlight
lighting gouraud
grid on
```

After running this script, we get the same output data with the exception that the triangles are saved in a different order. But, we basically have the same triangles as before (Figure 7.11).

7.4.3   Time Profiling

Let us now perform time profiling on this new, optimized code. Go back to the Profiler and run testSurfaceWithOpt.m (Figure 7.12).

This time, the new function, getSurfaceWithOpt, took only 0.029 seconds, compared to 1.9 seconds with no optimization. This is huge improvement over the straightforward implementation. We saved most of the time by getting rid of triple nested for-loops.

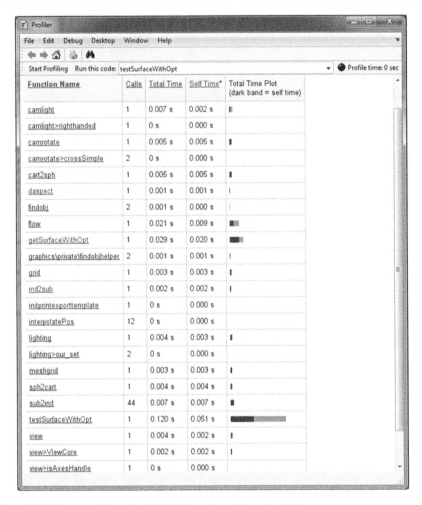

Figure 7.12 Time profiling for MATLAB codes with optimization.

7.5   Implementation Using c-mex and GPU

Without even introducing GPU and c-mex, we can gain huge improvement in speed if we carefully design using vectorization and preallocation techniques, as we have seen in the previous sections. In this section, we further explore how much speed we can squeeze out if we use c-mex and the GPU in our implementation. Overall, we follow our first implementation with no optimization and replace all the operations in the innermost loops with CUDA functions.

7.5.1   Step 1

Create a gateway routine for the c-mex function and fill the main function body as follows. We save this as getSurfaceCuda.cpp.

getSurfaceCuda.cpp

```cpp
#include "mex.h"
#include <vector>
#include <cuda_runtime.h>
#include "MarchingCubes.h"

// [Vertices, Indices] = getSurface(X, Y, Z, V, isovalue)
void mexFunction(int nlhs, mxArray *plhs[], int nrhs, const mxArray *prhs[])
{
    if (nrhs != 5)
        mexErrMsgTxt("Invaid number of input arguments");

    if (nlhs != 2)
        mexErrMsgTxt("Invalid number of outputs");
    if (!mxIsSingle(prhs[0]) && !mxIsSingle(prhs[1]) &&
        !mxIsSingle(prhs[2]) && !mxIsSingle(prhs[3]) &&
        !mxIsSingle(prhs[4]))
        mexErrMsgTxt("input vector data type must be single");

    const mwSize* size = mxGetDimensions(prhs[3]);
    int sizeX = size[0];
    int sizeY = size[1];
    int sizeZ = size[2];

    float* X = (float*mxGetData(prhs[0]);
    float*Y = (float*mxGetData(prhs[1]);
    float*Z = (float*mxGetData(prhs[2]);
    float*V = (float*mxGetData(prhs[3]);
    float isovalue = *float*mxGetData(prhs[4]));

    float*vertices[3];
    unsigned int*indices[3];
    int numVertices = 0;
    int numTriangles = 0;

    marchingCubes(isovalue,
                  X, Y, Z, V,
                  sizeX, sizeY, sizeZ,
                  vertices, indices,
                  numVertices, numTriangles);
    cudaError_t error = cudaGetLastError();
    if (error != cudaSuccess)
    {
        mexPrintf("%s\n", cudaGetErrorString(error));
        mexErrMsgTxt("CUDA failed\n");
    }

    mexPrintf("numVertices = %d\n", numVertices);
    mexPrintf("numTriangles = %d\n", numTriangles);

    plhs[0] = mxCreateNumericMatrix(numVertices, 3, mxSINGLE_CLASS, mxREAL);
    plhs[1] = mxCreateNumericMatrix(numTriangles, 3, mxUINT32_CLASS, mxREAL);
```

```
float*Vertices = (float*mxGetData(plhs[0]);
unsigned int*Indices = (unsigned int*mxGetData(plhs[1]);

for (int i = 0; i < 3; ++i)
{
    memcpy(Vertices + i *numVertices, vertices[i], numVertices
    *sizeof(float));
    free(vertices[i]);
}
for (int i = 0; i < 3; ++i)
{
    memcpy(Indices + i *numTriangles, indices[i], numTriangles
    *sizeof(unsigned int));
    free(indices[i]);
}
}
```

As usual, we check the input data type first. We call the marchingCubes(...) function and copy the results back to our MATLAB arrays.

7.5.2 Step 2

The function marchingCubes(...) is declared in the header file, MarchingCubes.h. Create this header file as follows and save it.

```
MarchingCubes.h
#ifndef __MARCHINGCUBES_H__
#define __MARCHINGCUBES_H__

#include <vector>

extern void marchingCubes(float isovalue,
                    float*X, float*Y, float*Z, float*V,
                    int sizeX, int sizeY, int sizeZ,
                    float*vertices[],
                    unsigned int*indices[],
                    int& numVertices, int& numTriangles);

#endif // __MARCHINGCUBES_H__
```

7.5.3 Step 3

We now implement the marchingCubes(...) function in MarchingCubes.cu using a CUDA kernel and runtime libraries. Here, again, we show only the partial table values. The full table values can be found in MarchingCubes.cu.

```
MarchingCubes.cu
#include "MarchingCubes.h"

__constant__ unsigned int edgeTable[256] =
{
```

```
        0,   265,   515,   778, 1030, 1295, 1541, 1804,
    2060, 2309, 2575, 2822, 3082, 3331, 3593, 3840,
    ...
    ...
    1804, 1541, 1295, 1030, 778, 515, 265, 0
};

__constant__ int triTable[256][16] =
{
    { -1, -1, -1, -1, -1, -1, -1, -1, -1, -1, -1, -1, -1, -1, -1, -1 },
    { 0, 8, 3, -1, -1, -1, -1, -1, -1, -1, -1, -1, -1, -1, -1, -1 },
    ...
    ...
    { -1, -1, -1, -1, -1, -1, -1, -1, -1, -1, -1, -1, -1, -1, -1, -1 }
};

__device__ float3 interpolatePos(float isovalue, float4 voxel1, float4 voxel2)
{
    float scale = (isovalue - voxel1.w) / (voxel2.w - voxel1.w);
    float3 pos;
    pos.x = voxel1.x + scale *(voxel2.x - voxel1.x);
    pos.y = voxel1.y + scale *(voxel2.y - voxel1.y);
    pos.z = voxel1.z + scale *(voxel2.z - voxel1.z);
    return pos;
}

#define MAX_VERTICES 15
__global__ void getTriangles(float isovalue,
                             float*X, float*Y, float*Z, float*V,
                             int sizeX, int sizeY, int sizeZ,
                             float3*vertexBin, int*triCounter)
{
    int i = blockIdx.x *blockDim.x + threadIdx.x;
    // compute capability >= 2.x
    //int j = blockIdx.y *blockDim.y + threadIdx.y;
    //int k = blockIdx.z *blockDim.z + threadIdx.z;

    // compute capability < 2.x
    int gy = (sizeY + blockDim.y - 1) / blockDim.y;
    int j = (blockIdx.y % gy) *blockDim.y + threadIdx.y;
    int k = (blockIdx.y / gy) *blockDim.z + threadIdx.z;

    if (i >= sizeX - 1 || j >= sizeY - 1 || k >= sizeZ - 1)
        return;

    float4 voxels[8];
    float3 isoPos[12];

    int idx[8];
    idx[0] = sizeX *(sizeY *k + j) + i;
    idx[1] = sizeX *(sizeY *k + j + 1) + i;
    idx[2] = sizeX *(sizeY *k + j + 1) + i + 1;
```

```
idx[3] = sizeX *(sizeY *k + j) + i + 1;
idx[4] = sizeX *(sizeY *(k + 1) + j) + i;
idx[5] = sizeX *(sizeY *(k + 1) + j + 1) + i;
idx[6] = sizeX *(sizeY *(k + 1) + j + 1) + i + 1;
idx[7] = sizeX *(sizeY *(k + 1) + j) + i + 1;

// cube
for (int n = 0; n < 8; ++n)
{
    voxels[n].w = V[idx[n]];
    voxels[n].x = X[idx[n]];
    voxels[n].y = Y[idx[n]];
    voxels[n].z = Z[idx[n]];
}

// find the cube index
unsigned int cubeIndex = 0;
for (int n = 0; n < 8; ++n)
{
    if (voxels[n].w >= isovalue)
    cubeIndex |= (1 << n);
}

// get edges from edgeTable
unsigned int edges = edgeTable[cubeIndex];
if (edges == 0)
    return;

// check 12 edges
if (edges & 1)
    isoPos[0] = interpolatePos(isovalue, voxels[0], voxels[1]);
if (edges & 2)
    isoPos[1] = interpolatePos(isovalue, voxels[1], voxels[2]);
if (edges & 4)
    isoPos[2] = interpolatePos(isovalue, voxels[2], voxels[3]);
if (edges & 8)
    isoPos[3] = interpolatePos(isovalue, voxels[3], voxels[0]);
if (edges & 16)
    isoPos[4] = interpolatePos(isovalue, voxels[4], voxels[5]);
if (edges & 32)
    isoPos[5] = interpolatePos(isovalue, voxels[5], voxels[6]);
if (edges & 64)
    isoPos[6] = interpolatePos(isovalue, voxels[6], voxels[7]);
if (edges & 128)
    isoPos[7] = interpolatePos(isovalue, voxels[7], voxels[4]);
if (edges & 256)
    isoPos[8] = interpolatePos(isovalue, voxels[0], voxels[4]);
if (edges & 512)
    isoPos[9] = interpolatePos(isovalue, voxels[1], voxels[5]);
```

```
      if (edges & 1024)
         isoPos[10] = interpolatePos(isovalue, voxels[2], voxels[6]);
      if (edges & 2048)
         isoPos[11] = interpolatePos(isovalue, voxels[3], voxels[7]);

      // walk through the triTable and get the triangle(s) vertices
      float3 vertices[15];
      int numTriangles = 0;
      int numVertices = 0;

      for (int n = 0; n < 15; n + = 3)
      {
          int edgeNumger = triTable[cubeIndex][n];
          if (edgeNumger < 0)
             break;
          vertices[numVertices++] = isoPos[edgeNumger];
          vertices[numVertices++] = isoPos[triTable[cubeIndex][n + 1]];
          vertices[numVertices++] = isoPos[triTable[cubeIndex][n + 2]];
          ++numTriangles;
      }

      triCounter[idx[0]] = numTriangles;
      for (int n = 0; n < numVertices; ++n)
          vertexBin[MAX_VERTICES *idx[0] + n] = vertices[n];
}

void marchingCubes(float isovalue,
                   float*X, float*Y, float*Z, float*V,
                   int sizeX, int sizeY, int sizeZ,
                   float*vertices[],
                   unsigned int*indices[],
                   int& numVertices, int& numTriangles)
{
    float*devX = 0;
    float*devY = 0;
    float*devZ = 0;
    float*devV = 0;
    float3*devVertexBin = 0;
    int*devTriCounter = 0;

    int totalSize = sizeX *sizeY *sizeZ;
    cudaMalloc(&devX, sizeof(float) *totalSize);
    cudaMalloc(&devY, sizeof(float) *totalSize);
    cudaMalloc(&devZ, sizeof(float) *totalSize);
    cudaMalloc(&devV, sizeof(float) *totalSize);
    cudaMemcpy(devX, X, sizeof(float) *totalSize, cudaMemcpyHostToDevice);
    cudaMemcpy(devY, Y, sizeof(float) *totalSize, cudaMemcpyHostToDevice);
    cudaMemcpy(devZ, Z, sizeof(float) *totalSize, cudaMemcpyHostToDevice);
    cudaMemcpy(devV, V, sizeof(float) *totalSize, cudaMemcpyHostToDevice);

    cudaMalloc(&devVertexBin, sizeof(float3) * totalSize *MAX_VERTICES);
```

```
cudaMemset(devVertexBin, 0, sizeof(float3) *totalSize *MAX_VERTICES);
cudaMalloc(&devTriCounter, sizeof(int) *totalSize);
cudaMemset(devTriCounter, 0, sizeof(int) *totalSize);

dim3 blockSize(4, 4, 4);

// compute capability >= 2.x
//dim3 gridSize((sizeX + blockSize.x - 1) / blockSize.x,
//              (sizeY + blockSize.y - 1) / blockSize.y,
//              (sizeZ + blockSize.z - 1) / blockSize.z);

// compute capabiltiy < 2.x
int gy = (sizeY + blockSize.y - 1) / blockSize.y;
int gz = (sizeZ + blockSize.z - 1) / blockSize.z;
dim3 gridSize((sizeX + blockSize.x - 1) / blockSize.x,
              gy *gz,
              1);

getTriangles << < gridSize, blockSize >> > (isovalue,
                                            devX, devY, devZ, devV,
                                            sizeX, sizeY, sizeZ,
                                            devVertexBin,
                                            devTriCounter);
float3*vertexBin = (float3*malloc(sizeof(float3) *totalSize
                    *MAX_VERTICES);
cudaMemcpy(vertexBin, devVertexBin, sizeof(float3) *totalSize
           *MAX_VERTICES, cudaMemcpyDeviceToHost);
int*triCounter = (int*malloc(sizeof(int) *totalSize);
cudaMemcpy(triCounter, devTriCounter, sizeof(int) *totalSize,
           cudaMemcpyDeviceToHost);

numTriangles = 0;
for (int i = 0; i < totalSize; ++i)
    numTriangles + = triCounter[i];
numVertices = 3 *numTriangles;

for (int i = 0; i < 3; ++i)
{
    vertices[i] = (float*malloc(sizeof(float) *numVertices);
    indices[i] = (unsigned int*malloc(sizeof(unsigned int) *numTriangles);
}

int tIdx = 0, vIdx = 0;
for (int i = 0; i < totalSize; ++i)
{
    int triCount = triCounter[i];
    if (triCount < 1)
        continue;

    int binIdx = i *MAX_VERTICES;
    for (int c = 0; c < triCount; ++c)
    {
```

```
            for (int v = 0; v < 3; ++v)
            {
                vertices[0][vIdx] = vertexBin[binIdx].x;
                vertices[1][vIdx] = vertexBin[binIdx].y;
                vertices[2][vIdx] = vertexBin[binIdx].z;
                indices[v][tIdx] = 3 *tIdx + v + 1;
                ++vIdx;
                ++binIdx;
            }
            ++tIdx;
        }
    }

    cudaFree(devX);
    cudaFree(devY);
    cudaFree(devZ);
    cudaFree(devV);
    cudaFree(devVertexBin);
    cudaFree(devTriCounter);
}
```

The basic structure of the algorithm is same as in the straightforward MATLAB implementation. Here, we do not see the nested for-loops. Instead, we assign each voxel to a thread. In the marchingCubes(...) function, we first allocate memory in the GPU device for all the input and output data using CUDA functions. Then, we copy all the input data from the host to the GPU device. We assign a block size to be $4 \times 4 \times 4$ three dimensional. This gives us a total of 64 threads per block. Once we determine the block size, we determine the grid size using the block size. Depending on the GPU's computing capability, a grid size could be three- or two-dimensional. In this example, we assume the computing capability is less than 2.x. The grid size and block size are then used in the CUDA kernel to determine the position of the voxel of interest.

In the marchingCubes(...) function, the grid sizes of y and z are combined as

```
// compute capability >= 2.x
//dim3 gridSize((sizeX + blockSize.x - 1) / blockSize.x,
//             (sizeY + blockSize.y - 1) / blockSize.y,
//             (sizeZ + blockSize.z - 1) / blockSize.z);

// compute capabiltiy < 2.x
int gy = (sizeY + blockSize.y - 1) / blockSize.y;
int gz = (sizeZ + blockSize.z - 1) / blockSize.z;
dim3 gridSize((sizeX + blockSize.x - 1) / blockSize.x,
              gy *gz,
              1);
```

Then, in the getTriangles kernel(...), the y and z grid dimensions are recovered as

```
int i = blockIdx.x *blockDim.x + threadIdx.x;

// compute capability >= 2.x
//int j = blockIdx.y *blockDim.y + threadIdx.y;
//int k = blockIdx.z *blockDim.z + threadIdx.z;

// compute capability < 2.x
int gy = (sizeY + blockDim.y - 1) / blockDim.y;
int j = (blockIdx.y % gy) *blockDim.y + threadIdx.y;
int k = (blockIdx.y / gy) *blockDim.z + threadIdx.z;
```

Once we determine the voxel position using thread and block indexes, the rest of the body follows exactly as in MATLAB.

7.5.4　Step 4

When the code is ready, we can compile and generate the c-mex file as

```
buildSurfaceCuda.m
system('nvcc -c MarchingCubes.cu -Xptxas -v');
mex getSurfaceCuda.cpp MarchingCubes.obj -lcudart -L"C:\Program Files
\NVIDIA GPU Computing Toolkit\CUDA\v5.0\lib\x64" -I"C:\Program Files
\NVIDIA GPU Computing Toolkit\CUDA\v5.0\include" -v
```

In nvcc, we add the option -Xptxas. This option prints additional information that is useful for determining how much memory the kernel will consume. This option can come in handy when we get an error message from CUDA regarding memory resources. The following is a sample printouts using −Xptxas:

```
ptxas : info : 0 bytes gmem, 17408 bytes cmem[0]
ptxas : info : Compiling entry function '_Z12getTrianglesfPfS_S_
iiiP6float3Pi' for 'sm_10'
ptxas : info : Used 38 registers, 88 bytes smem, 68 bytes cmem[1], 324 bytes
lmem
```

After running this MATLAB code, we get the c-mex file that we call from the MATLAB command window.

7.5.5　Step 5

Now, modify the test MATLAB code as follows and run it:

```
% generate sample volume data
[X, Y, Z, V] = flow;
X = single(X);
Y = single(Y);
Z = single(Z);
V = single(V);
isovalue = single(-3);
```

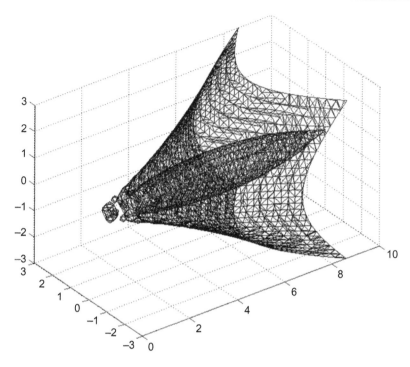

Figure 7.13 Isosurface at isovalue $= -3$ with c-mex and GPU.

```
[Vertices3, Indices3] = getSurfaceCuda(X, Y, Z, V, isovalue);

% visualize triangles
figure
p = patch('Faces', Indices3, 'Vertices', Vertices3);
set(p, 'FaceColor', 'none', 'EdgeColor', 'blue');
daspect([1,1,1])
view(3);
camlight
lighting gouraud
grid on
```

This brings up the new figure with triangles we calculated using GPU
(Figure 7.13).

7.5.6 Time Profiling

Let us do the time profile and see how much improvement we added using GPU.
Run testSurfaceCuda.m in Profile (Figure 7.14).

—

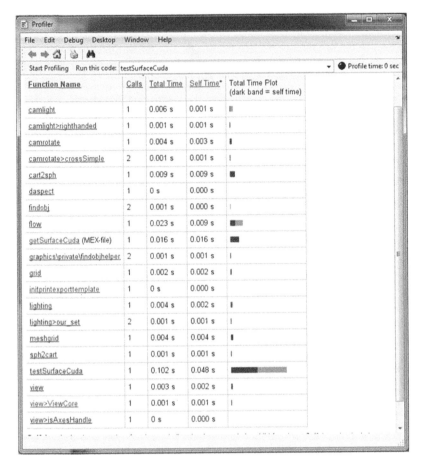

Figure 7.14 Time profiling for c-mex with GPU.

Now, with GPU, we are able to compute all the triangles in getSurfaceCuda
(...) within 0.016 seconds. This is roughly twice as fast as the second
implementation.

7.6 Conclusion

We explore three ways of implementing the marching cubes algorithm. First is the
straightforward implementation of the algorithm with no optimization.

In the second implementation, we try to improve the speed by using the concept
of vectorization and preallocation. In this implementation, we get rid of the triple
nested for-loops, and the speed improvement is pretty huge. But, be mindful that
we may encounter a memory resource issue, as the volume data grow.

Third, we introduce GPU to the first implementation. We replace all the operations in the innermost loop with a CUDA kernel. We assign each thread in GPU to compute triangles for each voxel. Then, all the output data are copied back to MATLAB arrays.

Overall, we achieve speed gains as we try each optimization technique, for example, as shown in the table that follows:

Functions	Time in Seconds
getSurfaceNoOpt	1.9
getSurfaceWithOpt	0.029
getSurfaceCuda	0.016

8 CUDA Conversion Example: 3D Image Processing

8.1 Chapter Objectives

Three-dimensional medical image processing is one of the computationally intensive fields, with huge amount of data. Through a 3D medical image processing example, we experience a practical CUDA conversion process from MATLAB code and gain real speed boost in performance. In this chapter, we discuss the following:

- A CUDA converting example with `c-mex` code.
- Analyzing the profiling results and planning a CUDA conversion.
- Practical CUDA conversion of big files.

8.2 MATLAB Code for Atlas-Based Segmentation

8.2.1 Background of Atlas-Based Segmentation

In various clinical and research medical imaging studies, accurate delineation of target anatomy from 3D patient image data is very useful. For large-scale patient studies, reliable automatic segmentation for target organs is critical, because manual processing of such a large data set is time consuming, tedious, and subject to high inter-observer variability. Therefore, automatic organ segmentation from a 3D medical image is one of hot topics in medical image processing.

Atlas-based segmentation is widely used in medical image analysis. The atlas-based segmentation method propagates the segmentation of an atlas image using the image registration technique. An atlas data set is composed of two images: a patient intensity image and the corresponding binary segmentation mask. The binary segmentation mask is manually created (Figure 8.1).

Figure 8.2 shows the concept of a single atlas-based segmentation. When we have new image data that needs to be segmented, we run the image registration from the atlas intensity image to the new target image. From the image registration, we obtain a transformation T to map from the atlas intensity image to the new target image. We can generate a new segmentation mask for the new target image by applying the transformation T to the atlas segmentation mask.

The atlas-based segmentation has advantages, because this method can generate segmentation result even for the challenging target objects with very ambiguous

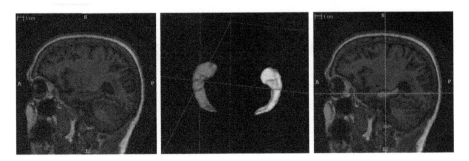

Figure 8.1 One atlas set: patient MRI image (left), its corresponding segmentation mask (middle), and its overlaid image (right).

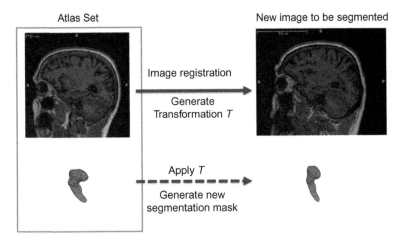

Figure 8.2 Concept behind the single atlas-based segmentation.

and complicated boundaries. One of disadvantage of the atlas-based segmentation method is that it requires a high computational power, because 3D image registration is used during the segmentation process. Since the 3D image registration is a computationally expensive iterative process, it is very slow when we use the original size of medical image.

8.2.2 MATLAB Codes for Segmentation

Let us start with pure m codes to do atlas-based hippocampus segmentation. In the m_code_Only example folder, the main module atlasSeg_Main.m, begins with loading a data file medical3D_data.mat, which includes one atlas set (atlasVol, atlasSegVol) and a target image (targetVol). Figures 8.3 and 8.4 show the whole intensity images for both the atlasVol data and targetVol data. The displaying planes can be adjusted by viewBx, viewBy, and viewBz values in line 6 at atlasSeg_Main.m.

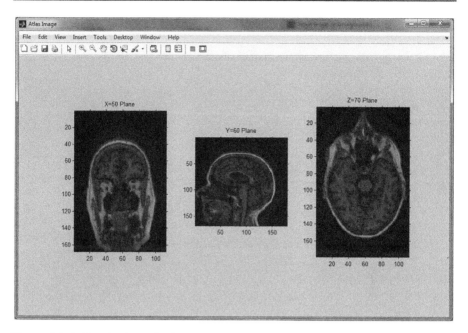

Figure 8.3 A 3D atlas intensity image (`atlasVol` data) on the $X = 50$, $Y = 60$, $Z = 70$ planes.

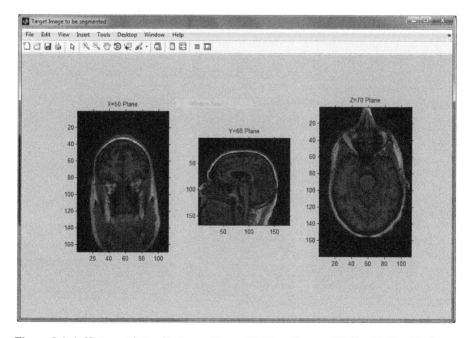

Figure 8.4 A 3D target intensity image (`targetVol`) on the $X = 50$, $Y = 60$, $Z = 70$ planes.

```
 1 % atlasSeg_Main.m
 2 % Single-Atlas-Based Hippocampus Segmentation

 3 clear all;
 4 close all;
 5 load('medical3D_data');

 6 viewBx = 50; viewBy = 60; viewBz = 70;
 7 myView2('Atlas Image',atlatVol, viewBx, viewBy, viewBz);
 8 myView2('Target Image to be segmented',targetVol,viewBx,viewBy,
   viewBz);

 9 viewLHippoX = 30; viewLHippoY = 28; viewLHippoZ = 25;
10 viewRHippoX = 28; viewRHippoY = 24; viewRHippoZ = 23;

11 % cropping margin around manual segmentation in atlas image
12 margin = 20;
13 iterLimit = 1000;

14 % objNum = 1 for left, objNum = 2 for right
15 tic

16 %
17 % For Left Hippocampus
18 %
19 objNum = 1;
20 [cropMovVol_Left, minPosX, maxPosX, minPosY, maxPosY, minPosZ,
   maxPosZ ] = ...
21 crop_around_ROI(atlatVol, atlasSegVol, objNum, margin);
22 cropTargetVol_Left = targetVol(minPosX - margin:maxPosX + margin,
   ...
23 minPosY - margin:maxPosY + margin, ...
24 minPosZ - margin:maxPosZ + margin);
25 myView2('Target Image around Left ROI',cropTargetVol_Left,
   viewLHippoX, viewLHippoY, viewLHippoZ);

26 movSeg_Left = atlasSegVol(minPosX - margin:maxPosX + margin, ...
27 minPosY - margin:maxPosY + margin, ...
28 minPosZ - margin:maxPosZ + margin);

29 % if the cropped region may include right segment by margin, we clean
   it up here.
30 movSeg_Left = double(movSeg_Left = = 1);
```

```
31 myView_overlap_red('Atlas Set (Moving Intensity Image and its
   manuaal segmentation) around left ROI',...
32 cropMovVol_Left, viewLHippoX,viewLHippoY,viewLHippoZ,
movSeg_Left);

33 % Make similar range of intensities for both 3D image for better
registration
34 movVol_org = cropMovVol_Left;
35 refVol_org = cropTargetVol_Left;
36 [adjMov, adjRef, adjMovRatio, maxOrgMov, minOrgMov] = rough_int_
adjust3(movVol_org, refVol_org);

37 movVol = adjMov;
38 refVol = adjRef;

39 % 3D deformable registration
40 [movVol_updated, Tx, Ty, Tz] = deformableRegister3D(movVol, 41
   refVol, iterLimit);

41 intAdjustBackMov = rough_int_adjustBack(movVol_updated,
   adjMovRatio, maxOrgMov, minOrgMov);
42 movSegVol_updatedNN = interp3(movSeg_Left, Ty, Tx, Tz, 'nearest');

43 myView_overlap_red('Registration Result from Left ROI of Atlas
set',...
44 intAdjustBackMov, viewLHippoX,viewLHippoY,viewLHippoZ,
   movSegVol_updatedNN);
45 myView_overlap_red('Segmentation Result for Left ROI of Target
   Image',...
46 cropTargetVol_Left, viewLHippoX,viewLHippoY,viewLHippoZ,
   movSegVol_updatedNN);

47 %
48 % For Right Hippocampus
49 %
50 objNum = 2;
51 [cropMovVol_Right, minPosX, maxPosX, minPosY, maxPosY, minPosZ,
   maxPosZ ] = ...
52 crop_around_ROI(atlatVol, atlasSegVol, objNum, margin);

53 cropTargetVol_Right = targetVol(minPosX - margin:maxPosX + margin,
...
54 minPosY − margin:maxPosY + margin, ...
55 minPosZ − margin:maxPosZ + margin);
```

```matlab
56 myView2('Target Image around Right ROI',cropTargetVol_Right,
   viewRHippoX, viewRHippoY, viewRHippoZ);

57 movSeg_Right = atlasSegVol(minPosX - margin:maxPosX + margin, ...
58 minPosY - margin:maxPosY + margin, ...
59 minPosZ - margin:maxPosZ + margin);
60 % if the cropped region may include right segment by margin, we clean
it up here.

61 movSeg_Right = double(movSeg_Right == 2);
62 myView_overlap_green('Atlas Set (Moving Intensity Image and its
   manuaal segmentation) around Right ROI',...
63 cropMovVol_Right, viewRHippoX,viewRHippoY,viewRHippoZ,
   movSeg_Right);

64 % Make similar range of intensities for both 3D image for better
   registration
65 movVol_org = cropMovVol_Right;
66 refVol_org = cropTargetVol_Right;
67 [adjMov, adjRef, adjMovRatio, maxOrgMov, minOrgMov] = ...
68 rough_int_adjust3(movVol_org, refVol_org);

69 movVol = adjMov;
70 refVol = adjRef;

71 % 3D deformable registration
72 [movVol_updated, Tx, Ty, Tz] = deformableRegister3D(movVol, refVol,
   iterLimit);

73 intAdjustBackMov = rough_int_adjustBack(movVol_updated,
   adjMovRatio, maxOrgMov, minOrgMov);
74 movSegVol_updatedNN = interp3(movSeg_Right, Ty, Tx, Tz, 'nearest');

75 myView_overlap_green('Registration Result from Right ROI of Atlas
   set',...
76 intAdjustBackMov, viewRHippoX,viewRHippoY,viewRHippoZ,
   movSegVol_updatedNN);
77 myView_overlap_green('Segmentation Result for Right ROI of Target
   Image',...
78 cropTargetVol_Right, viewRHippoX,viewRHippoY,viewRHippoZ,
   movSegVol_updatedNN);
79 toc
```

To reduce the computation during registration, we use an image cropped to the region of interest (ROI) in line $20 \sim 24$ within atlasSeg_Main.m. Since each brain has two hippocampi, we crop two regions of left and right ROI for the atlas image and target image. The cropping regions are chosen based on the atlas manual segmentation masks with margins.

Figure 8.5 shows the cropping results from the atlas image around left hippocampus segmentation mask with 20 pixel margins for each x, y, and z. The first row in Figure 8.5 shows the intensity atlas image in ROI, the second row shows the manual segmentation image corresponding intensity atlas ROI, and the third row shows the overlaid image. The left hippocampus mask value is set as 1 (objNum = 1 in line 19), while the right hippocampus mask value is set as 2 (objNum = 2 in line 50), so we can easily classify them as the right and left ROIs, based on their mask values. Figure 8.6 shows the cropping results around the right hippocampus segmentation mask.

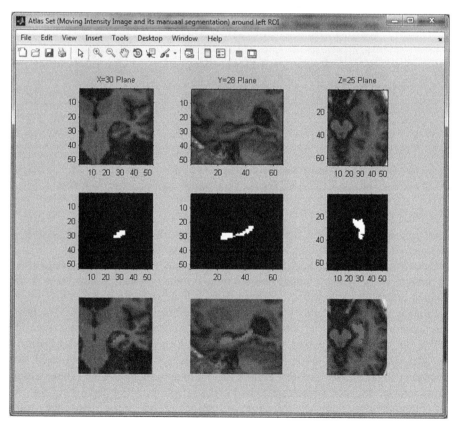

Figure 8.5 **Left ROI of atlas image set (**cropMovVol_Left**) on the $X = 30$, $Y = 28$, $Z = 25$ planes. The mask value is 1 for the left hippocampus (shown in bottom row).**

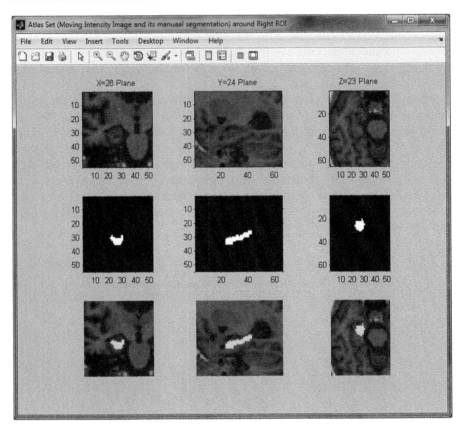

Figure 8.6 Right ROI of atlas image set (`cropMovVol_Right`) on the $X = 28$, $Y = 24$, $Z = 23$ planes. The mask value is 2 for the right hippocampus (shown in bottom row).

Figures 8.7 and 8.8 show the cropping results from the target image, which have the same coordinate bounding box as those of the cropped atlas image.

Since we are going to transform the cropped atlas image into the cropped target image, we call the cropped atlas image a *moving image* (line 34) and the cropped target image a *reference image* (line 35). After making the similar intensity ranges between the moving image and the reference image for easy registration process (`rough_int_adjust3` in line 36), we do the "`deformableRegister3D`" in line 40. From the 3D transformation (`Tx, Ty, Tz`), we apply this transform to the atlas segmentation mask (line 42) to get the final segmentation mask for the target image. We see the results in Figures 8.9 and 8.10. These result planes can be adjusted by setting `viewLHippoX,viewLHippoY,viewLHippoZ` for the left hippocampus and `viewRHippoX,viewRHippoY,viewRHippoZ` for the right hippocampus.

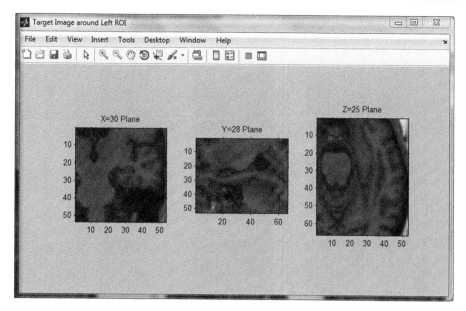

Figure 8.7 Left ROI of target image (`cropTargetVol_Left`) on the $X = 30$, $Y = 28$, $Z = 25$ planes.

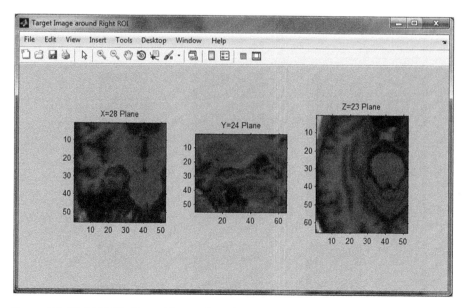

Figure 8.8 Right ROI of target image (`cropTargetVol_Right`) on the $X = 28$, $Y = 24$, $Z = 23$ planes.

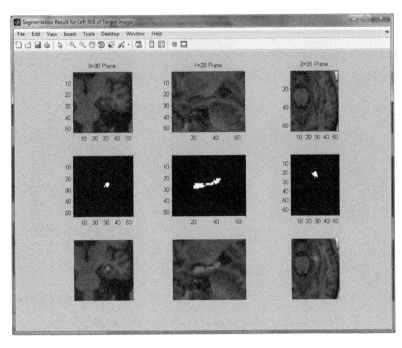

Figure 8.9 Target segmentation result for the left hippocampus.

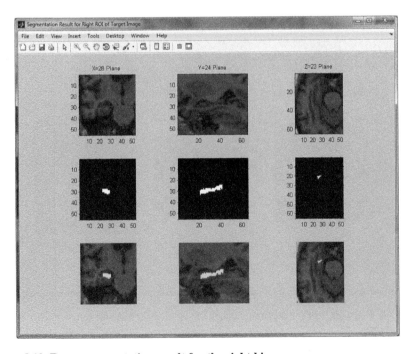

Figure 8.10 Target segmentation result for the right hippocampus.

```
iter =

    998

iter =

    999

iter =

    1000

Elapsed time is 609.036528 seconds.
```

Figure 8.11 The elapsed time for atlasSeg_Main.m.

Although the segmentation results in Figures 8.9 and 8.10 look decent, the elapsed time of atlasSeg_Main.m is around 609 seconds for both the left and right hippocampus processing (Figure 8.11). Let us analyze which are the most computationally busy submodules during this process through profiling.

8.3 Planning for CUDA Optimization Through Profiling

8.3.1 Profiling MATLAB Code

Now, we profile our implementation using Profiler in MATLAB. Then, we enter the main top file name, atlasSeg_Main, and run it. Figure 8.12 shows the profiling result of it. We clearly find that 99.5% of total processing time comes from the function deformableRegiser3D. If we click on the deformableRegiser3D link in the summary, we see the more detailed results shown in Figure 8.13.

```
1   function [movVol_updated, Tx, Ty, Tz] = deformableRegister3D
    (movVol, refVol, iterLimit)
2   [refX, refY, refZ] = size(refVol)
3   [Ty,Tx,Tz] = meshgrid(1:refY,1:refX,1:refZ);

4   % calculate gradient for moving volume
5   [movX, movY, movZ] = size(movVol)
6   movXGrad_Org = zeros(movX, movY, movZ);
7   movYGrad_Org = zeros(movX, movY, movZ);
8   movZGrad_Org = zeros(movX, movY, movZ);

9   movXGrad = zeros(movX, movY, movZ);
10  movYGrad = zeros(movX, movY, movZ);
11  movZGrad = zeros(movX, movY, movZ);
```

atlasSeg_Main (1 call, 793.349 sec)
Generated 13-Jul-2013 10:53:57 using cpu time.
script in file C:\Users\jsuh\Documents\MATLAB_sample\m_code_Only\atlasSeg_Main.m
Copy to new window for comparing multiple runs

This function changed during profiling or before generation of this report. Results may be incomplete or inaccurate.

[Refresh]

☑ Show parent functions   ☑ Show busy lines   ☑ Show child functions
☑ Show Code Analyzer results   ☑ Show file coverage   ☑ Show function listing

Parents (calling functions)
No parent

Lines where the most time was spent

Line Number	Code	Calls	Total Time	% Time	Time Plot
79	[movVol_updated, Tx, Ty, Tz] =...	1	395.382 s	49.8%	▬▬▬▬
45	[movVol_updated, Tx, Ty, Tz] =...	1	393.943 s	49.7%	▬▬▬▬
21	[cropMovVol_Left, minPosX, max...	1	0.547 s	0.1%	
55	[cropMovVol_Right, minPosX, ma...	1	0.541 s	0.1%	
3	load('medical3D_data');	1	0.462 s	0.1%	
All other lines			2.474 s	0.3%	
Totals			793.349 s	100%	

Children (called functions)

Function Name	Function Type	Calls	Total Time	% Time	Time Plot
deformableRegister3D	function	2	789.321 s	99.5%	▬▬▬▬▬▬
crop_around_ROI	function	2	1.085 s	0.1%	
myView2	function	4	0.761 s	0.1%	
myView_overlap_green	function	3	0.739 s	0.1%	
myView_overlap_red	function	3	0.731 s	0.1%	
close	function	1	0.146 s	0.0%	

Figure 8.12 Profiling the results of the top main function (atlasSeg_Main.m).

```
12 movXGrad_Org(2:end-1,2:end-1,2:end-1) = movVol(3:end,2:end-1,2:
end-1) - movVol(1:end-2,2:end-1,2:end-1);
13 movYGrad_Org(2:end-1,2:end-1,2:end-1) = movVol(2:end-1,3:end,2:
end-1) - movVol(2:end-1,1:end-2,2:end-1);
14 movZGrad_Org(2:end-1,2:end-1,2:end-1)=movVol(2:end-1,2:end-1,3:
end) - movVol(2:end-1,2:end-1,1:end-2);

15 forceX = zeros(refX, refY, refZ);
16 forceY = zeros(refX, refY, refZ);
17 forceZ = zeros(refX, refY, refZ);

18 regX = zeros(refX, refY, refZ);
19 regY = zeros(refX, refY, refZ);
20 regZ = zeros(refX, refY, refZ);

21 delta_Tx = zeros(refX, refY, refZ);
```

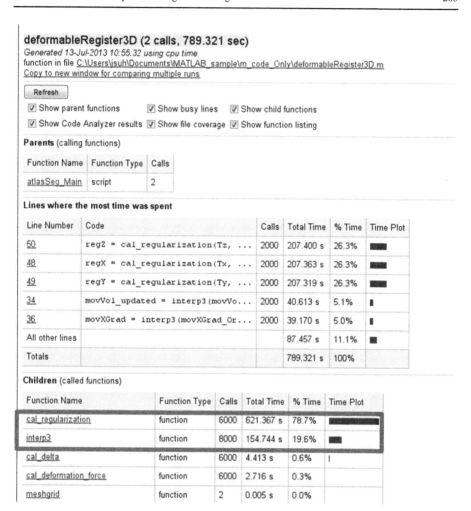

Figure 8.13 **Profiling the result of the** `deformableRegister3D` **module, which consumes most of the computational time of the parent main function.**

```
22 delta_Ty = zeros(refX, refY, refZ);
23 delta_Tz = zeros(refX, refY, refZ);

24 for iter = 1:iterLimit

25 iter
26 movVol_updated = interp3(movVol, Ty, Tx, Tz); % make movVol in the ref
   space
```

```
27 movXGrad = interp3(movXGrad_Org, Ty, Tx, Tz);
28 movYGrad = interp3(movYGrad_Org, Ty, Tx, Tz);
29 movZGrad = interp3(movZGrad_Org, Ty, Tx, Tz);
30 % calculate deformation force
31 forceX = cal_deformation_force(refVol, movVol_updated, movXGrad);
32 forceY = cal_deformation_force(refVol, movVol_updated, movYGrad);
33 forceZ = cal_deformation_force(refVol, movVol_updated, movZGrad);
34 % Regularization
35 % Regularization makes the registration smoother warps.
36 regulFactor = 0.1;
37 regX = cal_regularization(Tx, regulFactor);
38 regY = cal_regularization(Ty, regulFactor);
39 regZ = cal_regularization(Tz, regulFactor);
40
41 stepSize = 1.0;
42 delta_Tx = cal_delta(forceX, regX, stepSize);
43 delta_Ty = cal_delta(forceY, regY, stepSize);
44 delta_Tz = cal_delta(forceZ, regZ, stepSize);
45 Tx = Tx + delta_Tx;
46 Ty = Ty + delta_Ty;
47 Tz = Tz + delta_Tz;
48 Tx = max(min(Tx, refX), 1);
49 Ty = max(min(Ty, refY), 1);
50 Tz = max(min(Tz, refZ), 1);
51 end
```

Within the detailed profiling result of the deformableRegister3D module, we see that cal_regularization is the busiest submodule and interp3 is the second busiest submodule. Figure 8.14 describes the computationally busy modules with shading in the deformableRegister3D.

Let us dig into more about the cal_regularization submodule. If we click on the cal_regularization link in the summary, we see more detailed results, as in Figures 8.15 and 8.16. According to the profiler results, we spend most of the time in the simple subtraction of gradient values from surrounding (front, back, top, bottom, right, and left) gradient values to get the regularization of deformation (Figure 8.16).

In Figure 8.13, the interp3 is the second busiest submodule. When we click on interp3 in Figure 8.13, we get a profiling screen, as in Figure 8.17. Since the interp3 we use within the deformableRegister3D module is a MATLAB built-in function, it is not easy to find the computational bottleneck of that code clearly, because MATLAB built-in functions usually contain many hierarchies with various options and are highly optimized.

```
          2    20  forceY = zeros(refX, refY, refZ);
< 0.01    2    21  forceZ = zeros(refX, refY, refZ);
               22
          2    23  regX = zeros(refX, refY, refZ);
< 0.01    2    24  regY = zeros(refX, refY, refZ);
< 0.01    2    25  regZ = zeros(refX, refY, refZ);
               26
          2    27  delta_Tx = zeros(refX, refY, refZ);
< 0.01    2    28  delta_Ty = zeros(refX, refY, refZ);
< 0.01    2    29  delta_Tz = zeros(refX, refY, refZ);
               30
          2    31  for iter = 1:iterLimit
               32
0.17     2000  33      iter
40.61    2000  34      movVol_updated = interp3(movVol, Ty, Tx, Tz);  % make movVol in the ref space
               35
39.17    2000  36      movXGrad = interp3(movXGrad_Org, Ty, Tx, Tz);   %f_r => dr_img2
37.95    2000  37      movYGrad = interp3(movYGrad_Org, Ty, Tx, Tz);
37.79    2000  38      movZGrad = interp3(movZGrad_Org, Ty, Tx, Tz);
               39
               40      % calculate deformation force
1.22     2000  41      forceX = cal_deformation_force(refVol, movVol_updated, movXGrad);
1.18     2000  42      forceY = cal_deformation_force(refVol, movVol_updated, movYGrad);
1.01     2000  43      forceZ = cal_deformation_force(refVol, movVol_updated, movZGrad);
               44
               45      % Regularization
               46      % Regularization makes the registration smoother warps.
< 0.01   2000  47      regulFactor = 0.1;
207.36   2000  48      regX = cal_regularization(Tx, regulFactor);
207.32   2000  49      regY = cal_regularization(Ty, regulFactor);
207.40   2000  50      regZ = cal_regularization(Tz, regulFactor);
               51
               52  %    stepSize = 0.5;
         2000  53      stepSize = 1.0;
1.95     2000  54      delta_Tx = cal_delta(forceX, regX, stepSize);
1.80     2000  55      delta_Ty = cal_delta(forceY, regY, stepSize);
1.80     2000  56      delta_Tz = cal_delta(forceZ, regZ, stepSize);
               57
0.44     2000  58      Tx = Tx + delta_Tx;
0.52     2000  59      Ty = Ty + delta_Ty;
0.49     2000  60      Tz = Tz + delta_Tz;
               61
0.36     2000  62      Tx = max(min(Tx, refX), 1);
```

Figure 8.14 Profiling the result of deformableRegister3D **also shows that the highlighted submodules take most of the computation time.**

8.3.2   Analyze the Profiling Results and Planning CUDA Optimization

From the profiling results, we could find that the cal_regularization is the busiest submodule and interp3 is the second busiest submodule. Definitely, those two modules should be replaced by c-mex with CUDA to speed up the whole process of segmentation. But, let us carefully look at the deformableRegister3D module again. In the deformableRegister3D code, which follows, the cal_regularization and interp3 submodules are located within the iteration loop, and a few other modules within that loop precede and follow those modules.

```
1    function [movVol_updated, Tx, Ty, Tz] = deformableRegister3D
     (movVol, refVol, iterLimit)
2
     .
     .
     .
```

cal_regularization (6000 calls, 621.367 sec)
Generated 13-Jul-2013 10:56:11 using cpu time.
function in file C:\Users\jsuh\Documents\MATLAB_sample\m_code_Only\cal_regularization.m
Copy to new window for comparing multiple runs

[Refresh]

☑ Show parent functions   ☑ Show busy lines   ☑ Show child functions
☑ Show Code Analyzer results ☑ Show file coverage ☑ Show function listing

Parents (calling functions)

Function Name	Function Type	Calls
deformableRegister3D	function	6000

Lines where the most time was spent

Line Number	Code	Calls	Total Time	% Time	Time Plot
13	regularization(i,j,k) =(gradIm...	1000242000	514.208 s	82.8%	▅▅▅▅▅▅
20	end	1000242000	100.289 s	16.1%	▆
11	for k=2:(sizeZ-1)	19242000	3.510 s	0.6%		
21	end	19242000	1.626 s	0.3%	
7	regularization = zeros(sizeX, ...	6000	1.607 s	0.3%	
All other lines			0.127 s	0.0%	
Totals			621.367 s	100%	

Figure 8.15 Profiling summary of the `cal_regularization` **submodule.**

```
24 for iter = 1:iterLimit

25 iter
26 movVol_updated = interp3(movVol, Ty, Tx, Tz); % make movVol in the ref
   space
27 movXGrad = interp3(movXGrad_Org, Ty, Tx, Tz);
28 movYGrad = interp3(movYGrad_Org, Ty, Tx, Tz);
29 movZGrad = interp3(movZGrad_Org, Ty, Tx, Tz);
30 % calculate deformation force
31 forceX = cal_deformation_force(refVol, movVol_updated,
   movXGrad);
32 forceY = cal_deformation_force(refVol, movVol_updated,
   movYGrad);
33 forceZ = cal_deformation_force(refVol, movVol_updated,
   movZGrad);
34 % Regularization
35 % Regularization makes the registration smoother warps.
36 regulFactor = 0.1;
37 regX = cal_regularization(Tx, regulFactor);
38 regY = cal_regularization(Ty, regulFactor);
```

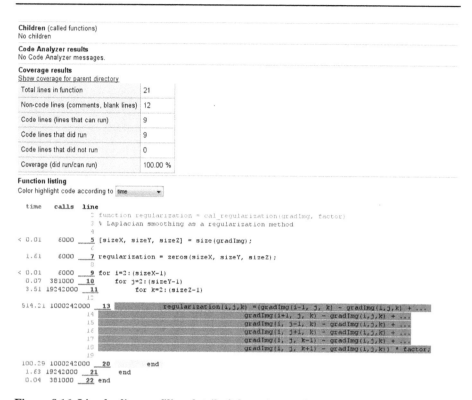

Figure 8.16 **Line-by-line profiling detail of the** `cal_regularization` **submodule.**

```
39 regZ = cal_regularization(Tz, regulFactor);
40
41 stepSize = 1.0;
42 delta_Tx = cal_delta(forceX, regX, stepSize);
43 delta_Ty = cal_delta(forceY, regY, stepSize);
44 delta_Tz = cal_delta(forceZ, regZ, stepSize);
45 Tx = Tx + delta_Tx;
46 Ty = Ty + delta_Ty;
47 Tz = Tz + delta_Tz;
48 Tx = max(min(Tx, refX), 1);
49 Ty = max(min(Ty, refY), 1);
50 Tz = max(min(Tz, refZ), 1);
51 end
```

So, if we replace only those two modules with the CUDA-enabled c-mex functions, then data transfers between the CPU and GPU memory are required before and after those two modified modules (shaded in the boxed code) within the

interp3 (8002 calls, 153.612 sec)
Generated 15-Jul-2013 14:20:46 using cpu time.
function in file C:\Program Files\MATLAB\R2012a\toolbox\matlab\polyfun\interp3.m
Copy to new window for comparing multiple runs

[Refresh]

☑ Show parent functions   ☑ Show busy lines   ☑ Show child functions
☑ Show Code Analyzer results   ☑ Show file coverage   ☑ Show function listing

Parents (calling functions)

Function Name	Function Type	Calls
deformableRegister3D	function	8000
atlasSeg_Main	script	2

Lines where the most time was spent

Line Number	Code	Calls	Total Time	% Time	Time Plot
170	Vq = F(Xq,Yq,Zq); % NDGRID fo...	8002	118.181 s	76.9%	▬▬▬▬▬
167	Xq = permute(Xq,p);	8002	5.598 s	3.6%	▮
168	Yq = permute(Yq,p);	8002	5.365 s	3.5%	▮
103	V = permute(V,p);	8002	5.287 s	3.4%	▮
169	Zq = permute(Zq,p);	8002	5.148 s	3.4%	▮
All other lines			14.033 s	9.1%	▪
Totals			153.612 s	100%	

Figure 8.17 Profiling summary of the `interp3` **submodule.**

iteration. These data transfers require a lot of overhead in processing and make the overall process very inefficient.

Therefore, the best way to reduce the data transfer between the CPU and GPU memory is to convert all parts within the iteration loop into GPU code, so that we can avoid all data transfer between the CPU and GPU device within the iterations.

8.4   CUDA Conversion 1 - Regularization

Let us start to convert the `cal_regularization`, which was revealed to be the busiest function during the profiling. In the `m_code_partialCuda` example folder, the main module `atlasSeg_PartialCuda.m` has almost same structure as the previous `atlasSeg_Main.m`.

    `cal_regularization_cuda.cpp`

```
1 #include "mex.h"
2 #include <cuda_runtime.h>
3 #include "cal_regularization_cuda.h"
4
5 // function regularization = cal_regularization(gradImg, factor);
```

```
6  void mexFunction(int nlhs, mxArray *plhs[], int nrhs, const mxArray
   *prhs[])
7  {
8     if (nrhs != 2)
9        mexErrMsgTxt("Invalid number of input arguments");
10
11    if (nlhs != 1)
12       mexErrMsgTxt("Invalid number of outputs");
13
14    for (int i = 0; i < nrhs; ++i)
15    {
16       if (!mxIsDouble(prhs[i]))
17       {
18          mexErrMsgTxt("input vector data type must be double");
19          break;
20       }
21    }
22
23    const mwSize* size = mxGetDimensions(prhs[0]);
24    int sizeX = size[0];
25    int sizeY = size[1];
26    int sizeZ = size[2];
27
28    // inputs
29    double* gradImg = (double*)mxGetData(prhs[0]);
30    double factor = *((double*)mxGetData(prhs[1]));
31
32    // outputs
33    plhs[0] = mxCreateNumericArray(3, size, mxDOUBLE_CLASS, mxREAL);
34    double* regularization = (double*)mxGetData(plhs[0]);
35
36    // calRegularization cuda
37    calRegularization(gradImg, factor, regularization, sizeX, sizeY,
   sizeZ);
38
39    cudaError_t error = cudaGetLastError();
40    if (error != cudaSuccess)
41    {
42       mexPrintf("%s\n", cudaGetErrorString(error));
43       mexErrMsgTxt("CUDA failed\n");
44    }
45 }
```

cal_regularization_cuda.h

```
1  #ifndef __CALREGULARIZATION_H__
2  #define __CALREGULARIZATION_H__
3
4  extern void calRegularization(double* in, double factor, double* out,
```

```
5                          int sx, int sy, int sz);
6
7 #endif // __CALREGULARIZATION_H__
```

calRegularization.cu

```
1  __global__ void calRegularizationKernel(double* in, double factor,
                                            double* out,
2                                           int sx, int sy, int sz)
3  {
4      int i = blockIdx.x * blockDim.x + threadIdx.x;
5      // compute capability >= 2.x
6      //int j = blockIdx.y * blockDim.y + threadIdx.y;
7      //int k = blockIdx.z * blockDim.z + threadIdx.z;
8      // compute capability < 2.x
9      int gy = (sy + blockDim.y - 1) / blockDim.y;
10     int j = (blockIdx.y % gy) * blockDim.y + threadIdx.y;
11     int k = (blockIdx.y / gy) * blockDim.z + threadIdx.z;
12
13     if (i < 1 || i >= sx - 1 ||
14         j < 1 || j >= sy - 1 ||
15         k < 1 || k >= sz - 1)
16         return;
17
18     int idx = sx * (sy * k + j) + i;
19     double org = in[idx];
20     out[idx] = (in[sx * (sy * k + j) + i - 1] - org +
21                 in[sx * (sy * k + j) + i + 1] - org +
22                 in[sx * (sy * k + j - 1) + i] - org +
23                 in[sx * (sy * k + j + 1) + i] - org +
24                 in[sx * (sy * (k - 1) + j) + i] - org +
25                 in[sx * (sy * (k + 1) + j) + i] - org) * factor;
26 }
27
28 void calRegularization(double* in, double factor, double* out,
29                        int sx, int sy, int sz)
30 {
31     int totalSize = sx * sy * sz;
32     double* devT = 0;
33     cudaMalloc(&devT, sizeof(double) * totalSize);
34     cudaMemcpy(devT, in, sizeof(double) * totalSize,
           cudaMemcpyHostToDevice);
35
36     // temps
37     double* devReg = 0;
38     cudaMalloc(&devReg, sizeof(double) * totalSize);
39     cudaMemset(devReg, 0, sizeof(double) * totalSize);
40
```

```
41    dim3 blockSize(4, 4, 4);
42    // compute capability >= 2.x
43    //dim3 gridSize((sx + blockSize.x - 1) / blockSize.x,
44    //              (sy + blockSize.y - 1) / blockSize.y,
45    //              (sz + blockSize.z - 1) / blockSize.z);
46    // compute capabiltiy < 2.x
47    int gy = (sy + blockSize.y - 1) / blockSize.y;
48    int gz = (sz + blockSize.z - 1) / blockSize.z;
49    dim3 gridSize((sx + blockSize.x - 1) / blockSize.x, gy * gz, 1);
50
51    calRegularizationKernel <<< gridSize,    blockSize >>> (devT,
      factor, devReg,
52    sx, sy, sz);
53
54    cudaMemcpy(out, devReg, sizeof(double) * totalSize,
      cudaMemcpyDeviceToHost);
55    cudaFree(devReg);
56    cudaFree(devT);
57 }
```

You can create a c-mex file from the MATLAB command window using the mex command. But, first, we compile the CUDA functions using the nvcc compiler and link its object when calling mex. We can create a c-mex file, for example, as

- In Mac OS X,

```
% mac
system('/Developer/NVIDIA/CUDA-5.0/bin/nvcc -c calRegularization.cu
-m64 -Xptxas -v');
mex cal_regularization_cuda.cpp calRegularization.o -lcudart -L"/
Developer/NVIDIA/CUDA-5.0/lib" -I"/Developer/NVIDIA/CUDA-5.0/
include" -v
```

- In Windows 64,

```
% MS Windows
system('nvcc -c calRegularization.cu -Xptxas -v');
mex cal_regularization_cuda.cpp calRegularization.obj -lcudart -L"C:
\Program Files\NVIDIA GPU Computing Toolkit\CUDA\v5.0\lib\x64" -I"C:
\Program Files\NVIDIA GPU Computing Toolkit\CUDA\v5.0\include" -v
```

If we have trouble setting a path for the Microsoft C compiler, then we can explicitly set the compiler path as follows:

```
% MS Windows
system('nvcc -c calRegularization.cu -Xptxas -v -ccbin "C:\Program Files
(x86)\Microsoft Visual Studio 10.0\VC\bin"');
```

Then, we slightly modify the deformableRegister3D(...) function to call the c-mex version. The modified function is

```
deformableRegister3D_partialCuda.m
```

```
1  function [movVol_updated, Tx, Ty, Tz] = deformableRegister3D_partial
   Cuda(movVol, refVol, iterLimit)
2  [refX, refY, refZ] = size(refVol)
3  [Ty,Tx,Tz] = meshgrid(1:refY,1:refX,1:refZ);
4
5  % calculate gradient for moving volume
6  [movX, movY, movZ] = size(movVol)
7  movXGrad_Org = zeros(movX, movY, movZ);
8  movYGrad_Org = zeros(movX, movY, movZ);
9  movZGrad_Org = zeros(movX, movY, movZ);

10 movXGrad = zeros(movX, movY, movZ);
11 movYGrad = zeros(movX, movY, movZ);
12 movZGrad = zeros(movX, movY, movZ);

13 movXGrad_Org(2:end-1,2:end-1,2:end-1) = movVol(3:end,2:end-1,2:
   end-1) - movVol(1:end-2,2:end-1,2:end-1);
14 movYGrad_Org(2:end-1,2:end-1,2:end-1) = movVol(2:end-1,3:end,
   2:end-1) - movVol(2:end-1,1:end-2,2:end-1);
15 movZGrad_Org(2:end-1,2:end-1,2:end-1) = movVol(2:end-1,2:end-1,
   3:end) - movVol(2:end-1,2:end-1,1:end-2);

16 forceX = zeros(refX, refY, refZ);
17 forceY = zeros(refX, refY, refZ);
18 forceZ = zeros(refX, refY, refZ);

19 regX = zeros(refX, refY, refZ);
20 regY = zeros(refX, refY, refZ);
21 regZ = zeros(refX, refY, refZ);

22 delta_Tx = zeros(refX, refY, refZ);
23 delta_Ty = zeros(refX, refY, refZ);
24 delta_Tz = zeros(refX, refY, refZ);

25 for iter = 1:iterLimit
26 iter
27 movVol_updated = interp3(movVol, Ty, Tx, Tz); % make movVol in the ref
   space

28 movXGrad = interp3(movXGrad_Org, Ty, Tx, Tz);
29 movYGrad = interp3(movYGrad_Org, Ty, Tx, Tz);
30 movZGrad = interp3(movZGrad_Org, Ty, Tx, Tz);

31 % calculate deformation force
32 forceX = cal_deformation_force(refVol, movVol_updated, movXGrad);
33 forceY = cal_deformation_force(refVol, movVol_updated, movYGrad);
34 forceZ = cal_deformation_force(refVol, movVol_updated, movZGrad);
```

```
35 % Regularization
36 % Regularization makes the registration smoother warps.
37 regulFactor = 0.1;
38 regX = cal_regularization_cuda(Tx, regulFactor);
39 regY = cal_regularization_cuda(Ty, regulFactor);
40 regZ = cal_regularization_cuda(Tz, regulFactor);

41 % stepSize = 0.5;
42 stepSize = 1.0;
43 delta_Tx = cal_delta(forceX, regX, stepSize);
44 delta_Ty = cal_delta(forceY, regY, stepSize);
45 delta_Tz = cal_delta(forceZ, regZ, stepSize);

46 Tx = Tx + delta_Tx;
47 Ty = Ty + delta_Ty;
48 Tz = Tz + delta_Tz;

49 Tx = max(min(Tx, refX), 1);
50 Ty = max(min(Ty, refY), 1);
51 Tz = max(min(Tz, refZ), 1);
52 end
```

After converting `cal_regularization` to the CUDA version, the total elapsed time for both the right and left hippocampus segmentation is 182 seconds (Figure 8.18), which is about 3.34 times faster than `atlasSeg_Main.m`. As mentioned previously, data transfer between the CPU and GPU memory within the loop in the single CUDA conversion of `cal_regularization` are too frequent. In the next section, we see the CUDA conversions of whole operations.

8.5   CUDA Conversion 2 - Image Registration

In this section, we try to replace the whole iteration loop in `deformableRegister3D` (...) with a `c-mex` and CUDA function. To minimize data transfer between the host

```
iter =

    999


iter =

    1000

Elapsed time is 182.141124 seconds.
```

Figure 8.18 The elapsed time for `atlasSeg_PartialCuda.m`.

and device, we replace every operation inside the loop with CUDA calls. We create
five CUDA kernels:

MATLAB	CUDA Kernels
interp3(...)	calInterp3 <<<...>>>
cal_deformation_force	calDeformationForce <<<...>>>
cal_delta	calDelta <<<...>>>
cal_regularization	calRegularization <<<...>>>
Tx = Tx + delta_Tx;	updatePos <<<...>>>
...	
Tx = max(min(Tx, refX), 1);	

Our block is $4 \times 4 \times 4$ threads, giving us a total of 64 threads per block. The
grid size is based on this block size and volume size. We determine the grid and
block size as

```
dim3 blockSize(4, 4, 4);

// compute capability >= 2.x
//dim3 gridSize((sx + blockSize.x - 1) / blockSize.x,
//     (sy + blockSize.y - 1) / blockSize.y,
//     (sz + blockSize.z - 1) / blockSize.z);

// compute capabiltiy < 2.x
int gy = (sy + blockSize.y - 1) / blockSize.y;
int gz = (sz + blockSize.z - 1) / blockSize.z;
dim3 gridSize((sx + blockSize.x - 1) / blockSize.x,
              gy * gz,
              1);
```

Note that, depending on the computing capability of your GPU, a grid size may or
may not support three dimensions. When a three-dimensional grid size is not supported,
we pass as two dimensions and then we recover them in the kernel as we did in Chapter 7

```
int i = blockIdx.x * blockDim.x + threadIdx.x;

// compute capability >= 2.x
//int j = blockIdx.y * blockDim.y + threadIdx.y;
//int k = blockIdx.z * blockDim.z + threadIdx.z;

// compute capability < 2.x
int gy = (sy + blockDim.y - 1) / blockDim.y;
int j = (blockIdx.y % gy) * blockDim.y + threadIdx.y;
int k = (blockIdx.y / gy) * blockDim.z + threadIdx.z;
```

Once we determine a grid and a block size from our volume, we allocate memory for the inputs and outputs on the GPU device. Then, we copy data from the

host to the device using `cudaMemcpy(...)`. We call our kernels in an iteration loop. After the specified number of iterations, we copy the results back to the host.

There are two major files: `register3D.cpp` and `register3D_cuda.cu`. The `register3D.cpp` implements a gateway routine for the `c-mex` and calls the `register3D(...)` function. The `register3D_cuda.cu(...)` implements all the necessary CUDA kernels and memory operations with GPU.

When defining a CUDA kernel, the kernel may not accept double precision floating point operations based on your GPU computing capability. Make sure that your GPU computing capability supports double precision. Otherwise, we need to convert the data to single precision. Our example assumes that double precision is supported.

`registger3D.cpp`

```
58 #include "mex.h"
59 #include <cuda_runtime.h>
60 #include "register3D_cuda.h"
61
62 // funciton [movVol_updated, Tx, Ty, Tz] = register3D(movVol, refVol,
                                      ...
63 //                       movXGrad_Org, movYGrad_Org, movZGrad_Org, ...
64 //                          Tx, Ty, Tz, ...
65 //                          iterLimit, regulFactor, stepSize);
66 void mexFunction(int nlhs, mxArray *plhs[], int nrhs, const mxArray
*prhs[])
67 {
68    if (nrhs != 11)
69       mexErrMsgTxt("Invaid number of input arguments");
70
71    if (nlhs != 4)
72       mexErrMsgTxt("Invalid number of outputs");
73
74    for (int i = 0; i < nrhs; ++i)
75    {
76       if (!mxIsDouble(prhs[i]))
77       {
78          mexErrMsgTxt("input vector data type must be double");
79          break;
80       }
81    }
82
83    const mwSize* size = mxGetDimensions(prhs[0]);
84    int sx = size[0];
85    int sy = size[1];
86    int sz = size[2];
87
88    // inputs
89    double* movVol = (double*)mxGetData(prhs[0]);
```

```
90    double* refVol = (double*)mxGetData(prhs[1]);
91    double* movXGrad_Org = (double*)mxGetData(prhs[2]);
92    double* movYGrad_Org = (double*)mxGetData(prhs[3]);
93    double* movZGrad_Org = (double*)mxGetData(prhs[4]);
94    double* TxIn = (double*)mxGetData(prhs[5]);
95    double* TyIn = (double*)mxGetData(prhs[6]);
96    double* TzIn = (double*)mxGetData(prhs[7]);
97    double iterLimit = *((double*)mxGetData(prhs[8]));
98    double regulFactor = *((double*)mxGetData(prhs[9]));
99    double stepSize = *((double*)mxGetData(prhs[10]));
100
101   // outputs
102   plhs[0] = mxCreateNumericArray(3, size, mxDOUBLE_CLASS, mxREAL);
103   double* movVol_updated = (double*)mxGetData(plhs[0]);
104   plhs[1] = mxCreateNumericArray(3, size, mxDOUBLE_CLASS, mxREAL);
105   double* Tx = (double*)mxGetData(plhs[1]);
106   plhs[2] = mxCreateNumericArray(3, size, mxDOUBLE_CLASS, mxREAL);
107   double* Ty = (double*)mxGetData(plhs[2]);
108   plhs[3] = mxCreateNumericArray(3, size, mxDOUBLE_CLASS, mxREAL);
109   double* Tz = (double*)mxGetData(plhs[3]);
110
111   // register3D cuda
112   register3D_cuda(movVol,
113                        refVol,
114                        movXGrad_Org,
115                        movYGrad_Org,
116                        movZGrad_Org,
117                        TxIn, TyIn, TzIn,
118                        movVol_updated,
119                        Tx, Ty, Tz,
120                        sx, sy, sz,
121                        (int)iterLimit, regulFactor, stepSize);
122
123   cudaError_t error = cudaGetLastError();
124   if (error != cudaSuccess)
125   {
126       mexPrintf("%s\n", cudaGetErrorString(error));
127       mexErrMsgTxt("CUDA failed\n");
128   }
129 }
```

register3D_cuda.h

```
1 #ifndef __DEFORMABLEREGISTER3D_H__
2 #define __DEFORMABLEREGISTER3D_H__
3
4 extern void register3D_cuda(double* movVol, // in
5                              double* refVol, // in
```

```
6                              double* movXGrad_Org, // in
7                              double* movYGrad_Org, // in
8                              double* movZGrad_Org, // in
9                              double* TxIn,  // in
10                             double* TyIn,  // in
11                             double* TzIn,  // in
12                             double* movVol_updated, // out
13                             double* Tx,  // out
14                             double* Ty,  // out
15                             double* Tz,  // out
16                             int sx, int sy, int sz,
17                             int iterLimit,
18                             double regulFacotr,
19                             double stepSize);
20
21 #endif // __DEFORMABLEREGISTER3D_H__


register3D_cuda.cu

22 #include "register3D_cuda.h"
23
24 __global__ void calInterp3(double* Vin,
25                            double* Tx, double* Ty, double* Tz,
26                            double* Vout,
27                            int sx, int sy, int sz)
28 {
29     int i = blockIdx.x * blockDim.x + threadIdx.x;
30     // compute capability >= 2.x
31     //int j = blockIdx.y * blockDim.y + threadIdx.y;
32     //int k = blockIdx.z * blockDim.z + threadIdx.z;
33     // compute capability < 2.x
34     int gy = (sy + blockDim.y - 1) / blockDim.y;
35     int j = (blockIdx.y % gy) * blockDim.y + threadIdx.y;
36     int k = (blockIdx.y / gy) * blockDim.z + threadIdx.z;
37
38     if (i >= sx - 1 || j >= sy - 1 || k >= sz - 1)
39         return;
40
41     int idx = sx * (sy * k + j) + i;
42
43     double tx = Tx[idx];
44     double ty = Ty[idx];
45     double tz = Tz[idx];
46     int ix = (int)tx - 1;
47     int iy = (int)ty - 1;
48     int iz = (int)tz - 1;
49     int idx0 = sx * (sy * iz + iy) + ix;
50     int idx1 = sx * (sy * iz + iy) + ix + 1;
```

```
51     int idx2 = sx * (sy * iz + iy + 1) + ix;
52     int idx3 = sx * (sy * iz + iy + 1) + ix + 1;
53     int idx4 = sx * (sy * (iz + 1) + iy) + ix;
54     int idx5 = sx * (sy * (iz + 1) + iy) + ix + 1;
55     int idx6 = sx * (sy * (iz + 1) + iy + 1) + ix;
56     int idx7 = sx * (sy * (iz + 1) + iy + 1) + ix + 1;
57
58     // along x
59     double wd = floor(tx + 1.0) - tx;
60     double wu = 1.0 - wd;
61     double R00 = wd * Vin[idx0] + wu * Vin[idx1];
62     double R10 = wd * Vin[idx2] + wu * Vin[idx3];
63     double R01 = wd * Vin[idx4] + wu * Vin[idx5];
64     double R11 = wd * Vin[idx6] + wu * Vin[idx7];
65
66     // along y
67     wd = floor(ty + 1.0) - ty;
68     wu = 1.0 - wd;
69     double R0 = wd * R00 + wu * R10;
70     double R1 = wd * R01 + wu * R11;
71
72     // along z
73     wd = floor(tz + 1.0) - tz;
74     wu = 1.0 - wd;
75
76     Vout[idx] = wd * R0 + wu * R1;
77 }
78
79 __global__ void calDeformationForce(double* refImg, double* movImg,
80                                      double*    gradientImg,    double*
                                         forceImg,
81                                      int sx, int sy, int sz)
82 {
83     int i = blockIdx.x * blockDim.x + threadIdx.x;
84     // compute capability >= 2.x
85     //int j = blockIdx.y * blockDim.y + threadIdx.y;
86     //int k = blockIdx.z * blockDim.z + threadIdx.z;
87     // compute capability < 2.x
88     int gy = (sy + blockDim.y - 1) / blockDim.y;
89     int j = (blockIdx.y % gy) * blockDim.y + threadIdx.y;
90     int k = (blockIdx.y / gy) * blockDim.z + threadIdx.z;
91
92     if (i >= sx || j >= sy || k >= sz)
93         return;
94
95     int idx = sx * (sy * k + j) + i;
96     forceImg[idx] = (refImg[idx] - movImg[idx]) * gradientImg[idx];
97 }
98
```

```
99 __global__ void calDelta(double* deformForce, double* resistance,
100                          double* delta, double stepSize,
101                          int sx, int sy, int sz)
102 {
103     int i = blockIdx.x * blockDim.x + threadIdx.x;
104     // compute capability >= 2.x
105     //int j = blockIdx.y * blockDim.y + threadIdx.y;
106     //int k = blockIdx.z * blockDim.z + threadIdx.z;
107     // compute capability < 2.x
108     int gy = (sy + blockDim.y - 1) / blockDim.y;
109     int j = (blockIdx.y % gy) * blockDim.y + threadIdx.y;
110     int k = (blockIdx.y / gy) * blockDim.z + threadIdx.z;
111
112     if (i >= sx || j >= sy || k >= sz)
113         return;
114
115     int idx = sx * (sy * k + j) + i;
116
117     double temp = (deformForce[idx] + resistance[idx]) * stepSize;
118     temp = (temp > -1.0) ? temp : -1.0; // max
119     delta[idx] = (temp < 1.0) ? temp : 1.0; // min
120 }
121
122 __global__ void updatePos (double* deltaX, double* deltaY, double*
                              deltaZ,
123                           double* Tx, double* Ty, double* Tz,
124                           int sx, int sy, int sz)
125 {
126     int i = blockIdx.x * blockDim.x + threadIdx.x;
127     // compute capability >= 2.x
128     //int j = blockIdx.y * blockDim.y + threadIdx.y;
129     //int k = blockIdx.z * blockDim.z + threadIdx.z;
130     // compute capability < 2.x
131     int gy = (sy + blockDim.y - 1) / blockDim.y;
132     int j = (blockIdx.y % gy) * blockDim.y + threadIdx.y;
133     int k = (blockIdx.y / gy) * blockDim.z + threadIdx.z;
134
135     if (i >= sx || j >= sy || k >= sz)
136         return;
137
138     int idx = sx * (sy * k + j) + i;
139
140     double tempX = Tx[idx] + deltaX[idx];
141     double tempY = Ty[idx] + deltaY[idx];
142     double tempZ = Tz[idx] + deltaZ[idx];
143
144     tempX = (tempX < sx) ? tempX : sx; // min
145     tempY = (tempY < sy) ? tempY : sy; // min
146     tempZ = (tempZ < sz) ? tempZ : sz; // min
```

```
147
148    Tx[idx] = (tempX > 1.0) ? tempX : 1.0; // max
149    Ty[idx] = (tempY > 1.0) ? tempY : 1.0; // max
150    Tz[idx] = (tempZ > 1.0) ? tempZ : 1.0; // max
151 }
152
153 __global__ void calRegularization(double* in, double factor, double*
                                      out,
154                                      int sx, int sy, int sz)
155 {
156    int i = blockIdx.x * blockDim.x + threadIdx.x;
157    // compute capability >= 2.x
158    //int j = blockIdx.y * blockDim.y + threadIdx.y;
159    //int k = blockIdx.z * blockDim.z + threadIdx.z;
160    // compute capability < 2.x
161    int gy = (sy + blockDim.y - 1) / blockDim.y;
162    int j = (blockIdx.y % gy) * blockDim.y + threadIdx.y;
163    int k = (blockIdx.y / gy) * blockDim.z + threadIdx.z;
164
165    if (i < 1 || i >= sx - 1 ||
166        j < 1 || j >= sy - 1 ||
167        k < 1 || k >= sz - 1)
168        return;
169
170    int idx = sx * (sy * k + j) + i;
171    double org = in[idx];
172    out[idx] = (in[sx * (sy * k + j) + i - 1] - org +
173               in[sx * (sy * k + j) + i + 1] - org +
174               in[sx * (sy * k + j - 1) + i] - org +
175               in[sx * (sy * k + j + 1) + i] - org +
176               in[sx * (sy * (k - 1) + j) + i] - org +
177               in[sx * (sy * (k + 1) + j) + i] - org) * factor;
178 }
179
180
181 void register3D_cuda(double* movVol, // in
182                      double* refVol, // in
183                      double* movXGrad_Org, // in
184                      double* movYGrad_Org, // in
185                      double* movZGrad_Org, // in
186                      double* TxIn,  // in
187                      double* TyIn,  // in
188                      double* TzIn,  // in
189                      double* movVol_updated, // out
190                      double* Tx,  // out
191                      double* Ty,  // out
192                      double* Tz,  // out
193                      int sx, int sy, int sz,
```

```
194                         int iterLimit,
195                         double regulFactor,
196                         double stepSize)
197 {
198     int totalSize = sx * sy * sz;
199
200     // inputs
201     double* devMovVol = 0;
202     double* devRefVol = 0;
203     double* devMovXGrad_Org = 0;
204     double* devMovYGrad_Org = 0;
205     double* devMovZGrad_Org = 0;
206     cudaMalloc(&devMovVol, sizeof(double) * totalSize);
207     cudaMalloc(&devRefVol, sizeof(double) * totalSize);
208     cudaMalloc(&devMovXGrad_Org, sizeof(double) * totalSize);
209     cudaMalloc(&devMovYGrad_Org, sizeof(double) * totalSize);
210     cudaMalloc(&devMovZGrad_Org, sizeof(double) * totalSize);
211     cudaMemcpy(devMovVol, movVol, sizeof(double) * totalSize,
                    cudaMemcpyHostToDevice);
212     cudaMemcpy(devRefVol, refVol, sizeof(double) * totalSize,
                    cudaMemcpyHostToDevice);
213     cudaMemcpy(devMovXGrad_Org, movXGrad_Org, sizeof(double) *
                    totalSize, cudaMemcpyHostToDevice);
214     cudaMemcpy(devMovYGrad_Org, movYGrad_Org, sizeof(double) *
                    totalSize, cudaMemcpyHostToDevice);
215     cudaMemcpy(devMovZGrad_Org, movZGrad_Org, sizeof(double) *
                    totalSize, cudaMemcpyHostToDevice);
216
217     // temps
218     double* devMovXGrad = 0;
219     double* devMovYGrad = 0;
220     double* devMovZGrad = 0;
221     double* devForceX = 0;
222     double* devForceY = 0;
223     double* devForceZ = 0;
224     double* devRegX = 0;
225     double* devRegY = 0;
226     double* devRegZ = 0;
227     double* devDeltaTx = 0;
228     double* devDeltaTy = 0;
229     double* devDeltaTz = 0;
230     cudaMalloc(&devMovXGrad, sizeof(double) * totalSize);
231     cudaMalloc(&devMovYGrad, sizeof(double) * totalSize);
232     cudaMalloc(&devMovZGrad, sizeof(double) * totalSize);
233     cudaMalloc(&devForceX, sizeof(double) * totalSize);
234     cudaMalloc(&devForceY, sizeof(double) * totalSize);
235     cudaMalloc(&devForceZ, sizeof(double) * totalSize);
236     cudaMalloc(&devRegX, sizeof(double) * totalSize);
```

```
237     cudaMalloc(&devRegY, sizeof(double) * totalSize);
238     cudaMalloc(&devRegZ, sizeof(double) * totalSize);
239     cudaMalloc(&devDeltaTx, sizeof(double) * totalSize);
240     cudaMalloc(&devDeltaTy, sizeof(double) * totalSize);
241     cudaMalloc(&devDeltaTz, sizeof(double) * totalSize);
242     cudaMemset(devMovXGrad, 0, sizeof(double) * totalSize);
243     cudaMemset(devMovYGrad, 0, sizeof(double) * totalSize);
244     cudaMemset(devMovZGrad, 0, sizeof(double) * totalSize);
245     cudaMemset(devForceX, 0, sizeof(double) * totalSize);
246     cudaMemset(devForceY, 0, sizeof(double) * totalSize);
247     cudaMemset(devForceZ, 0, sizeof(double) * totalSize);
248     cudaMemset(devRegX, 0, sizeof(double) * totalSize);
249     cudaMemset(devRegY, 0, sizeof(double) * totalSize);
250     cudaMemset(devRegZ, 0, sizeof(double) * totalSize);
251     cudaMemset(devDeltaTx, 0, sizeof(double) * totalSize);
252     cudaMemset(devDeltaTy, 0, sizeof(double) * totalSize);
253     cudaMemset(devDeltaTz, 0, sizeof(double) * totalSize);
254
255     // outputs
256     double* devMovVol_updated = 0;
257     double* devTx = 0;
258     double* devTy = 0;
259     double* devTz = 0;
260     cudaMalloc(&devMovVol_updated, sizeof(double) * totalSize);
261     cudaMalloc(&devTx, sizeof(double) * totalSize);
262     cudaMalloc(&devTy, sizeof(double) * totalSize);
263     cudaMalloc(&devTz, sizeof(double) * totalSize);
264     cudaMemcpy(devMovVol_updated, movVol, sizeof(double) *
    totalSize, cudaMemcpyHostToDevice);
265
266     // init Tx, Ty, Tz
267     cudaMemcpy(devTx, TxIn, sizeof(double) * totalSize,
                     cudaMemcpyHostToDevice);
268     cudaMemcpy(devTy, TyIn, sizeof(double) * totalSize,
                     cudaMemcpyHostToDevice);
269     cudaMemcpy(devTz, TzIn, sizeof(double) * totalSize,
                     cudaMemcpyHostToDevice);
270
271     dim3 blockSize(4, 4, 4);
272     // compute capability >= 2.x
273     //dim3 gridSize((sx + blockSize.x - 1) / blockSize.x,
274     //  (sy + blockSize.y - 1) / blockSize.y,
275     //  (sz + blockSize.z - 1) / blockSize.z);
276     // compute capabiltiy < 2.x
277     int gy = (sy + blockSize.y - 1) / blockSize.y;
278     int gz = (sz + blockSize.z - 1) / blockSize.z;
279     dim3 gridSize((sx + blockSize.x - 1) / blockSize.x,
280                   gy * gz,
281                   1);
```

```
282
283    calInterp3 << <gridSize, blockSize>> >(devMovVol, devTx,
       devTy, devTz,
284     devMovVol_updated, sx, sy, sz);
285
286 for (int i = 0; i < iterLimit; ++i)
287 {
288     // interpolation
289     calInterp3 << <gridSize, blockSize>> >(devMovVol, devTx,
        devTy, devTz,
290     devMovVol_updated, sx, sy, sz);
291     calInterp3 << <gridSize, blockSize>> >(devMovXGrad_Org,
        devTx, devTy, devTz,
292     devMovXGrad, sx, sy, sz);
293     calInterp3 << <gridSize, blockSize>> >(devMovYGrad_Org,
        devTx, devTy, devTz,
294     devMovYGrad, sx, sy, sz);
295     calInterp3 << <gridSize, blockSize>> >(devMovZGrad_Org,
        devTx, devTy, devTz,
296     devMovZGrad, sx, sy, sz);
297
298     // deformation force
299     calDeformationForce << <gridSize, blockSize>> >(devRefVol,
        devMovVol_updated,
300     devMovXGrad, devForceX,
301     sx, sy, sz);
302     calDeformationForce << <gridSize, blockSize>> >(devRefVol,
        devMovVol_updated,
303     devMovYGrad, devForceY,
304     sx, sy, sz);
305     calDeformationForce << <gridSize, blockSize>> >(devRefVol,
        devMovVol_updated,
306     devMovZGrad, devForceZ,
307     sx, sy, sz);
308
309     // Regularization
310     calRegularization << <gridSize, blockSize>> >(devTx,
        regulFactor, devRegX, sx, sy, sz);
311     calRegularization << <gridSize, blockSize>> >(devTy,
        regulFactor, devRegY, sx, sy, sz);
312     calRegularization << <gridSize, blockSize>> >(devTz,
        regulFactor, devRegZ, sx, sy, sz);
313
314     // Calculate delta
315     double stepSize = 1.0;
316     calDelta << <gridSize, blockSize>> >(devForceX, devRegX,
        devDeltaTx, stepSize, sx, sy, sz);
317     calDelta << <gridSize, blockSize>> >(devForceY, devRegY,
        devDeltaTy, stepSize, sx, sy, sz);
```

```
318     calDelta<<<gridSize, blockSize>>>(devForceZ, devRegZ,
        devDeltaTz, stepSize, sx, sy, sz);
319
320     // Update pos
321     updatePos<<<gridSize, blockSize>>>(devDeltaTx, devDeltaTy,
        devDeltaTz,
322     devTx, devTy, devTz, sx, sy, sz);
323
324     //error = cudaGetLastError();
325     //if (error != cudaSuccess)
326     // exit(-1);
327 }
328
329
330     // copy outputs
331     cudaMemcpy(movVol_updated, devMovVol_updated, sizeof(double) *
        totalSize, cudaMemcpyDeviceToHost);
332     cudaMemcpy(Tx, devTx, sizeof(double) * totalSize,
        cudaMemcpyDeviceToHost);
333     cudaMemcpy(Ty, devTy, sizeof(double) * totalSize,
        cudaMemcpyDeviceToHost);
334     cudaMemcpy(Tz, devTz, sizeof(double) * totalSize,
        cudaMemcpyDeviceToHost);
335
336     // free resources
337     cudaFree(devMovVol);
338     cudaFree(devRefVol);
339     cudaFree(devMovXGrad_Org);
340     cudaFree(devMovYGrad_Org);
341     cudaFree(devMovZGrad_Org);
342
343     cudaFree(devMovXGrad);
344     cudaFree(devMovYGrad);
345     cudaFree(devMovZGrad);
346     cudaFree(devForceX);
347     cudaFree(devForceY);
348     cudaFree(devForceZ);
349     cudaFree(devRegX);
350     cudaFree(devRegY);
351     cudaFree(devRegZ);
352     cudaFree(devDeltaTx);
353     cudaFree(devDeltaTy);
354     cudaFree(devDeltaTz);
355
356     cudaFree(devMovVol_updated);
357     cudaFree(devTx);
358     cudaFree(devTy);
359     cudaFree(devTz);
```

```
360 }
```

You can create a c-mex file from the MATLAB command window using the mex command. But, first, we compile our CUDA functions using the nvcc compiler and link its object when calling mex. You can initiate c-mex, for example, as follows:

- In Mac OS X,

```
% mac
system('/Developer/NVIDIA/CUDA-5.0/bin/nvcc  -c  register3D_cuda.cu
-m64 -Xptxas -v');
mex register3D.cpp register3D_cuda.o -lcudart -L"/Developer/NVIDIA/
CUDA-5.0/lib" -I"/Developer/NVIDIA/CUDA-5.0/include" -v
```

- In Windows 64,

```
% MS Windows
system('nvcc -c register3D_cuda.cu -Xptxas -v');
mex register3D.cpp register3D_cuda.obj -lcudart -L"C:\Program Files
\NVIDIA GPU Computing Toolkit\CUDA\v5.0\lib\x64" -I"C:\Program Files
\NVIDIA GPU Computing Toolkit\CUDA\v5.0\include" -v
```

Then, we slightly modify the deformableRegister3D(...) function to call the c-mex version. The modified function is

```
deformableRegister3D_cuda.m

function [movVol_updated, Tx, Ty, Tz] = deformableRegister3D_cuda
(movVol, refVol, iterLimit)
[refX, refY, refZ] = size(refVol)
[Ty,Tx,Tz] = meshgrid(1:refY,1:refX,1:refZ);

% calculate gradient for moving volume
[movX, movY, movZ] = size(movVol)
movXGrad_Org = zeros(movX, movY, movZ);
movYGrad_Org = zeros(movX, movY, movZ);
movZGrad_Org = zeros(movX, movY, movZ);

movXGrad_Org(2:end-1,2:end-1,2:end-1) = movVol(3:end,2:end-1,2:
end-1) - movVol(1:end-2,2:end-1,2:end-1);
movYGrad_Org(2:end-1,2:end-1,2:end-1) = movVol(2:end-1,3:end,2:
end-1) - movVol(2:end-1,1:end-2,2:end-1);
movZGrad_Org(2:end-1,2:end-1,2:end-1) = movVol(2:end-1,2:end-1,3:
end) - movVol(2:end-1,2:end-1,1:end-2);
regulFactor = 0.1;
stepSize = 1.0;
[movVol_updated, Tx, Ty, Tz] = register3D(movVol, refVol,...
                        movXGrad_Org, movYGrad_Org, movZGrad_Org,...
                        Tx, Ty, Tz,...
                        iterLimit, regulFactor, stepSize);
```

8.6 CUDA Conversion Results

Let us perform the time profile to see how much improvement we added using GPU. Run `atlasSeg_Cuda.m` in the `Profiler` (Figure 8.19).

After CUDA conversion, the elapsed time of `atlasSeg_Cuda.m` is around 26 seconds for both left and right hippocampus processing, which is about 24 times faster than `atlasSeg_Main.m`. Let us see how the profiling results are changed after CUDA conversion (Figure 8.20).

Compared to the profiling results of `atlasSeg_Main.m` (Figure 8.12), the profiling results of `atlasSeg_Cuda.m` have much smaller time in the `deformableRegister3D_cuda` function. Figure 8.21 shows that the `register3D` function still takes 99.8% of the total processing time within the `deformableRegister3D_cuda` function, but the total time is 22.792 seconds. Figure 8.22 shows the profiling result of the `register3D` module. Since the `register3D` module is a `c-mex` module, MATLAB profiler does not show much information on the code profiling.

8.7 Conclusion

From the CUDA conversion of the single function revealed to be the busiest function during the profiling, we improve the speed about 3.3 times faster than the pure `m` codes for 3D medical image segmentation. However, the CUDA-converted function gives rise to too frequent data transfer between CPU and GPU memory before and after the modified module within the iteration. This makes the overall process inefficient. In the final CUDA conversion of all operations within the loop, we could run the algorithm about 24 times faster than the pure m codes for 3D medical image segmentation.

The first thing to do for speed optimization is profiling, from which we can identify the target modules to be converted to CUDA functions. Second, when we

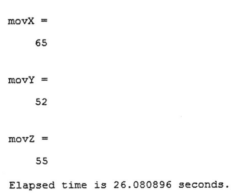

Figure 8.19 The elapsed time for `atlasSeg_Cuda.m`.

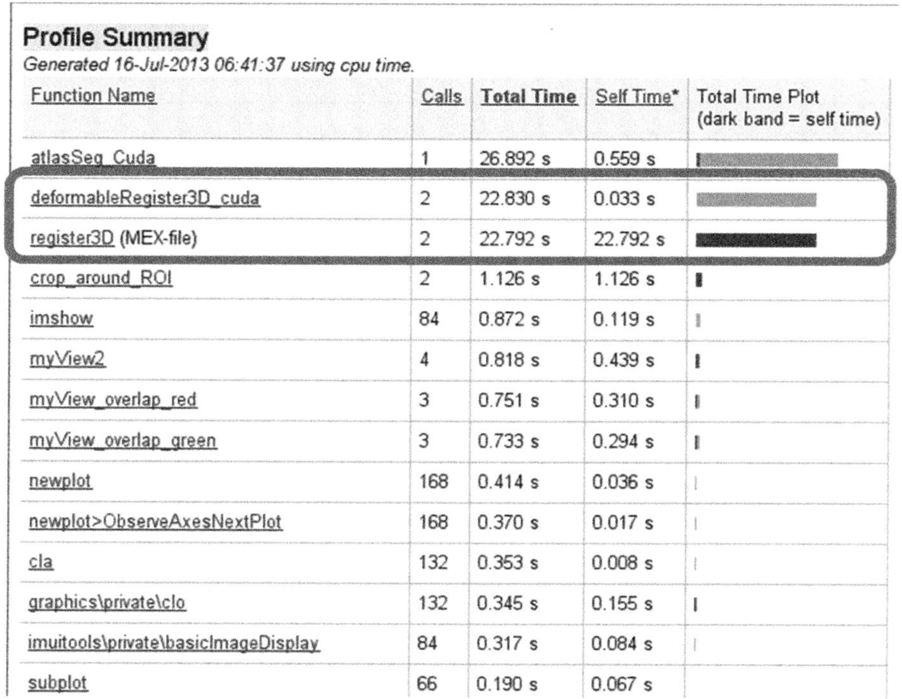

Profile Summary

Generated 16-Jul-2013 06:41:37 using cpu time.

Function Name	Calls	Total Time	Self Time*	Total Time Plot (dark band = self time)
atlasSeg_Cuda	1	26.892 s	0.559 s	
deformableRegister3D_cuda	2	22.830 s	0.033 s	
register3D (MEX-file)	2	22.792 s	22.792 s	
crop_around_ROI	2	1.126 s	1.126 s	
imshow	84	0.872 s	0.119 s	
myView2	4	0.818 s	0.439 s	
myView_overlap_red	3	0.751 s	0.310 s	
myView_overlap_green	3	0.733 s	0.294 s	
newplot	168	0.414 s	0.036 s	
newplot>ObserveAxesNextPlot	168	0.370 s	0.017 s	
cla	132	0.353 s	0.008 s	
graphics\private\clo	132	0.345 s	0.155 s	
imuitools\private\basicImageDisplay	84	0.317 s	0.084 s	
subplot	66	0.190 s	0.067 s	

Figure 8.20 Profiling the results of the top main function (atlasSeg_Cuda.m) after CUDA conversion.

deformableRegister3D_cuda (2 calls, 22.830 sec)

Generated 16-Jul-2013 06:45:47 using cpu time.
function in file C:\Users\sun\Documents\Books\Chapters\Ch8\codes\m_code_Cuda\deformableRegister3D_cuda.m
Copy to new window for comparing multiple runs

[Refresh]

☑ Show parent functions ☑ Show busy lines ☑ Show child functions
☑ Show Code Analyzer results ☑ Show file coverage ☑ Show function listing

Parents (calling functions)

Function Name	Function Type	Calls
atlasSeg_Cuda	script	2

Lines where the most time was spent

Line Number	Code	Calls	Total Time	% Time	Time Plot
17	[movVol_updated, Tx, Ty, Tz] =...	2	22.795 s	99.8%	▬
3	[Ty,Tx,Tz] = meshgrid(1:refY,1...	2	0.010 s	0.0%	
13	movZGrad_Org(2:end-1,2:...	2	0.005 s	0.0%	
12	movYGrad_Org(2:end-1,2:...	2	0.005 s	0.0%	
11	movXGrad_Org(2:end-1,2:...	2	0.004 s	0.0%	
All other lines			0.011 s	0.0%	
Totals			22.830 s	100%	

Children (called functions)

Function Name	Function Type	Calls	Total Time	% Time	Time Plot
register3D	MEX-file	2	22.792 s	99.8%	▬
meshgrid	function	2	0.005 s	0.0%	
Self time (built-ins, overhead, etc.)			0.033 s	0.1%	
Totals			22.830 s	100%	

Figure 8.21 Profiling the result of the deformableRegister3D_cuda module.

register3D (2 calls, 22.792 sec)

MEX-file in file C:\Users\jsuh\Documents\Books\Chapters\Ch8\codes\m_code_Cuda\register3D.mexw64

Copy to new window for comparing multiple runs

[Refresh]

☑ Show parent functions   ☑ Show busy lines   ☑ Show child functions

☑ Show Code Analyzer results ☑ Show file coverage ☑ Show function listing

Parents (calling functions)

Function Name	Function Type	Calls
deformableRegister3D_cuda	function	2

Lines where the most time was spent
No MATLAB code to display

Children (called functions)
No children

Code Analyzer results
No MATLAB code to display

Coverage results
No MATLAB code to display

Function listing
No MATLAB code to display

Figure 8.22 Profiling result of the c-mex register3D **module.**

plan to convert from MATLAB m codes to GPU-enabled c-mex codes, we should carefully consider the size of the data and the frequency of data transfer between CPU memory and GPU device memory. Introducing too many and unnecessary data transfers with big data may actually defeat the purpose of speed optimization for host-device data transfer is the slowest data movement in GPU computing.

Appendix 1: Download and Install the CUDA Library

A1.1 CUDA Toolkit Download

To get started with CUDA on our system, we first need to install the CUDA development tools and ensure the correct operation of these tools. We can download the CUDA toolkit from the NVIDIA website at http://www.nvidia.com/content/cuda/cuda-downloads.html (Figure A1.1).

A1.2 Installation

You choose and download the installer for the system you use from the link in Figure A1.1. Once the download is complete, you can start installing by executing the installer and following the on-screen prompts, for example,

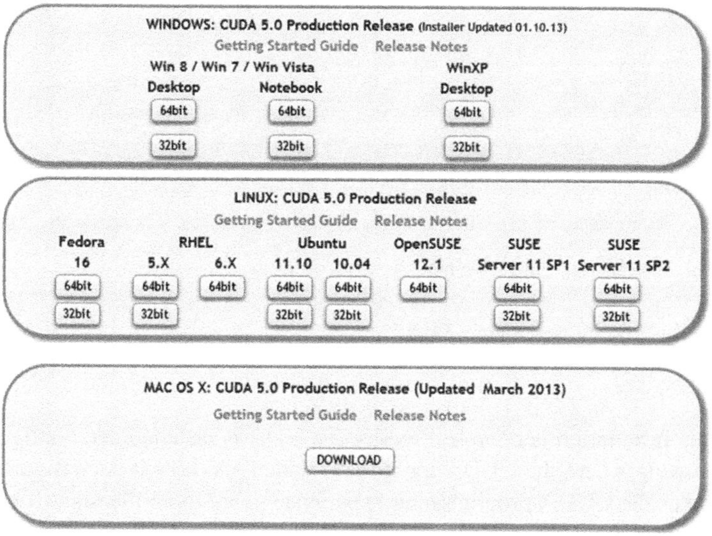

Figure A1.1 CUDA downloads for various systems.

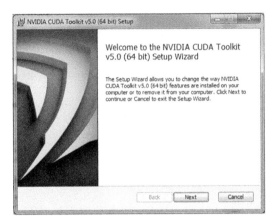

Figure A1.2 Windows CUDA Installer.

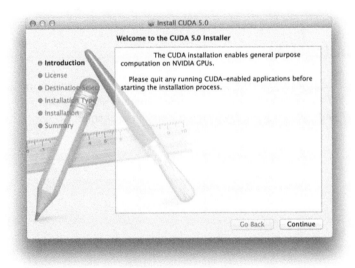

Figure A1.3 Mac OS X CUDA Installer.

- For Widows 7 64 bit, see Figure A1.2.
- For Mac OS X, see Figure A1.3.
- For Linux, see Figure A1.4.

Once the installation is complete, verify if CUDA is installed and configured correctly. Knowing where the CUDA toolkit is installed and how it is configured on the system makes the CUDA programming experience much more pleasant. If we follow the default installation options, we have CUDA installed for each system as follows:

- For Window 7 64 bit, `C:\Program Files\NVIDIA GPU Computing Toolkit\CUDA \v5.0` (Figure A1.5).

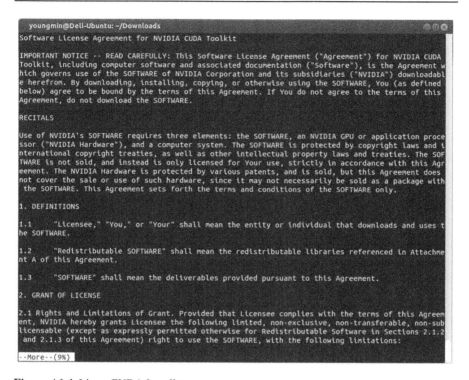

Figure A1.4 Linux CUDA Installer.

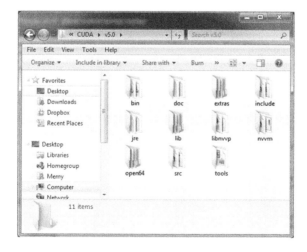

Figure A1.5 Windows CUDA Default Installation Directory.

- For Mac OS X, /Developer/NVIDIA/CUDA-5.0 (Figure A1.6).
- For Linux, /usr/local/cuda-5.0 (Figure A1.7).

For each system, try to identify the following files in the following subdirectories.

- nvcc.exe or nvcc at bin.
- cuda_runtime.h at include.
- cudart.lib at lib\64 for Windows 7 64 bit.
- libcudart.so at lib for Linux.
- libcudart.dylib at lib for Mac OS X.

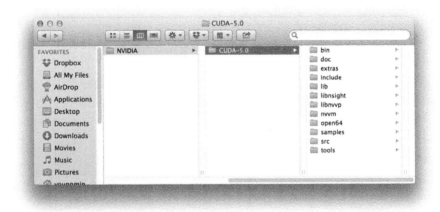

Figure A1.6 Mac OS X Default Installation Directory.

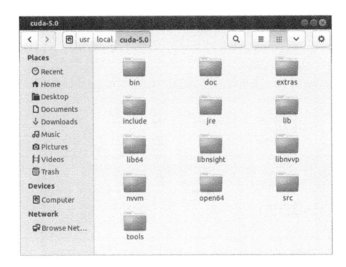

Figure A1.7 Linux Default Installation Directory (Ubuntu, in this example).

A1.3   Verification

Now, the most important thing is to be able to execute the CUDA compiler, nvcc, from the command prompt. Open the command prompt window in Windows or shell in Linux or Mac OS X. Try to execute the command in Figure A1.8 at the prompt. If you are unable to run nvcc at the command prompt, make sure the bin directory of the installed CUDA toolkit is in your system environment.

- For Windows 7 64 bit, enter PATH at the prompt and see if the directory that has nvcc is specified as in Figure A1.9.
- For Mac OS X and Linux, type in echo $PATH at the prompt in the shell and make sure the path to nvcc is specified Figures A1.10 and A1.11).

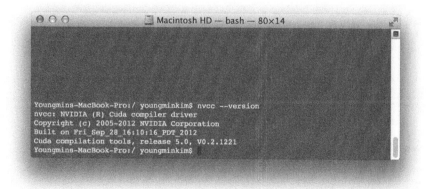

Figure A1.8 The nvcc version verification.

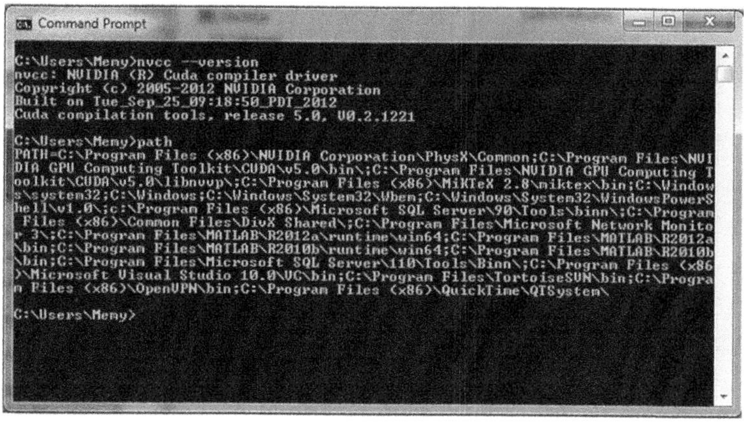

Figure A1.9 The nvcc PATH in the Windows environment.

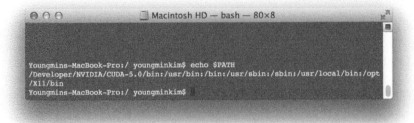

Figure A1.10 The nvcc PATH in the Mac OS X.

Figure A1.11 The nvcc PATH in the Linux environment.

Appendix 2: Installing NVIDIA Nsight into Visual Studio

NVIDIA Nsight, Visual Studio Edition, is a development environment for CUDA. NVIDIA Nsight, Visual Studio Edition, provides strong debugging and profiling functions, which are very efficient for CUDA code development. Although the NVIDIA Nsight is free, you need to register yourself to download the tool.

1. Access NVIDIA Nsight (http://www.nvidia.com/object/nsight.html) for user registration. You will see the screen in Figure A2.1.
2. After registration, download the tool corresponding to your system, as shown in Figure A2.2.
3. Install the Nsight Visual Studio Edition as shown in Figure A2.3.
4. After finishing the installation, find the Nsight menu in your Microsoft Visual Studio. If you see this menu (Figure A2.4), all the installation process for Nsight is successfully done.

Figure A2.1 NVIDIA Nsight website. Select Download Nsight Visual Studio Edition for Visual Studio.

Figure A2.2 Download website after registration. You can select the version for your system.

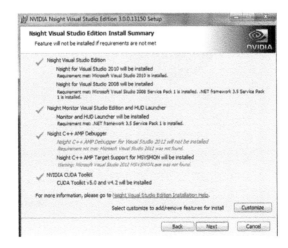

Figure A2.3 Installing window for NVIDIA Nsight, Visual Studio Edition.

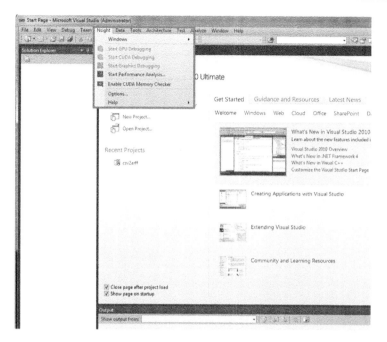

Figure A2.4 Check the Nsight menu in the Microsoft Visual Studio after successful installation.

Bibliography

Bourke, P. (2013). Polygonising a scalar field. Available at <http://paulbourke.net/geometry/polygonise>.

Burkardt, J., Cliff, G., & Krometis, J. (2011). Parallel MATLAB: Single program multiple data. Available at <http://www.icam.vt.edu/Computing/vt_2011_spmd.pdf>.

CUDA toolkit documentation, NVIDIA. 2013. Available at <http://docs.nvidia.com/cuda/index.html>.

CUFFT Library. (2013). Available at <http://docs.nvidia.com/cuda/pdf/CUDA_CUFFT_Users_Guide.pdf>, NVIDIA.

Davidge, H. (2012). 2D and 3D symmetric registration using CUDA. Available at <http://www.mathworks.com/matlabcentral/fileexchange/37685-2d-and-3d-symmetric-registration-using-cuda>.

Dean, L. (2010). GPU computing with MATLAB. Available at <http://www.nvidia.com/content/GTC-2010/pdfs/2267_GTC2010.pdf>, MathWorks.

Kirk, D. B., & Hwu, W. W. (2010). *Programming massively parallel processors: A hands-on approach*. San Mateo, CA: Morgan Kaufmann.

Marching cubes, Wikipedia, The Free Encyclopedia, 2013. Available at <http://en.widipedia.org/wiki/Marching_cubes>.

MATLAB GPU computing support for NVIDIA CUDA-enabled GPUs. Available at <http://www.mathworks.com/discovery/matlab-gpu.html>.

NVIDIA developer zone: CUDA toolkit documentation—CUBLAS, 2013. Available at <http://docs.nvidia.com/cuda/cublas/index.html>.

NVIDIA developer zone: CUDA toolkit documentation—Thrust. Available at https://developer.nvidia.com/thrust, NVIDIA. (last accessed in July 18, 2013).

NVIDIA's next generation CUDA compute architecture: Kepler GK110, NVIDIA, 2013. Available at <http//www.nvidia.com/content/PDF/kepler/NVIDIA-Kepler-GK110-Architecture-Whitepaper.pdf>.

Profiling for improving performance. Available at <http://www.mathworks.com/help/matlab/matlab_prog/profiling-for-improving-performance.html>.

Sanders, J., & Kandrot, E. (2010). *CUDA by example: An introduction to general-purpose GPU programming*. Reading, MA: Addison-Wesley Professional.

Suh, J. W., Kwon, O. K., Scheinost, D., Sinusas, A. J., Cline, G. W., & Papademetris, X. (2012). CT-PET weighted image fusion for separately scanned whole body rat. *Medical Physics*, 39(1), 533−542.

Suh, J. W., Scheinost, D., Dione, D. P., Dobrucki, L. W., Sinusas, A. J., & Papademetris, X. (2011). A non-rigid registration method for serial lower extremity hybrid SPECT/CT imaging. *Medical Image Analysis*, 15(1), 96−111.

Suh, J. W., & Yushkevich, P. A. (2011). AHEAD: Automatic hippocampal estimator using atlas-based delineation. Available at <http://www.nitrc.org/projects/ahead/>.

Tagare, H. D., Groisser, D., & Skrinjar, O. (2009). Symmetric non-rigid registration: A Geometric theory and some numerical techniques. *Journal of Mathematical Imaging and Vision* (May).

Techniques for improving performances. Available at <http://www.mathworks.com/help/matlab/matlab_prog/techniques-for-improving-performance.html>.

Vectorization. Available at <http://www.mathworks.com/help/matlab/matlab_prog/vectorization.html>.

Wang, H., Suh, J. W., Das, S. R., Pluta, J., Altinay, M., Craige, C., et al. (2013). Multi-atlas segmentation with joint label fusion. *IEEE Transactions on Pattern Analysis and Machine Intelligence, PAMI-5*(3) (March), pp. 611−623.

Index

Note: Page numbers followed by "*f*" and "*b*" refers to figures and boxes respectively.

Essential Matlab for Engineers and Scientists
Brian Hahn and David Valentine
ISBN: 9780123943989

Programming Massively Parallel Processors, 2nd Edition
A Hands-on Approach
David Kirk and Wen-mei Hwu
ISBN: 9780124159921

CUDA Application Design and Development
Rob Farber
ISBN: 9780123884268

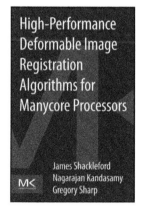

High Performance Deformable Image Registration Algorithms for Manycore Processors
James Shackleford,
Nagarajan Kandasamy, Gregory Sharp
ISBN: 9780124077416

Intel Xeon Phi Coprocessor High Performance Programming
Jim Jeffers and James Reinders
ISBN: 9780124104143

The Art of Multiprocessor Programming, Revised Reprint
Maurice Herlihy and Nir Shavit
ISBN: 9780123973375

mkp.com

Printed and bound by CPI Group (UK) Ltd, Croydon, CR0 4YY

03/10/2024

01040423-0004